The Same Thing Over and Over

The Same Thing Over and Over

How School Reformers Get Stuck in Yesterday's Ideas

Frederick M. Hess

Harvard University Press • Cambridge, Massachusetts • London, England • 2010

Library of Congress Cataloging-in-Publication Data

Hess, Frederick M.
The same thing over and over : how school reformers get stuck
in yesterday's ideas / Frederick M. Hess.
p. cm.
Includes bibliographical references and index.
ISBN 978-0-674-05582-7 (alk. paper)
1. School improvement programs—United States.
2. Educational change—United States.
3. Public schools—United States. 4. Education—
Aims and objectives—United States. 5. Education—
United States—Evaluation. I. Title.

LB2822.82.H492 2010
371.2′070973—dc22 2010013274

Contents

We have witnessed decade after decade of hyped reforms found by decorated academics and bombastic advocates. Yet,
while we have nearly tripled real per pupil spending since 1970, student achievement has barely budged and a superintendent who nod-
ded off in 1950 would feel almost uncannily at home in most of today's school districts. What's the deal?

In the pages that follow, I argue that, while we reform at a frenzied pace, we have rarely dug deeply enough into the underlying
system of districts, schools, and teachers to start reshaping the educational landscape. As Albert Einstein so eloquently put it, "The definition of insanity is doing the same thing over and over again and expecting different results." Escaping that fate begins by understanding
why all of our seemingly varied reform strategies add up to little
more than doing the same thing over and over again. We do this by,
for once, not focusing on the hot reforms of the moment, but by asking what we are trying to accomplish, whether today's schools are
equipped for that task, and how we might use twenty-first century
tools and talent to do better.

We need to emancipate ourselves from the institutions and habits of mind that make school reform a pointless, aimless charade.
Doing this requires distinguishing the purpose of schooling from its
established practice so as to determine where today's means do not
serve our ends. This exercise is a task best accomplished by looking
in the rearview mirror.

I am a political scientist, a policy thinker, and occasionally a
pamphleteer. I am no historian. Yet, this book required that I spend

more than a little time dabbling in the typically tranquil groves of history. Some fair-minded readers may be moved to ask why.

Nearly a decade ago, I penned a white paper on teacher licensure for the Progressive Policy Institute, the Democratic think tank led in the 1980s and 1990s by the likes of then governor Bill Clinton and then senator Al Gore. Titled "Tear Down This Wall: The Case for a Radical Overhaul of Teacher Certification," the paper contended that the rationale for our established system of teacher licensure systems did not stand up under scrutiny. I argued that the system built upon education schools and paper-driven state certification—which may have worked passably well in an earlier era when plenty of talented women wanted to teach and no other mechanism of quality control was feasible—had now become a hindrance. I argued that it discouraged potentially promising applicants and propped up mediocre teacher-training programs. Much to my surprise, the piece drew substantial popular interest, receiving enthusiastic receptions from U.S. Education Secretary Rod Paige and the editorial page of *USA Today,* among others. All of this attention was new to me and enormously educational.

As I spoke about the piece in various forums, I soon realized that the strengths and frailties of my argument typically received far less scrutiny than did my motives. I grew accustomed to critics casually depicting me (a former high school teacher and, at that point, a professor of education) as hostile to teachers and an implacable enemy of education schools. It became clear that, whatever the finer points of the issue, the failure to address those concerns directly meant that I would find myself brushed aside as a gadfly mounting an ideological assault on the public education community.

While frustrating, the experience sparked a useful insight: the pushback from my critics was most dismissive when I failed to provide a broader context for my interest and for the argument. I found, however, that listeners were more receptive when I began not with bullet points, statistics, or blanket indictments, but by explaining why I thought that familiar, long-standing arrangements no longer served our needs. In discussing where licensure came from and why it no longer made much sense given the tools at our disposal and the shape of the contemporary labor force, I found that many listeners seemed more inclined to at least consider ideas they might have otherwise rejected out of hand. Addressing these issues helped to temper concerns about my agenda and established common ground for reasoned debate.

In the years since, I have found this to be true again and again, on issues ranging from teacher pay to school governance. We are mired in static organizational arrangements, which may have sprung from perfectly sensible roots but are now an obstacle to promoting excellence in teaching and learning. Because we're so used to these practices and institutions, though, we have difficulty seeing them as problematic.

While this book ranges over much of K–12 schooling, the value of looking backward is tellingly illustrated in the case of school leadership. The question of how to train school leaders is often framed as a contest between education professionals and corporate stooges seeking to impose private-sector management practices upon K–12 schooling, especially by the self-proclaimed champions of "schoolhouse leadership." As popular author Alfie Kohn and his colleague Patrick Shannon thundered in *Education, Inc.*, "The problem is that people in the public sector are uncritically adopting the worldview of the private sector—and applying it to schools."[1]

The Kohn-Shannon stance reflects the established schooling community's determined disinterest in thinking from outside the sector. For instance, today's most widely assigned education leadership texts treat education as a unique pursuit, embracing variations of the assertion that: "We [must] accept the reality that leadership for the schoolhouse should be different, and . . . we [need to] begin to invent our own practice."[2] Almost entirely absent from the syllabi of education leadership classes are seminal thinkers like Michael Porter, Jim Collins, Clayton Christensen, Tom Peters, Peter Drucker, and Warren Bennis, whose work has helped to inform management and governance in fields ranging from telecommunications to health care.[3] This glaring absence, unfortunately, doesn't raise even one eyebrow among leading education professors and practitioners, who regard such blind spots in curriculum as unremarkable. (One ironic consequence of this lack of exposure is that thinkers like Collins and Christensen can become objects of faddish fascination when educators are finally exposed to them. Having been given no opportunity to scrutinize the thinking or assess how it translates to K–12 schooling, education leaders misapply sensible insights, swallow pat but misguided prescriptions, and mistake jargon for action.)

The widespread distrust of such thinking is symptomatic of the status quo's white-knuckled grip on the ways of the past. Defenders of the status quo imply that today's model of governance and leadership is a model borne of deeply held values, enlightened pedagogy, and a principled resistance to business thinking. Such claims are fatuous. Rather, the status quo represents *a bastardized application of early-twentieth-century "best practices" management.* It is the result of Progressive era reformers applying Frederick Taylor's industrial vision of rigid, hierarchical, and bureaucratic "scientific management" to schooling. Indeed, today's best-managed public and private ventures are managed in ways that are far more collaborative, participatory, and energizing than are most schools or school systems.

Ellwood Cubberley, longtime dean of the Stanford Graduate School of Education and in many ways the father of modern school administration, wrote approvingly in 1947, "The condition of our schools before about 1900 . . . was that of a manufacturing establishment running at a low grade of efficiency," but since that time, "we have been engaged in improving the business by speeding it up, supplying it with new and specialized machinery, saving wastes, and increasing the rate and the value to society of the output." By "revising our manufacturing specifications," he and his fellow Progressive reformers were bringing to schooling "the same principles of specialized production and manufacturing efficiency which control in other parts of the manufacturing world."[4]

The way businesses are managed has changed profoundly since Cubberley's musings on the virtues of manufacturing-style schooling. Diane Ravitch spoke for the educational consensus in 2010 when she opined, "Our schools will not improve if we expect them to act like private, profit-seeking enterprises. Schools are not businesses; they are public services. . . . The best principals have had a long apprenticeship as educators, first as teachers, then as assistant principals, and finally as principals."[5] Many in education regard any intimations of embracing business practices as an existential threat while ascribing ethereal virtues to the assembly-line arrangements of schooling.

And yet today's educational leadership debate should not be understood as a battle between defenders of public education and those laying siege to it, but as a clash between two schools of thought. One is an established educational management practice that's arguably anachronistic and better suited to factory management than to the rigors of a knowledge-based profession. The other is a more nimble school of professional management that has evolved in nearly every other sector of the economy. The debate over the sanctity of "schoolhouse leadership," then, is really a debate between the defenders of early-twentieth-century management practices and those championing the management practices devised by leading public and private organizations in recent decades.

The reflexive denunciation of nontraditional measures is ultimately destructive to reasoned debate. Several years ago I engaged in a protracted discussion in the pages of *Phi Delta Kappan* over precisely this question: what is it that is "public" about public schooling? In that exchange, Evans Clinchy, the founder of Educational Planning Associates, illustrated the perils of the "it's not public" claim. After making the reasonable but arguable assertion that educational management organizations (EMOs) had an "educationally and economically dismal" track record, Clinchy went on to make the troubling declaration that EMOs are not "morally acceptable in any fair, just, and equitable system of democratic government."[6]

While Clinchy's first assertion is susceptible to reasoned debate, his second—positing one ethically permissible approach to school governance—seeks to stifle rational argument and turns school reform into a clash of absolutes. Such rhetoric labels all those opposed to the speaker's prescriptions as enemies of public schooling. In twenty-first-century America, I will argue in the pages to follow, a sensible conception of public schooling does not require that a singular orthodoxy must hold sway when it comes to questions of who should run schools, what role for-profits might play, or how teachers should be paid. Many different arrangements may be consistent with our notions of public schooling. It is not that charter schools ought to be preferred to district schools, that schools ought to employ fewer traditional teachers, or that students should make more use of online tutoring—it is only that such arrangements *are not inconsistent with a sensible rendering of public schooling.*

Rather than debate what arrangements and practices are most likely to serve our needs, how to promote them, or how to leverage newly available tools and talent, we find ourselves trapped in heated debates about whether rethinking the status quo amounts to abandoning the principles of public education. Obeisance to familiar practices—no matter how problematic, ineffective, or anachronistic—has become a proxy for a commitment to schooling. In this book, I seek to help us shift away from grim debates over whether fresh thinking is permissible so that we might more constructively focus on its merits and practical challenges. On that score, I'll note that this focus and a taste for brevity dictated eschewing more contemporary educational history for the period in which American schooling took shape.

This is not intended to be and should not be read as a historical work. Rather, it is a book that strolls back into the precincts of history to help us understand the source of contemporary policy and practice, so that we might better address the challenges of twenty-first-century schooling. Shall we get started?

The Same Thing Over and Over

Ideas Equal to Our Ambitions

"For this is the tragedy of man—circumstances change, but he does not."

—Niccolò Machiavelli

How would you respond if asked for a plan to transform America's schools into a world-class, twenty-first-century system? Now imagine that there is one condition: you must retain the job descriptions, governance arrangements, management practices, compensation strategies, licensure requirements, and calendar of the existing system. Hopefully, you would flee just as fast as you possibly could and if so, you would be way ahead of the rest of us, who have spent decades slogging through that dismal scenario.

Wave upon wave of reformers seeking to better serve the 50 million students in K–12 schooling have met with disappointment as they struggled to reconcile demands that they simultaneously "change" and "protect" public schooling. The default response has been decades of frenzied tinkering. The result is a wealth of clumsy, half-baked reform proposals that ask schools to do the same thing they've always done, except to do more of it and to do it better. As *Life* magazine so aptly put it in 1948, "A basic principle of American democracy is the more education, the better,"[1] but the "more is better" approach has distracted us from asking the key question: Are our schools as they are now configured capable of accomplishing what we now ask of them?

This book proceeds from the assumption that the answer is "no." When pursued with sufficient genius, energy, and advantages, our system of schooling can deliver in some places, at some times, and for some children, but the architecture of schooling makes it extraordinarily difficult to sustain or extend such successes. The result is a shelf's worth of depressing postmortems with titles like *So Much Reform, So Little Change*[2]; *Tinkering toward Utopia*[3]; *Spinning Wheels*[4]; and *Left Back*.[5] Current arrangements don't preclude isolated successes, but they do make these efforts so exhausting and dependent on individual genius that systemic excellence seems to be an unreachable, ghostly mirage. Even the boldest proposals have not amounted to much. As Chester Finn Jr., a prominent advocate of ambitious reforms like accountability and charter schooling, argued in 2010, "The education reform debate as we have known it for a generation is creaking to a halt. . . . The problem is not that [standards, testing, and choice] are misguided. Rather, they are just not powerful enough to force the rusty infrastructure of American primary and secondary education to undergo meaningful change."[6]

Let me start by being perfectly clear about my own biases. I generally favor structural reforms such as merit pay, school vouchers, charter schooling, alternative teacher licensure, and educational accountability. I endorse these ideas not because there is anything magical about the measures or because they are "proven" to work, but because it makes good sense to pay good employees more than mediocre ones, to allow a variety of schools to serve children, to tap a larger pool of instructional talent, and to emphasize results rather than paperwork. This book is an attempt to persuade readers that ideas like these are useful responses to the demands of twenty-first-century schooling and consistent with the principles of public schooling. Looking backward to more clearly see the roots of our educational system as they took shape and grew can help us see that much which we regard as sacrosanct is the legacy of happenstance, inertia, or innovations that once made sense but have outlived their usefulness.

Such a view suggests that we have a long-standing habit of getting unduly attached to the fads of the day. Today, jargon, platitudes, and brow-knitting too often stand in for creative problem solving. We invest terms like "master teacher," "site-based management," "data-driven decision-making," "human capital," "online instruction," and "school turnaround" with talismanic significance. These measures are hyped, only to be gradually discarded when they don't live up to the grand promises. In the late 1980s and through much of the 1990s, the alluring if vaguely incoherent decentralization strategy of "site-based management" (SBM) enjoyed a pleasant run—until disappointing results and confusion about how it should actually work led reformers to look elsewhere. SBM didn't vanish, of course, but left a detritus of school management councils scattered in districts across the land. In the first years of this past decade, another case study played out when the Gates Foundation led a national charge on behalf of "small high schools." The effort engendered much enthusiasm and consumed vast sums before petering out amid uncertain results and practical challenges.

These and other peddled fixes are sold with promises that they won't entail anything more jarring or disruptive than more training, collaboration, parental involvement, and remembering to love kids a whole lot. The notion that real improvement will require dramatic or painful change is barely evident. The need for more substantial change is made clear when we consider the sea change in American education over the past century. In 1900, less than 6 percent of seventeen-year-olds had even completed high school.[7] By the end of the twentieth century, more than 80 percent of those over age twenty-five had earned at least a high school degree.[8]

In other words, the arrangements first crafted over a century ago are enormously successful—if the criteria are ensuring that every child has a school, a principal, a teacher, transportation, a schedule, a report card, and receives their diploma on time. Over the years, however, as historian Christopher Lucas has noted, schools have also been asked to "teach order, discipline, and democracy, the virtues of thrift, cleanliness, and honest labor, the evils of alcohol, tobacco, atheism, drugs, war, peace, sex, and communism; and they have been asked to help acculturate immigrants, to foster patriotism, tolerance, and, above all, to produce a universally high standard of literacy."[9]

Teachers ultimately do a lot more than just, you know, teach. In fact, the National Center for Education Statistics has reported that in 2003–2004, teachers spent only 54 percent of their total working hours instructing students.[10] Accomplishing all of this is no small feat and required the construction of elaborate, jury-rigged federal, state, and local bureaucracies in a nation characterized by its federal system and attachment to localism. Today, as we make new demands, we should hardly be shocked to learn that these systems are clumsy and ill equipped to promote widespread academic excellence.[11]

And that means we are stuck. If one set out in the twenty-first century to design a system capable of fostering world-class teaching and learning for all of our nation's 50 million students, the challenges would be staggering. In answering that heady call, one would be well advised to employ personnel strategies geared to today's labor market and not that of a half-century or a century ago; to utilize contemporary management strategies to coordinate far-flung and specialized organizations in smarter ways; and to leverage new technologies to deliver and configure schooling in a fashion not feasible when distance education entailed texts and essays transported by the U.S. Postal Service. Perhaps most important would be the need to abandon the one-size-fits-all ethos that held sway in the industrial era.

In short, you would not rely upon outdated tools to confront new challenges and opportunities. The first step in responding would be to emancipate your thinking from ossified mantras long enough to simply ask: Given the tools and resources available, what are the smartest, most promising ways to answer the challenges?

ESCAPING OLD ORTHODOXIES . . . AND NOT JUST ENSHRINING NEW ONES

In considering how to cast off these shackles of once useful routines, norms, and habits of mind, we routinely make one of two mistakes. The first, and more prevalent by far, is made by those who fail to distinguish between the principles of democratic schooling and the rusty bureaucracies erected to deliver them. Rather than the legacy of democratic public schooling, they end up defending aged orthodoxies and familiar but creaky machinery. These defenders of the status quo misguidedly regard proposals to rethink the architecture of schooling as assaults on education. The second kind of mistake belongs to those would-be reformers who insist upon doing what "works." Rather than ask whether school districts are still a sensible way to organize schooling, how to rethink the job of teaching, or how to foster a diverse array of excellent schools, these reformers, whom I like to call "New Progressives," seem to take much of the familiar machinery for granted.[12] Much like the reform-minded and self-confident Progressives who did so much to build our system of schooling in the early twentieth century, the New Progressives have an exaggerated faith in the power of science to issue definitive answers to thorny questions and the ability of government to design and execute complex solutions.

Champions of the Status Quo

Proponents of the status quo, while regarding themselves as defenders of public schools, are too often defending familiar *institutions* rather than the *mission* of providing outstanding teaching and learning. Those in this camp are frequently unwilling to consider the possibility that our familiar schools and school systems may be incapable of meeting today's goals, or that familiar practices governing teacher pay or school governance may be incompatible with fulfilling our new ambitions. In fall 2009, for instance, while working upon this book, I visited with a gathering of state educational leaders. The head of one state organization opened the conference with a slide showing the cover of a then recent issue of *The Louisiana Boardmember*, featuring the bold headline, "Louisiana School Boards Association Fought Off a National War on Public Schools" emblazoned over a glaring boxer with raised gloves. The "war" he referred to entailed efforts to promote charter schooling, to restrict the ability of school boards to remove superintendents and influence district hiring, and to give the state authority over low-performing schools. Indeed, we saw this rhetoric take on a new vehemence in early 2010, when historian Diane Ravitch heatedly charged that proposals like charter schooling, mayoral control, and test-based accountability constituted an assault that influential business leaders and philanthropists were mounting on public education. Now, these ideas may or may not be good ones, but the notion that they constitute an assault on public schooling raises an insuperable barrier to reimagining how to answer the challenges of a new century.

Of course, as matters stand, public schooling in practice often falls short of its reputed virtues. A public school is open only to families that can afford a residence in the local district, and some districts operate schools that limit admission based on grades, exams, or ability. Traditional districts accept these inequities and differences in opportunity, but decry that same possibility in alternative arrangements as a betrayal of public schooling. Indeed, many alternative solutions are intended to address these very inequities. Charter schools, for instance, are required to admit students by lottery and without regard to place of residence. It is a bizarre double standard when such objectionable outcomes are not thought to threaten the "publicness" of public schools when they transpire in traditional districts—while efforts to reimagine the familiar system to address those very issues are pilloried as efforts to abandon a sacred covenant.

The New Progressives

While defenders of the status quo reject the case for radical change, the New Progressives talk of unprecedented challenges, heightened expectations, and the need for transformation, but then marry these calls with underwhelming proposals. This is a mismatch of ends and means, of ambition and imagination. At the same time, the New Progressives are eager to establish new orthodoxies in place of (or atop) the old. Even after taking advantage of the opportunities presented by charter schooling or more flexible licensure systems, they now hustle to impose new prescriptive, test-reliant policies regarding teacher evaluation and pay, interventions for low-performing schools, leadership preparation, and much else.

The perils of the New Progressivism are particularly evident when it comes to using "value-added" assessments to gauge teacher performance. The impatient rush to "fix" teacher quality in one furious burst of legislating amounts to troubling overreaching; it is a case of putting the cart before the horse. As a result, promising efforts to uproot outdated and stifling arrangements get enveloped in sketchily considered, potentially self-destructive efforts to mandate the use of systems that are crudely drawn and not yet equal to the technical or practical burden they are being asked to bear. Early problems risk discrediting these systems, even as advocates skip past the inconvenient fact that systems based too narrowly on individual value-added calculations can stifle smart efforts to use teachers more effectively. Principals who rotate their faculty based on individual strengths, or who augment classroom teachers with guest instructors or online lessons, are going to clash with a system predicated on linking each student's annual test scores to a single teacher. Nonetheless, impassioned progressives frustrated with stagnant results and teachers-union obstruction have trouble accepting that unwinding a century's worth of accumulated detritus and replacing it with a functioning system will take time.

Similarly, New Progressive proposals for "alternative licensure" go only so far as recruiting a slightly different pool of people to go through slightly modified training, but then have them proceed into positions and along career paths that have changed little in the past century. Having witnessed some of the promising results posted by Teach For America (TFA), a terrific venture that selectively recruits new college graduates to teach for a couple of years in high-poverty schools, the New Progressives have decided that TFA should be the new model and its corps members the gold standard. I'm as enthusiastic a booster of TFA as one is likely to find, but its critical lesson is that there are vast pools of talent that our traditional licensing and training system is missing—not that TFA's focus and approach are the optimal way to tackle the challenge. An agenda less wedded to establishing a new orthodoxy would take more care to regard alternative licensure models like TFA as initial, stumbling steps in an effort to reimagine a system that currently is ill equipped to attract, utilize, or retain excellent teachers. Instead, in far too many cases and places, TFA-style alternative licensure has become *the* program that supportive foundations and public officials eagerly embrace, while other models—to recruit professionals into part-time teaching duty, to recruit retired professionals into teaching, to tap graduate students and stay-at-home parents as tutors or teaching assistants—go largely unexplored.

Another Route?

The struggles of these competing camps serve to enmesh us ever more deeply into ceaseless, unending debates that have been playing out for centuries. Current practices that may have once made sense need to be reevaluated and refashioned or discarded in light of new demands and opportunities. We will fail, however, if this becomes an exercise in peddling favored fixes of the moment rather than an opportunity to clear the way for creative problem-solving or if we substitute inspiring oratory for bold action.

BRASH CALLS FOR CHANGE . . . BUT BASHFUL REMEDIES

More than a quarter-century ago, in the influential Reagan-era report *A Nation at Risk*, which many regard as the starting gun for modern school reform efforts, a panel of leading thinkers declared, "The educational foundations of our society are presently being eroded by a rising tide of mediocrity that threatens our very future as a Nation and a people." They proclaimed, "If an unfriendly foreign power had attempted to impose on America the mediocre educational performance that exists today, we might well have viewed it as an act of war."[13] Decades later, the rhetoric has remained equally emphatic.

- In a 2005 speech to the nation's governors, Microsoft chairman Bill Gates declared, "America's high schools are obsolete. By obsolete, I don't just mean that our high schools are broken, flawed, and under-funded . . . I mean that our high schools—even when they're working exactly as designed—cannot teach our kids what they need to know today. Training the workforce of tomorrow with the high schools of today is like trying to teach kids about today's computers on a fifty-year-old mainframe. It's the wrong tool for the times."[14]
- Speaking to the Hispanic Chamber of Commerce in 2009, President Barack Obama asserted, "We've let our grades slip, our schools crumble, our teacher quality fall short, and other nations outpace us. . . . The relative decline of American education is untenable for our economy, it's unsustainable for our democracy, it's unacceptable for our children—and we can't afford to let it continue. What's at stake is nothing less than the American Dream."[15]
- In submitting his blueprint for No Child Left Behind to Congress in 2001, former president George W. Bush declared, "We must confront the scandal of illiteracy in America, seen most clearly in high poverty schools where nearly 70 percent of fourth graders are unable to read at a basic level. We must address the low standing of America's test scores amongst industrialized nations in math and science. . . . We must focus the spending of Federal tax dollars on things that work. Too often, we have spent without regard for results."[16]
- The U.S. Chamber of Commerce, in the 2007 report *Leaders and Laggards,* declared, "Despite decades of reform efforts and many trillions of dollars in public investment, U.S. schools are not equipping our children with the skills and knowledge they—and the nation—so badly need." The report continued, "Throughout that period, education spending has steadily increased and rafts of well-intentioned school reforms have come and gone. But student achievement has remained stagnant, and our K–12 schools have stayed remarkably

unchanged—preserving, as if in amber, the routines, culture, and operations of an obsolete 1930s manufacturing plant."[17]

Despite the thunderous critiques, the proposed remedies are notable for their timidity. They tend to color safely within the lines— largely, it often seems, because those lines are so taken for granted that would-be reformers don't realize there is an alternative. After proclaiming high schools obsolete in 2005, Gates declared it vital to give all students "a challenging curriculum," "courses and projects that clearly relate to their lives and their goals," and "adults who know them, look out for them, and push them to achieve."[18]

Pledging to reverse school decline and restore the "American Dream," President Obama has called for states to "raise the quality of [their] early learning programs," promote "better standards and assessments," recruit and reward good teachers, and add more charter schools and time in school.[19]

To combat concerns about illiteracy, low international rankings, and ineffectual school spending, President George W. Bush's solutions largely amounted to an effort to promote scientifically based reading materials in elementary schools, the insistence that "children must be tested every year in reading and math" in grades three through eight, and the requirement that schools be accountable for students being minimally proficient in learning reading and math.[20]

Even *A Nation at Risk*'s grand vision of a hostile invasion yielded relatively mild recommendations: that curricular content be strengthened; that more academic courses be required; that achievement tests be used more widely, grades be tougher, and textbooks be better; that the school day and school year be lengthened, students do more homework, and attendance policies be strengthened; that aspiring teachers should meet high standards; that career ladders and performance metrics should be utilized; and that local, state, and federal leaders needed to help support schools.[21]

Given the ferocity of the indictments, the familiar contours of these measures are striking. Seen from an arm's length removed, the diagnoses generally amount to a concession that everyone can more or less go on about their business, so long as we demand more, do more, and spend more. In response, educators, parents, and policy makers all pretty much nod their heads in assent, take care to shave the discordant edges off any reforms, and then wonder why decades of reform yield little evident change.

It's not that the proposed remedies are bad, per se, but that they are pretty slim pickings given the enumerated challenges. Rigor and relevance are good. More charter schooling and extended learning time make good sense, as does rewarding good teaching. The whole *Nation at Risk* litany seems reasonable enough. But to a striking extent, all of these remedies accept the existing edifice as it stands. After first condemning it as "obsolescent," "plagued by mediocrity," and "crumbling," they settle for fiddling with course requirements, attendance policies, pay schedules, and assessments while the familiar building blocks—schools, classrooms, districts, staffing, teacher training, state oversight, Carnegie Units, salary schedules—remain intact.

When a fresh idea does happen to come along, it is all too often oversold as a miracle cure rather than a useful tool. Advocates demand that favored measures be adopted everywhere, as rapidly as possible—until a sensible idea is turned into an ill-conceived fad that eventually loses favor, to be replaced by another. This tyranny of sequential orthodoxies yields a conventional wisdom that holds sway until it is displaced by a new conventional wisdom. As Chester Finn Jr. has argued, in his postmortem on the quarter-century of activity that followed *Nation at Risk* reform, reformers must move past paeans to choice or accountability and focus instead on "more fundamental questions, challenging long-held assumptions about how education is managed, funded, designed, and overseen."[22]

We've spent too many years trying to fix schools in a hurry. That very urgency tends to feed the search for quick, one-size-fits-all solutions. The key to real, lasting improvement may lie not in frenzied activity but in finding the will to loosen the grip of old dogmas and open our eyes to new solutions.

"BUT IT'S NOT PUBLIC!"

Any such effort at rethinking, however, quickly crashes into a pha-lanx of critics who denounce proposals to rethink the shape or struc-ture of schooling as antieducation and antiteacher. The list of mor-ally dubious measures is long and familiar: performance-based pay; charter schooling; efforts to modify or end teacher tenure; mayoral control of school districts; school vouchers; hiring principals and superintendents from outside K–12; and virtual schooling. Often, we never even get to Finn's "more fundamental questions" because the fights over these measures are so long and heated. Many times, more energy is devoted to debating whether a proposal comports with re-flexive notions of "public schooling" than to whether it solves prob-lems. I am not suggesting that we retreat from the ideal of public schooling, but I am calling for a hard look at what that ideal requires and implies.

Defenders of public schools are often vociferous even as they are more than a little vague about just what it is they are defending. Edu-cational author Gerald Bracey explained a few years ago, "A war is being waged on America's public schools. They are under siege. Many entrepreneurs and some former U.S. Department of Education offi-cials are out to destroy them."[23] Paul Houston, former chief at the American Association of School Administrators, has warned, "If common schools go, we are no longer America [and yet] the past few decades have seen a full-scale assault on the institution of public ed-ucation and its place in American life."[24] Even popular radio person-ality and commentator Garrison Keillor has waded in, asserting, "Education is an expensive proposition but there's no choice: nobody is born smart and we need good schools. . . . When you wage war on the public schools, you're attacking the mortar that holds the com-munity together. You're not a conservative, you're a vandal."[25] Such formulations lend enormous weight to familiar definitions of a pub-lic school, encouraging those with skin in the game to belittle any attempt to rethink these aged institutions.

In a world where charter schooling, distance education, and alternative teacher licensure no longer fit neatly into our conventional pigeonholes, the public school label is less and less useful. For instance, traditional public schools have always dealt with for-profit providers of textbooks, teaching supplies, and professional development. With profit-seeking ventures such as EdisonLearning now providing summer school for dozens of districts, or working with districts to address schools identified for restructuring under No Child Left Behind, does this mean that some summer school programs are less public than others? Or that schools restructured with for-profits involvement are less public than are other schools?

We have already answered this question in other sectors. The Environmental Protection Agency and the Department of Health and Human Services hire for-profit ventures to help tackle toxic waste or provide children with health care. All government agencies, including public hospitals and public transit systems, routinely harness the services of various private operators while maintaining their claim on being public, so it seems at odds with our experience that education would lose this moniker by taking advantage of similar public-private partnerships. Ultimately, there are many legitimate ways to provide public education. The key is not whether providers are arms of the state or staffed by state employees, but whether they are hired with public dollars, overseen by public officials, and charged with serving public ends.

The principles that public schooling embodies can accommodate a much broader set of arrangements than we sometimes think. That makes it important to distinguish between the ends of schooling and the familiar arrangements by which these are served.

If public schooling is consistent with a more diverse set of approaches, then what might be the core principles that can preserve core values? For our purposes, public schooling should be broadly defined by a commitment to equip students to become productive members of a social order, aware of their societal responsibilities and respectful of constitutional strictures, in addition to helping them master a body of knowledge and skills that will provide opportunities once they reach the age of maturity. Rendered slightly more concretely, this requires a system of schooling where each student is able to access at least a minimally appropriate instructional setting that promotes universal literacy, numeracy, and basic skills; nurtures skills and talents; prepares youth for work or postsecondary schooling; and cultivates a respect for the privileges and duties of American citizenship.

If this sounds like a pretty broad mission statement, *that's exactly the point*. Rather than presuming that public schooling supposes a pinched set of acceptable arrangements, an emancipatory approach embraces the opposite stance—presuming that anything not expressly at odds with these general principles deserves consideration. Now, some readers will deem this list of principles to be narrow or incomplete. That's perfectly appropriate. The challenge I'd extend, then, is to respond not by imagining that public schooling is whatever happens to be in place today, but by offering additional or alternative principles. Whatever the merits of one list or another, this approach is valuable because it offers a frame for debating just what the core principles of schooling are. In doing so, it gets away from the food-fight dynamic of merely asserting that some proposal is an "attack on schooling" or, alternatively, that we need not worry ourselves about principle because this or that reform "works."

Let's be clear. I am not arguing that private management firms are necessarily effective, that charter schools are necessarily good, or that teacher licensure ought to be radically downsized—only that that we allow ourselves to consider these possibilities.

Branding measures like these as attacks on public schooling has real costs. Doing so stifles exploration of promising departures and breeds culture wars where we might otherwise find measured debate. Taking care to define public schooling so that it protects the sacrosanct, yet is less sweeping in its claims, can create a sturdier institution—one that welcomes competing perspectives on how to best serve our children. The task in this volume is not to prescribe what transformed twenty-first-century schooling should look like, but only to argue that it may look profoundly different from what we're used to, and that this belief ought not to be presumed to be a retreat from essential values.

WHAT'S CHANGED

I have suggested that there have been profound changes in the mission and the context of schooling over time, and it is essential to understand these. Just what are they, exactly? There are at least six worth noting: what we hope to achieve, what we want graduates to know, what values we want schools to teach, the job market for graduates, our ability to recruit teachers, and the tools for delivering schooling.

The Importance We Accord to Schooling

A century ago, barely one American in ten finished high school. Reformers spent the first half of the twentieth century battling to make high school completion a norm, and by the 1960s, they had succeeded. Now, the new goal is not just high school completion but also to ensure that every student be academically proficient and graduate rigorously prepared for a career or postsecondary education. This is something new under the sun. It can be difficult to appreciate just how unprecedented such sentiments are and how little cause we have to imagine that our current system of schooling is equipped for such a charge. After all, it was Thomas Jefferson, champion of public schooling and firebrand egalitarian, who explained that the states in the new republic needed to promote schooling, not so that all might be educated, but so the "best geniuses [could be] raked from the rubbish annually."[26]

In 1894, the Committee of Ten, a group of education luminaries, convened to help standardize high school curricula, which we will discuss later in further detail, bluntly declared, "The secondary schools of the United States, taken as a whole, do not exist for the purpose of preparing boys and girls for the colleges. Only an insignificant percentage of the graduates of these schools go to colleges or scientific schools. . . . The preparation of a few pupils for college or scientific school should in the ordinary secondary school be the incidental, not the principal object."[27]

Even into the middle of the twentieth century, the notion that schools could or should educate all students to a high level was dismissed by most educational leaders. As Harvard University president James Bryant Conant advised in 1959, "I should start by questioning the dogma one often hears that all the youth, irrespective of academic ability and interest, should complete grade twelve. Above all, the relation of education to employment of youth sixteen and over must be constantly kept in mind."[28] Conant found the famed post–World War II GI Bill "distressing" because it "failed to distinguish between those who can profit most by advanced education and those who cannot."[29] Such concerns were once not only respectable but the very height of conventional wisdom. Today, however, when thinkers such as American Enterprise Institute scholar Charles Murray echo Conant by questioning the value of boosting graduation rates or the feasibility of "universal proficiency," they are denounced as racist, classist, and reactionary. A dramatic new consensus has taken hold.

Over the vast majority of time in the last three centuries, our educational goals remained generally modest and primarily focused on expanding basic literacy. We can see how expectations have evolved if we consider not only the number of those deemed literate, but also the shifting definitions of literacy over time. Three centuries ago, in 1700, about 50 percent of New Englanders were literate in the sense that they could sign their names—and New England was regarded as the most educated region in the American colonies. That figure had climbed to 88 percent in 1795,[30] and by 1900, 89 percent of American adults could write.[31] And in 2003, 88 percent of adults were able to read and comprehend textually based writing.[32] Over time, even as literacy has become nearly universal, our notion of what it entails has become increasingly more ambitious.

Beyond literacy, we can see the push for increasing levels of proficiency across all other subjects as well. The No Child Left Behind Act of 2001 wrote into federal statute the expectation that 100 percent of K–12 students would be "proficient" in reading and math by 2014 (though the meaning of "proficiency" was left to the individual states). In 1998, President Bill Clinton was even more ambitious, telling the Education International World Congress that in the twenty-first century we could and should "guarantee universal, excellent education for every child on our planet" by relying upon "the explosion of technology and . . . the dedication of teachers."[33] Ambitions that once would have been deemed nonsensical have now become the norm.

The expectations can be heady, indeed. Sonia Nieto, professor of language, literacy, and culture at the University of Massachusetts School of Education, has declared, "Even under difficult conditions— one might well say *especially* under these conditions—public schools are the best hope for realizing the utopian vision of a democratic society."[34] In the same spirit, influential advocacy groups like the Education Trust and the National Council of La Raza, and political leaders from the Reverend Al Sharpton to former Republican House Speaker Newt Gingrich have proclaimed education the "new civil right" and asserted that American prosperity rests on our ability to educate every child. Indeed, a quiet revolution in aims has fundamentally altered our expectations for schooling.

What We Want Graduates to Know

For most of Western history, basic literacy and numeracy were thought to be more than sufficient for the needs of most students. In 1918, the Cardinal Principles of Secondary Education, perhaps the clearest statement of progressive ambitions for universal high school, suggested that high school curricula be geared with an eye to seven standards: "Health; command of fundamental processes; worthy of home-membership; vocation; citizenship; worthy use of leadership; [and] ethical character."[35] Our ambitions have since soared. Today, reform organizations of various stripes, such as Achieve, Inc. and the Partnership for 21st Century Skills, sketch broad, ambitious visions of the skills and knowledge all students must master. The upshot is that we insist upon all students mastering academic material to an unprecedented degree *and* that new skills such as "media literacy" and "information literacy" be accorded their place alongside older conceptions of essential content.[36]

For example, Achieve, Inc. proposes that all eleventh- and twelfth-grade students should be able to "effectively and purpose-fully employ conventional and unconventional visual images, text, graphics, music and/or sound effects . . . to convey explicit and im-plicit messages and achieve the purposes in complex media presen-tations."[37] An American Diploma Project benchmark for algebra holds that all students should be able to "determine the 126th term of the arithmetic sequence whose third term is 5 and seventh term is 29."[38] Knowledge at this level is well above anything we've previously expected our schools to teach or expected all students to master.

Even if we could snap our fingers and ensure that all students could clear these ever-rising bars of achievement, however, it would have only limited benefit when it came to preparing students for life beyond graduation. It's already been more than a decade since Rich-ard Murnane of Harvard University and Frank Levy of MIT ex-plained in *Teaching the New Basic Skills,* "During the past twenty years, the skills required to succeed in the economy have changed radically, but the skills taught in most schools have changed very little. As a result . . . a U.S. high school diploma is no longer a ticket to the U.S. Middle Class."[39]

Murnane and Levy thought that even if schools did a much bet-ter job, it would be insufficient because "the issue is not that U.S. education has declined . . . but the economy is changing much faster than the schools have improved."[40] They identified a set of "New

Basic Skills"—what they thought was the necessary minimum to land a middle-class job—which included the ability to read and do math at the ninth-grade level, to solve semi-structured problems in which hypotheses must be formed and tested, to work in groups with persons of various backgrounds, and to communicate orally and in writing.[41] While the exact composition of any such list is debatable, it is now assumed that students must master more complex skills and content than in the past.

We now aim to educate not merely some but all students, and we stipulate that all these students be educated to a degree that was once the province of the few. Our ambitions may be socially desirable and economically vital, but we should consider the possibility that our institutions may not be equal to these new demands.

The Values We Want Schools to Promote

From the time of the Greeks through the early twentieth century, the values that schools were to inculcate seemed relatively clear. Religious schools were to train youth to be faithful to the church, and, more relevant for our purposes here, state-run schools were to teach children to be faithful to the state. As Plato famously explained, "The children must attend school, whether their parents like it or not; for they belong to the state more than to their parents," a conviction that would find staunch adherents millennia later in the American colonies.[42] Founding Father Benjamin Rush, about whom more will be said in the next chapter, asserted, "Let our pupil be taught that he does not belong to himself, but that he is public property . . . [and] must forsake and even forget [his family] when the welfare of his country requires it."[43] Horace Mann, long-serving president of the Massachusetts School Board and champion of the nineteenth-century Common School reform movement, charged in 1837, "The obligations of the future citizen [should be] sedulously inculcated upon all the children of this Republic."[44] Schooling, for these thinkers and the systems they conceived, was not about individual students or their career prospects; it was about forging students into the *right kind* of citizen.

Today, conventional notions of patriotism centered on fealty to country and flag—those once deemed the central mission of schooling—are controversial. Historian David Labaree has pointed out that the U.S. Supreme Court's seminal decision in *Brown v. Board of Education of Topeka* reflected a larger shift in attitudes toward the purpose of schooling, observing, "For the Common School movement, schools were critically important in the effort to build a republic; their purpose was political. But for the Civil Rights movement, schools were critically important as a mechanism of social opportunity."[45]

Proposals that schools should teach immigrant children to break free from their native culture, to be obedient and deferential, or to reject "un-American" religions are today regarded as wrongheaded by leading educational thinkers. Noted education author Alfie Kohn, for instance, has assailed the claim that children should be "diligent, obedient, and patriotic." He disputed "whether these traits really qualify as moral"[46] and derided the emphasis on concepts like respect, responsibility, and citizenship "as euphemisms for uncritical deference to authority."[47]

As schools have downshifted their attempts to preach patriotism and "traditional" American culture, there has been a corresponding drive to celebrate the virtues of cultural diversity. Helping children of different backgrounds assimilate into a white Protestant culture was once viewed as the *sine non qua* of good schooling; it is now widely deemed nefarious. Diana Selig, professor of history at Claremont McKenna College, has characterized this new sensibility as the "cultural gifts" movement: signaling the notion that each culture makes unique contributions to American life.[48] Across large swaths of schooling, and most prominently in many colleges of education, a new conception of American cultural identity and of the mission of schooling has taken hold. In a stark illustration of how thinking has changed, the University of Minnesota's College of Education proposed in 2009 to require all of its aspiring teachers to acknowledge that students suffer from "white privilege, hegemonic masculinity, heteronormativity, and internalized oppression."[49]

Even those skeptics who resist the contemporary celebration of multiculturalism are far less attached to traditional definitions of Americanization than previous generations. The teacher's role is now more contested, less clear-cut, and certainly far less subservient to promoting a belief in the rightness of American life and the established order. If the purpose of schools is not to teach particular values or fidelity to the state but to accept and nurture diversity and democratize opportunity—then schools erected to build "republican machines" and promote state-approved values may be ill configured for their new duties.

The Prospects for Graduates

The labor market that high school graduates enter today is profoundly unlike that of the late-nineteenth and early-twentieth centuries when features of schooling like Carnegie Units, school calendars, and school governance practices started to take on their modern shape. At that time, a high school diploma—or formal education at all—was generally regarded as a luxury of limited practical relevance. Indeed, universal schooling was first pursued as an important tool for getting children out of the labor force and off the streets; what they would learn once they were in a classroom was a secondary concern.[50]

During the twentieth century, the economic center of gravity shifted from farming and manual labor to sectors dominated by professional, technical, and service workers. In 1900, almost 40 percent of the labor force worked on farms.[51] By 2000, that number had dropped to less than 3 percent.[52] The same trend is evident in the number of workers engaged in mining, manufacturing, or construction; the share of workers in those industrial jobs declined from 31 percent in 1900 to 19 percent in 2000.[53] And formal schooling, irrelevant for most jobs in 1900, had become nearly essential for good jobs by the century's end. Indeed, the percentage of college graduates in today's workforce exceeds the share of workers in 1915 who had *even attended high school*.[54]

In the mid-twentieth century, signs of the coming divide between workers with high school diplomas and those without were already evident in emerging industries. In 1940, over half the hires at burgeoning high-tech industries like aircraft manufacturing were high school graduates, while just one-tenth of the employees carried this credential in the shrinking cotton manufacturing sector.[55] Increasing technological demands further sped this trend as new labor market conditions produced a growing return to those with competitive workforce skills. Harvard University economists Claudia Goldin and Lawrence Katz have reported that the returns for completing a college education rather than just a high school education, for example, doubled from 1980 to 2005.[56] During that same period, the number of employees using computers at work more than doubled, from 25 percent in 1984 to 57 percent in 2003.[57] Wages for the educated were climbing while the demand for those without such skills was not. British scholar Philip Brown has summarized the shift: "The exponential increase in scientific and technical knowledge" in post-industrial societies has spurred demand for "technical, professional, and managerial workers."[58]

A century ago, a high school diploma distinguished a graduate and served as a valued credential; today, it's regarded as a stepping-stone of little inherent value. The demands of the information economy, the emergence of new sectors like biotechnology and aerospace, and the disappearance of first agricultural and then manufacturing jobs have made a quality education—and, increasingly, a college degree—the key to professional opportunity.

The Pool of Available Teachers

A century ago, schools could be careless about hiring talent because educated women had nowhere else to turn. Most women didn't work, and those who did disproportionately entered teaching. In 1900, for instance, women constituted just 1 percent of the nation's lawyers and 6 percent of its physicians. Meanwhile, 81 percent of working-age women were not employed.[59] This created (to borrow Karl Marx's memorable phrase) a vast "reserve army of labor" that could be drawn on to staff the growing school system. By 1999, the situation looked much different. Sixty percent of working-age women were in the labor force, and women comprised 29 percent of lawyers and 24 percent of physicians.[60] As economists Sean Corcoran, William Evans, and Robert Schwab have noted, "employment opportunities for talented women outside of teaching have soared," which has meant that "the likelihood that a female from the top of her high school class will eventually enter teaching has fallen dramatically from 1964 to 1992—by our estimation, from almost 20 percent to under 4 percent."[61] In other words, schools could no longer count on an immense reservoir of talented, educated women with few other employment options.

Most of the women who received a teaching degree in the early 1900s accepted a local teaching job and planned on teaching until they got married (or, later in the twentieth century, until they reached retirement age). Future teachers attended a sprawling array of geographically dispersed teacher colleges that trained and certified them to work in area schools. As the century wore on, teachers in these ordered bureaucracies welcomed a seniority-driven system of pay and benefits that rewarded long service.

Today, the labor market has changed. Post–World War II America's comfortable promise of lifetime employment with a single company has given way to a "free agent nation," where college graduates expect to change jobs more frequently, to be courted by prospective employers, and to be rewarded for excellent performance. This evolution was accompanied in the private sector by more portable benefit plans, 401(k)s, and efforts to more thoughtfully woo and cultivate talent. Whereas the average college graduate in the 1960s could expect to hold five jobs in the course of his or her working life, the same individual today will typically hold six jobs by the age of thirty-two.[62] The pool of twenty-first-century college graduates who plan to stay in their first job for twenty-five or thirty years offers slim pickings; add the expectation that employees will stay in one community for most of their working lives, and the available talent is winnowed further still.

It should be no surprise that arrangements that delivered the teachers we needed in the 1950s, when the nation employed 1 million public school teachers a year, are working less well today, as the nation employs nearly 3.3 million such teachers each year and competes within a very different labor market. The proliferation of options for working women and the dynamism of modern career paths mean that schools can no longer rely on their traditional source of hires. Those realities, along with an increasing demand for effective teachers able to make use of new data systems and technological tools, require schools now to compete for college-educated talent against a variety of public and private employers. These competitors pursue the most motivated and energetic candidates by proffering professional opportunities, material rewards, and a variety of work arrangements. A teaching profession that worked well enough when fueled by a plentiful supply of careerist, captive educators is poorly equipped to compete with those offerings today.

The Tools at Our Disposal

Our assumptions about the organization of school systems, schools, classrooms, and teaching are inherited from a time when communications, computing, travel, and data management were primitive by contemporary standards. It is easy to forget, in a world of smartphones, videoconferencing, and the Internet, how profoundly different the world looked in 1900, when less than 10 percent of American homes had electricity and American life did not feature yet-to-be-invented advances such as the refrigerator and dishwasher—much less the photocopier, calculator, or airplane.[63] Since that time, a series of new technologies have upended old routines and created new ways of communicating, interacting, and learning that would have been unthinkable at the dawn of American schooling.

As recently as 1985, for instance, obtaining a particular book entailed visiting a bookstore or checking it out of the local library. Writing a book report required a student to get the requisite material at school, visit the community library, or rely on the family encyclopedia. Enrolling in distance education meant using the U.S. Postal Service to receive printed material and submit tests and essays. Long-distance phone calls were expensive, most Americans had never been on a plane, and attempting to deliver tutoring or to manage schools in multiple locations was a daunting proposition.

Those circumstances have changed. Dramatic advances in technology, transportation, and data storage have created new possibilities for autonomy, decentralization, and customization. In recent decades, cell phones, e-books, laptop computers, MP3 players, the Internet, and related advances have revolutionized our ability to store, share, convey, and access information. In 1993, the U.S. Census reported that just 23 percent of households owned a personal computer; today, computers are nearly as common as televisions.[64] The iPod didn't exist in 2000; by the end of 2009, more than 220 million had been sold.[65] In 1985, only a handful of Americans had sent an e-mail, and most still relied upon landlines and letters. Today, anyone under thirty is likely to regard e-mail as unduly constricting, preferring more recent innovations like Twitter, Facebook, or text messaging.

The potential of new tools and technologies to upend teaching and learning has not escaped notice. New technologies create unprecedented opportunities for curricular customization; for schools to escape geographic constraints; for students to interact with teachers and each other in new ways; for parents to be looped into school-student communications; for teachers to escape the confines of their classroom; and for data systems that permit granular monitoring and intervention on a previously impossible scale.[66] Harvard Business School professor Clay Christensen has argued that Web-based learning is so accessible, convenient, and cost-effective that it will inevitably start displacing traditional K–12 course instruction.[67]

Confronted with such claims, skeptics sometimes echo the late Daniel Patrick Moynihan, who was fond of saying that producing a Mozart quartet two centuries ago required four musicians, four stringed instruments, and, say, thirty-five minutes, and that today it requires the same four musicians, four instruments, and thirty-five minutes. However, Christensen argues this analogy is incomplete and even misleading in the case of schooling. In the arts, what has changed over two centuries is that because of new technologies like radio, CDs, television, and digital media, the number of people able to *hear and appreciate* a given performance has increased dramatically, at an ever decreasing cost. Most obviously, these new tools mean that a gifted lecturer can now speak to hundreds or thousands of students, or that a talented tutor in New York City or even Nepal can work one-on-one with a child in Topeka or Tampa Bay. Improved technology has now made available to the general public what was once the preserve of the elite.

The challenge is to not romanticize any given technological advance but to ask how it might be used to solve problems in smarter ways. The question is not "Does this technology make schools obsolete?" but instead "Can it be used to improve delivery of instruction, recruiting, professional development, assessments, or the organization of school systems?"

THE DIFFERENCE BETWEEN "SCHOOLS" AND "SCHOOLING"

These changes make it necessary to stretch our critical faculties and contemplate how we envision, organize, and operate schools with fresh eyes. As Charles Bidwell and John Kasarda elegantly observed in their seminal 1980 article, "Conceptualizing and Measuring the Effects of School and Schooling," we tend to mistake schools, which are organizations where schooling takes place, with schooling, "a process that individual students experience." They explain that "Schools are organizations that conduct instruction. Schooling is the process through which instruction occurs. Schooling, which is comprised of acts by students and teachers, is conditioned by the social organization of classrooms, curricular tracks, and other instructional units within schools."[68] The failure to appreciate this distinction has led us to conflate the schools we know with what schooling can and should be.

The result? Status quo *schools* have become the measure used to gauge whether proposed alternatives to *schooling* are acceptable or legitimate. Of course, this means that any number of routines fifty or a hundred or two hundred years ago, for reasons good and bad, have come to serve as the defining features of public schooling. We frequently make this same mistake when we conflate "teachers" and "teaching"—a point discussed at more length later. Our system of schooling was never designed to answer the burdens now being laid upon it. It would be a miraculous thing indeed if a system that grew haphazardly over the course of centuries *was* the optimal means of answering a new and different set of challenges.

Responding to those who confuse the principle of democratic schooling with the machinery of today's public schools, those championing change can too easily get caught up in overheated critiques of those defending the status quo, romanticizing proposed reforms, or scrambling to marshal evidence that will "prove" their proposals are superior to outdated practices. In each case, the back-and-forth can distract us from identifying the practices that no longer make sense and from the central question of whether proposed reforms hold promise.

Let's briefly take each of these distracting tendencies in turn.

Union Bashing and Ad Hominem Attack

The teacher unions, in particular, seem to have a knack for driving their critics to distraction. As a result, unions become an all-purpose whipping boy, used to excuse inept system management and making it more difficult to distinguish real problems from the litany of complaints. The sensible course is to call unions out on their self-interest and their defense of problematic arrangements, but to do so in a fashion that acknowledges legitimate concerns and does not blame unions for inept school and school district management.

Too often, criticism of unions can morph into shrill caricature, and critics can too readily slip into ad hominem, demonizing language that distracts attention from the need to update creaky systems. Peter Brimelow begins his book *Worm in the Apple* with a description of the National Education Association as "a parasite upon the body educational," and proceeds to call unions "extraordinarily fat, for a start."[69] In 2004 then Secretary of Education Rod Paige characterized the teachers unions as "terrorist organizations."[70] Such language is unfortunate, because it has repeatedly led the vast majority of parents, voters, and policy makers to line up with the unions, and thus the status quo, rather than with their critics. A more deliberate and less ham-fisted line of criticism can enable observers to distinguish sympathy for teachers from support for troubling policies. Similarly, the claim that the unions are to blame for the plight of our schools has too often allowed superintendents and school boards to skate by, freeing them of responsibility to rework problematic contracts or overhaul sputtering school systems.

Schools of education have received much the same treatment, as have local school boards. The result is that the real problems with teacher unions and colleges of education can too readily be lost amidst the appearance of ideological witch-hunting, while sensible reforms become mired in ideology and personalities.

Romanticizing Reforms

A second problematic habit, as noted earlier, is the tendency to oversell proposed reforms. Rather than explain what's wrong with the way we pay or hire teachers or with school governance, would-be reformers and snake oil salesmen promote wondrous new solutions.

For example, champions of magnet schooling, desegregation, detracking, whole language instruction, and an array of other reforms argue that their pet cause is the key piece of the puzzle. Some of these efforts are innocuous, while others are positively harmful. "Differentiated instruction," for instance, is a pleasant enough sentiment that ultimately requires teachers to simultaneously instruct a variety of students, with various needs and varying levels of achievement, in a single classroom. While laudable in theory, the problem is that such reforms set unrealistic expectations for what most teachers will be able to do. In the case of differentiated instruction, this disconnect between expectations and reality may unwittingly reduce teacher effectiveness while making it more difficult to attract and retain enough quality educators.

The most ardent advocates of school vouchers and charter schooling also routinely argue that these measures, all by themselves, will revolutionize American schooling. Two decades ago, scholars John Chubb and Terry Moe sounded the starting gun on choice-based reform when they famously argued in their seminal *Politics, Markets, and America's Schools,* "Without being too literal about it, we think reformers would do well to entertain the notion that choice is a panacea. . . . It has the capacity all by itself to bring about the kind of transformation that, for years, reformers have been seeking to engineer in myriad other ways."[71]

When the quick fixes fail to work as advertised, both the solution and the underlying insight are written off amidst the backlash, and would-be reformers rush off in another direction to identify a new flavor of the month. We have seen this play out in full force in the past decade, as sensible notions of accountability that enjoyed broad bipartisan support in the late 1990s have come in for disdain due to frustration with the overwrought and overly strident No Child Left Behind Act. A whole range of sensible ideas have suffered the same fate when deeply etched problems proved more complicated than advocates first suggested.

The Consequentialist Gambit

In the past, education debates have too often seemed frustratingly impervious to evidence, but when combating the status quo and faddism, today's would-be reformers have leaned heavily on evidence to make their case. This has had real benefits. Research documenting the efficacy of different approaches to reading instruction has been invaluable. However, data have also been stretched far beyond the breaking point, often in an attempt to promote new orthodoxies. President Obama illustrated this tendency in 2009 when he touted his administration's Race to the Top proposals for charter schooling and improved data systems as "evidence-based," despite the glaring lack of compelling research to support any of the various measures.[72]

Consider the case of merit pay for teachers. Most research seeks to determine whether test scores go up after merit pay is adopted. This consequentialism asks whether linking salaries to student test results produces a predictable change in teacher behavior. Often it does. (No surprise there.) However, that Pavlovian strategy—which is not a whole lot more sophisticated in its vision of incentives than training a hamster to hit a lever to release food pellets—has little or nothing to do with the more fundamental argument for rethinking teacher pay. Assuming that the goal is to attract and keep talent in schooling, studies examining whether merit pay is associated with short-term bumps in student test scores on reading and math tests may be fundamentally misleading—none of the results reveal much about how altering pay and professional norms could help attract and retain more talented educators.

Indeed, the notion that rewarding performance ought to be subject to scientific validation before adoption is akin to suggesting that the National Institutes of Health should determine permissible compensation systems for doctors. If we applied that logic elsewhere in state government, presuming that states should only embark upon reforms whose merits have been "scientifically" validated, we may well never have automated revenue departments, streamlined departments of motor vehicles, or adopted measures to control urban sprawl. A healthy concern for the impact of reforms is desirable. The risk is that proponents use short-term or partial outcomes that can serve as a way to short-circuit honest debate or to promote easy "guarantees" rather than more problem-oriented rethinking.

In the end, absent a more coherent rethinking of salary structure, most merit pay proposals merely stack new bonuses atop entrenched pay scales while celebrating a new orthodoxy. All the existing commitments are taken as a given—meaning that such reform only comes by piling new dollars atop the old. In an era of tighter purse strings and overextended government, this is hardly a recipe for bold change.

THIS IS NOT A CASE OF PICKING ON SCHOOLS

The challenge we've discussed is not unique to education. Far from it. It is not that schooling should lead the rethinking of old arrangements and adapt to changing circumstances, but that schooling has lagged decades behind other less crucial sectors in doing so. Schooling is not the only sector that requires these changes; however, the role of elected officials in funding, governing, and operating school systems means that educational transformation requires conscious efforts to change policy and practice and cannot rely upon market forces and private action.

Most sectors regenerate as a matter of course. Old firms are constantly pressed to keep up with new entrants, or give way if they fail to adapt. Indeed, the average life span of a Fortune 500 company, from conception to dissolution, is only fifty years.[73] While most Fortune 500 companies built before 1950 are no longer with us, almost all of our school systems were in place by 1950—and most are the direct descendants of organizations that took shape more than a century ago. For better or worse, in education we cannot rely on the Darwinian dynamic. We are forced to push, prod, nudge, and pull the sector along. And that's why our ability to reimagine and revisit old assumptions becomes so critical.

It is not that individuals in other sectors are smarter or can see farther than individuals in education; the sheer number of misfires and failed businesses is a reminder that no one is particularly good at imagining the future. The advantage of market-based sectors is not wisdom or virtue but the ability to enable evolutionary change. In sectors where private operators work more freely, it is less necessary for anyone to consciously unwind existing policies, negotiate legislative changes, or reroute an entire statewide system every time a course correction is required.

The very system of schools that Americans have spent centuries assiduously building and then systematizing has been an enormous source of good and a point of pride; however, its intricate rules governing finances, governance, attendance, and the rest have also become a velvet cage.

PATH DEPENDENCY CAN HAPPEN TO ANYONE

All that said, the problematic expectation that we should keep doing things in some fashion simply because that's the way they've always been done is hardly unique to education. The tendency to stay the course, termed "path dependency" by social scientists, is a familiar phenomenon; for a good illustration, you only need to look as far as your computer . . . or your cell phone.

The QWERTY Keyboard

Did you ever glance at your laptop's keyboard and wonder why the keys are arranged that way? Odds are you work on a keyboard in which the first six letters on the top line are QWERTY. This so-called QWERTY keyboard was configured so as to keep the newly invented typewriter from jamming too frequently. While such concerns have receded, QWERTY remains the standard despite the existence of more efficient and user-friendly alternatives. Stanford University economist Paul David wrote in his article "Clio and the Economics of QWERTY" that consumers and producers are "held fast in the grip of events long forgotten and shaped by circumstances in which neither they nor their interests figured."

The original keyboard model, patented in 1867 by Christopher Sholes, was predisposed to key jams, especially when the keys for frequently used letters would collide. Sholes reorganized the keyboard to separate commonly utilized letter pairs, like "TH," to minimize jamming. In doing so, he shifted the letters from their original alphabetical order to something resembling the modern QWERTY standard. One modification, made at the behest of typewriter salesmen, involved switching the positions of the period mark "." and the "R". This made possible a little gimmick that allowed salesmen demonstrating for potential buyers to type "TYPE WRITER" while using only the top row of keys.

Competing designs emerged but never took hold. Ever heard of the Blickensderfer keyboard? Created in 1893, it was termed the "ideal" because its home row included the letters "DHIATENSOR," with which one could compose over 70 percent of the words in the English language. In 1936, educational psychologist August Dvorak created the Dvorak Simplified Keyboard, which sensibly shifted the vowels "AEIOU" and the most commonly used consonants, "DHTNS," to the home row. By this time the typewriter was in wide use, however. People were used to the familiar keyboard, and the cost of retraining individuals and replacing QWERTY keyboards was deemed prohibitive.[74]

The QWERTY keyboard, developed to avoid jammed keys in nineteenth-century typewriters, remains, more than a century later, the default design for computer keyboards. When IBM introduced the first personal computer in 1981, one advertised highlight was its inclusion of a QWERTY keyboard.[75] In a world where almost as many Americans have accessed the Internet via their phone as through their laptop, cell phone keyboards have become ubiquitous.[76] Yet while keyboards on these new electronic devices no longer even involve a typing position, they have all adopted the QWERTY format.[77] As August Dvorak wryly observed decades ago, "Changing the keyboard format is like proposing to reverse the Ten Commandments and the Golden Rule, discard every moral principle, and ridicule motherhood!"[78]

Employer-Based Health Care

A more significant example of path dependency is the United States' employer-based health insurance system, which took shape during and in the years following World War II. Employer-based health care got its start when the War Labor Board that President Franklin Roosevelt established shortly after the attack on Pearl Harbor started to set and enforce strict wage controls. The board opted, however, not to limit fringe benefits if they amounted to less than 5 percent of a worker's salary.[79] Companies competing for workers in a strapped wartime labor market began offering health insurance as a fringe benefit. By the war's end, enrollment in group hospital plans had jumped almost fourfold, to 26 million.[80] The resulting system worked passably well during the middle of the twentieth century, at a time when giant American corporations were stable, workers tended to stay with a single employer, and only a small number of retirees were collecting corporate health benefits.

The situation has changed markedly. As Democratic U.S. Senator Ron Wyden has noted, Americans are "shackled by the employer/employee relationship in health care, which isn't much different in 2008 from what it was in 1948. But economic challenges for business and workers today are very different than they were in 1948 . . . [when] employees who went to work at twenty stuck around long enough to get a gold watch."[81] Giant U.S. firms, most famously General Motors, have also been handcuffed by expansive health care obligations.

Meanwhile, by making the costs of health care invisible to consumers, employer-based insurance has been blamed for boosting demand, promoting overutilization, and fueling inflation in the sector. As Pulitzer Prize–winning columnist Charles Krauthammer has observed, "There is no logical reason to get health insurance through your employer. This entire system is an accident of World War II wage and price controls. It's economically senseless. It makes people stay in jobs they hate."[82] While there are sharp disagreements as to what should be done, there is widespread agreement that these old arrangements no longer make sense.

A free people have no obligation to alter routines or overturn existing institutions merely because some researchers claim they should or because more promising alternatives emerge. If a free people prefer to retain the QWERTY keyboard, employer-based health care, or the familiar system of schooling for whatever reason, that is certainly their prerogative. But when the issue involves the future of critical national institutions, the plight of tens of millions of children, and the fate of generations yet unborn, we are obliged to deliberate with an appreciation for costs and benefits and to not simply swaddle ourselves in a reflexive deference to routine. Our new ambitions in education call for an equally bold commitment to rethinking. It is not enough to merely walk the old path more briskly.

THE BOOK FROM HERE

One advantage of a historical perspective is that it can help us to elongate our gaze and to think past the circumstances and the orthodoxy of the moment. This process can remind us how we got here, temper us for inevitable uncertainties and difficulties, and rein in our foolish enthusiasms and taste for the quick fix. Failure to heed history makes it too easy to get caught up in the conventions of the moment, leaving would-be reformers to exhaust themselves in pursuits that will one day look foolish.

This phenomenon is hardly unique to education. Painful but wonderfully illustrative analogies are always available in the world of investment and finance. Consider the plight of Susan York, a fifty-year-old telecom equipment representative from Naples, Florida, who was frustrated in early 2009 by the dismal performance of her 401(k). York told the *Washington Post* that, one Sunday morning, her husband saw an infomercial touting the benefits of trading stock options. York was intrigued. After attending a few seminars, York, who confessed to little prior investment knowledge, started trading at precisely the moment the market took off on a turbo-boosted ascent after a historic crash. Thrilled by her early returns, she quit her job to become a full-time trader. York marveled in late summer 2009 that she had made an average of 40 percent a month in her first few months, enthusing, "It's the best job I've ever had, not just for the enjoyment but from the compensation standpoint."[83] Of course, if Susan York had paid more attention over time, she might have recalled the eager stock traders who radiated similar enthusiasm during the late 1990s "dot-com" bubble, or the real estate investors who were similarly impressed by their good fortune during the 2001–2006 housing bubble, before seeing their fortunes later turn. If she had been paying attention, York might have thought to wonder whether she was misreading the signs and merely taking one more spin around a well-worn track.

Much like novice investors who have never learned the lessons of our boom-and-bust cycle, so new waves of bright-eyed would-be reformers can too readily imagine that their insights, strategies, and techniques are unlike anything that has come before. Just as those investors can only watch, puzzled, when their fortunes turn, so the champions of site-based management, block scheduling, small high schools, and the rest have watched seemingly surefire brainstorms fail to live up to their early billing. Grasping the lessons of the past can leave reformers better able to distinguish the important from the ephemeral and to gird themselves for the slow, patient, and difficult work of emancipating a hidebound system from its shackles.

Much of our energy in recent decades has been directed toward asking schools to do more things for more people, and to do them better. Our operative assumption has been that this demand will simply require more resources, expertise, and passion. However, the price for asking anyone—educator, engineer, or elephant trainer—to do lots of different things is that they will tend not to do them well. This posed little cause for concern in an earlier era, when the amount of schooling mattered more than its quality. But our priorities have changed.

Answering the call begins not by simply pledging "more, and better" or latching onto popular new orthodoxies, but by diagnosing the problems to be addressed. This book aims to help with that task. From here, chapter 2 briefly touches upon key issues regarding the birth of the American educational system. Chapter 3 will offer a bit of a time-out, as we take a step back into the broader Western educational tradition so as to gain useful perspective on a few key issues. Chapter 4 will consider the Common School project and the bureaucratic legacy that it bequeathed to us. Chapter 5 discusses the Progressives and the consequences of their successful push to universalize schooling, particularly the endless conflicts over instruction, the import of input-based metrics, and the crude attempts to quantify outputs. Be forewarned: the purpose of this effort means that I focus upon the eras in which American schooling took shape rather than the more familiar history of the post–civil rights era.

Chapters 6 and 7 shift gears to demonstrate more concretely why a variety of measures that once made sense deserve to be rethought and how the broader themes of the earlier chapters can be applied. Chapter 6 explains why a teaching profession shaped by the "best practices" of an earlier era is ill suited for the twenty-first century. In chapter 7, I similarly argue that various institutional arrangements that once made sense now impede more promising solutions. In chapter 8, I contend that much of what passes for reform today is hampered by a failure to fully understand the challenges we face, and I suggest that we forgo the pursuit of new orthodoxies in favor of a consciously diverse world of schooling that builds upon American traditions of decentralization, diversity, and dynamism. Finally, in a closing epilogue, I offer some thoughts on the challenges posed by our situation and how we might address them.

In a nation as dynamic and diverse as ours, is it ludicrous to think that dynamism and diversity should help to define our educational system? In a nation where public and private ventures commingle as they do nowhere else on earth, where individual initiative and entrepreneurial activity are hallmarks of our national character, why imagine that state-run bureaucracies should have a monopoly on running our schools? Rather than seek consensus and uniformity, let us revel in a world of schooling that embraces competing pedagogies, missions, and approaches. Instead of worrying that such diversity is a problem, let us recognize it as a strength, as an opportunity for a rich mix of educators to educate children with an enormous array of needs and skills.

Absent a willingness to rethink the shape of schooling, improvement fueled by instructional coaching and best practices will remain a frustrating, grinding attempt to push uphill even as our feet keep slipping beneath us. When the path ahead is treacherous or obstructed, it can help to take a step or two backward in search of a better route. Let's take that step.

2 The American Education Tradition

"The ultimate result of the whole scheme of education would be the teaching [of] all the children of the State reading, writing, and common arithmetic."

—Thomas Jefferson, *Notes on the State of Virginia*

"Should [learning] become universal it would be as destructive to civilization as universal barbarism."

—Benjamin Rush

A little more than a decade ago, David Stratman, former director of governmental relations of the National PTA and author of *On the Public Agenda,* delivered a heralded keynote address to the Massachusetts Association of School Superintendents. Stratman explained that the "education reform movement in Massachusetts and the nation is part of a decades-long corporate and government attack on public education and on our children. Its goal is . . . not to raise the hopes and expectations of our young people but to narrow them, stifle them, and crush them; [and] not to improve public education but to destroy it." This dastardly reform agenda included efforts to promote charter schooling, school choice, higher standards, testing, and accountability.

Stratman coolly revealed that "the aggressive effort . . . to discredit public education" stemmed from the fact that "our young people have more talent and intelligence and ability than the corporate system can ever use . . . [so] their expectations must be downsized and their sense of themselves restructured to fit into the new corporate order." In a state where less than 40 percent of fourth graders were proficient in reading or math according to the National Assessment of Educational Progress, Stratman told the superintendents,

"You are under attack not because you have failed—which is what the media and the politicians like to tell you. You are under attack because you have succeeded—in raising expectations which the corporate system cannot fulfill."

As noted already, Stratman's sentiments are hardly unique. Indeed, his concluding exhortation illuminates a vision of schooling that continues to shape the education debate: "At the heart of the public education system, there is a conflict over what goals it should pursue.... We can prepare students for unrewarding jobs in an increasingly unequal society, or we can prepare our young people to understand their world and to change it. The first is education to meet the needs of the corporate economy. The second is education for democracy."[1]

Critics of what we have termed "emancipatory" reforms are quick to play the "democracy" card, intimating that they are defending schools from structural changes designed to undermine institutions committed to democratic opportunity. But this presumes that today's system is actually fulfilling its mission. If it's not, then our choice is *either* to preserve the public institutions we know *or* to promote the public purposes of schooling. Indeed, defenders of the status quo wax rhapsodic about the majesty of our democratic schools without ever paying much attention to where they came from or what it is about them that is distinctively democratic. They impute an inevitability and high-mindedness to what are in fact makeshift responses to the exigencies of an earlier era.

When the rhetoric starts flying, we can too easily forget that contemporary American schooling was not born of *Brown v. Board of Education of Topeka* or *A Nation at Risk*. To understand how expectations have changed, and what purposes our institutions were designed to solve, it is useful to set down the bustle of moral urgency and take the time to glance backward. With that in mind, let us briefly visit the birth of the American educational tradition.

THE AMERICAN FOUNDING

The American Revolution severed the thirteen colonies from the monarchy, feudal society, and aristocratic social order that had shaped Europe. The Founders' experiment in republican government prompted them to question the role of schooling in shaping citizens. While they disagreed on much, they adamantly agreed that the new nation could not simply adopt European institutions but must instead create its own.

America's founders saw schools primarily as places to shape and mold citizens into "republican machines," in Benjamin Rush's none-too-delicate phrase. They had no illusions or expectation that democratic schools would yield equal citizens; they variously saw schools as sifting out the most talented youth or even as reinforcing wealth-based class distinctions. Historian Gerald Gutek has observed, "The colonists believed in a two-track system of schools—one for the poor and another for the wealthy." They envisioned a system where the children of workers and peasants would receive a basic primary education in reading, writing, arithmetic, and religion, while the upper classes' male children would begin their schooling at a Latin Grammar school, then proceed to a college preparatory institution, and finally to college.[2] The contrast with today's ambitions is stark.

With distinct ideas on what they didn't want to see replicated in American education, the colonists developed some loosely organized and locally funded "public" grammar schools, but generally only in the densely populated urban centers. Colony-wide laws mandating or regulating education were rare, with the exception of a few New England colonies.

Massachusetts was the first among these, as Bay State reformers led the gradual push for larger, more organized systems of state-run schools which became the cornerstones of our modern educational system. The steps that Massachusetts took in the 1630s and 1640s to provide a regular system of schools in all towns by mandating a system of local taxation were new measures in the English-speaking world. Perhaps the most important of these laws was the Massachusetts Law of 1647, also known as the "Old Deluder Satan Law," which mandated that "every town having fifty householders should at once appoint a teacher of reading and writing" or be assessed a financial penalty.[3]

Despite such efforts, most schooling was informal and far from systematic at the time of the Revolution; however, a rough hierarchy of institutions did emerge. Petty (or "dame") schools, much like modern preschool, taught young children the basics of spelling and reading and sometimes offered some training in skills like sewing. The only schools in which teachers were typically women, dame schools typically met in the woman's own home. In some cases, dame school completion was required for admission to the local grammar school.

It was in town grammar schools, the crude equivalent of today's public elementary schools, that local children were taught reading, writing, and some math. Instructors tended to be young men or those without better career options. Latin grammar schools, the closest thing to today's college preparatory school, were most common in New England and offered instruction to boys from about the age of eight to fifteen (corresponding to the equivalent of grades two through nine, or so). While graduates were usually ignorant of numbers and unable to write English with much fluency or accuracy, attendance at these schools was the path to a university education.[4]

Many children, especially those from families of modest means, were educated primarily through apprenticeships. This involved learning a craft under an established craftsman, typically a relation or family friend. These arrangements were sometimes voluntary and sometimes entailed indentured servitude, as when orphans would be forcibly placed by town officials. Laws often stipulated that apprentices receive basic instruction in reading and religion, though follow-through on this score was iffy.

Schools frequently convened in the local church, while local school affairs and spending were often coordinated by the head of the local church or the church elders. Parish elementary schools, similar to today's parochial schools, provided an educational alternative to the grammar school. These church-supported schools were typically led by a church leader and concentrated on teaching local children religion and reading. Historian David Tyack has observed that, in the early nineteenth century, there was no clear distinction between "public" and "private" education. Tyack notes, "States liberally subsidized 'private' academies and colleges while towns and cities helped to support 'private' charity schools" in the assumption "that institutions sponsored by individuals or sects would serve the public interest."[5]

The differentiation of American education from British traditions was paramount for many early reformers. Noah Webster, famed author of the first American dictionary, published a collection of essays in 1790 that included the influential "On the Education of Youth in America," in which he argued the importance of molding schools to fit the nation's new government. He thought it would be an "absurdity" for America to adopt its institutions from those of the monarchy.[6] The next year, Robert Coram, a schoolmaster in Delaware, would publish his "Plan for the General Establishment of Schools throughout the United States." Coram argued that American democracy required a form of schooling distinct from that practiced under Europe's monarchies. Coram wanted to see "no modes of faith, systems of manners, or foreign or dead languages" taught, but only the knowledge, skills, and habits of mind likely to produce good republicans.[7] He envisioned an outsized influence for these schools, with "A System of Equal Education" serving to "transmit light, life and harmony to all under its influence."[8] In the plan, Coram made clear his dissatisfaction with the status quo, devoting one chapter to the "Wretched State of the Country Schools, through the United States; and the Absolute Necessity of a Reformation."[9]

While many opined on the question of schooling in the Founding Era, I shall not try to survey the entire landscape; given our purpose, doing so would unduly and unnecessarily tax both the author and reader. Instead, we will be well-served to focus on the thinking of two men who were among the most influential early American advocates for public schooling: Benjamin Rush of Pennsylvania and Thomas Jefferson of Virginia.

Benjamin Rush

Twenty-one years old at the time of the Revolution, Rush was a signatory of the Declaration of Independence and a member of the Continental Congress in 1776 and in 1777.[10] In 1783, he founded Dickinson College, and prior to the Revolutionary War, he taught as a professor at the University of Pennsylvania (then the College of Philadelphia).[11] He would ultimately return to that position after serving as the surgeon general of the Continental Army.[12]

In 1786, Rush addressed the Pennsylvania legislature to deliver his essays "A Plan for the Establishment of Public Schools and the Diffusion of Knowledge in Pennsylvania" and "Thoughts upon the Mode of Education Proper in a Republic." Outlining the benefits of an educated citizenry, he argued that schooling would promote religion, liberty, good government, manners, agriculture, and industry. Schools were to be a means for supplying the new republic with a skilled and obeisant citizenry. Rush explained, "The business of education acquired a new complexion by the independence of our country," and "in laying the foundations for nurseries of wise and good men, [we need] to adapt our modes of teaching to the peculiar form of our government."[13]

Rush called for a free school to be established in every township, roughly one school for every one hundred families, and to provide universal education at the public's expense. All citizens—rich and poor—would attend tax-supported free schools. Rush reasoned that both rich and poor would have a say in choosing the nation's leaders and that all citizens should therefore receive a basic education (he was not concerned with the education of slaves, since they were not to have a voice in elections). All children would receive training in reading, writing, and arithmetic. However, Rush very deliberately sought to ensure that only a limited number of individuals would receive schooling beyond this minimal standard. Seeking to balance the need for "learning and labor," Rush suggested that education beyond basic schooling be provided publicly only to those whose parents could afford it.

Flatly rejecting the notion that schools should be engines of social leveling, Rush believed that class distinctions were necessary to maintain social order.[14] Indeed, he would have rejected the universalist impulses championed today by those who most eagerly celebrate the system of schooling he helped promote. As Rush wrote, "Should [learning] become universal it would be as destructive to civilization as universal barbarism."[15] Rush believed that a prosperous republic required social stability and that universal learning would breed dissatisfaction among the lower classes. He wanted schools to cultivate stability by imbuing students with the right sorts of republican notions, which included teaching those both of higher birth and of lower birth to embrace their lot in life. "From the observations that have been made it is plain," he explained, "that I consider it is possible to convert men into republican machines. This must be done, if we expect them to perform their parts properly, in the great machine of the government of the state."[16]

While Rush was unusual in his strong support for the schooling of women, he explained in a 1787 address to the Young Ladies' Academy in Philadelphia that he thought they required a distinctive education. Further, he believed that American girls needed to be educated quite differently from their British counterparts, in light of the differences in "society, manners, and government" between the two nations.[17] Rush thought it essential for American women to learn reading, grammar, handwriting, basic math, geography, history, basic science, vocal music, dancing, poetry, and religion; arguing that, if the women of a society were properly educated, prudence and wisdom would blossom throughout the citizenry.[18]

Concerned that Americans had retained many laws, opinions, and manners from Europe's corrupted monarchies, Rush thought it essential that schools also teach "the art of forgetting." The point for Rush was less the content and knowledge that students might master than it was the wiping away of Continental frailties and ingraining American sentiments. As he asserted with characteristic bluntness, "I wish to see a supreme regard to their country inculcated upon them."[19] Given the crucial formative role of schooling, Rush wanted teachers to be "exemplary in their morals, and of sound principles in religion and government" and thought they should be granted "liberal salaries" provided by the state.[20] In an argument that will be familiar to contemporary readers, Rush argued that this investment would pay for itself because an educated public would allow leaders to avoid expensive mistakes by learning from the experiences of the past and by reducing the crime rate.[21]

Thomas Jefferson

Thomas Jefferson, author of the Declaration of Independence, third president of the United States, and founder of the University of Virginia, played a seminal role in shaping American educational thought. In 1776, Jefferson turned down a seat in the Continental Congress to return to Virginia and sit in the state legislature, where his primary interest was reforming Virginia's education system. In 1779, Jefferson was part of a committee that put forward "A Bill for the More General Diffusion of Knowledge," which eventually served as a blueprint for the state's system of schooling.[22]

Jefferson believed that establishing some sort of public education system was essential to preserving American democracy, famously asserting, "If a nation expects to be ignorant and free, in a state of civilization, it expects what never was and never will be."[23] While deemed a radical egalitarian in his day, even Jefferson never imagined an agenda of universal schooling—much less the ambitions of those who today talk of universal proficiency and "college for all."

As American education historian Rush Welter dryly observed in 1962, "Although Jefferson's Bill for the More General Diffusion of Knowledge provided for three years of elementary public education for all children, it sought chiefly to arrange for the selection of potential leaders from the mass of the people—and Jefferson, after all, was a radical for his times."[24] When it came to women, Jefferson believed that a basic education was necessary but, as he observed in a letter to Nathaniel Burwell in 1818, "A plan of female education has never been a subject of systematic contemplation with me."[25]

Jefferson envisioned a system comprised of three levels of schooling: primary schools, grammar schools, and universities. Counties were to be divided into districts that would each have a primary school.[26] There, children would receive a basic education, consisting of the three Rs and obtained by reading from books that would teach them about Grecian, Roman, English, and American history. All free children in the district, male and female, would be entitled to three years of schooling at public expense; thereafter, the parents of students who wished to continue would pay a fee.[27] The universal education provided by primary schools was intended to "instruct the mass of our citizens in these, their rights, interests, and duties, as men and citizens."[28] Even when it came to elementary education, however, Jefferson did not champion compulsory schooling, arguing, "It is better to tolerate the rare instance of a parent refusing to let his child be educated, than to shock the common feelings and ideas by the forcible [transportation] and education of the infant against the will of the father."[29]

Jefferson thought two kinds of citizens would emerge from primary school education. He explained, "The mass of our citizens may be divided into two classes—the laboring and the learned. The laboring will need the first grade of education to qualify them for their pursuits and duties; the learned will need it as a foundation for further acquirements."[30] Those "destined for labor" would begin work in agriculture or enter apprenticeships. Members of the learned class would move on to a much smaller number of grammar schools, where they would be taught foreign languages, grammar, geography, and higher math.[31]

Because Jefferson desired to break down the birth-based aristocracy, he proposed a system designed for promising young boys from families that could not afford grammar school. Each year, overseers would pick one boy from each school who showed the "best and most promising genius and disposition" but whose parents were too poor to provide further education. The following year, they would be educated and boarded at public expense.[32] After one year of free education, inspectors would eject one-third of the scholarship students, weeding out those who appeared least promising. After two years, one scholarship student would be selected for further study.[33]

From the pool of twenty scholarship students who would graduate from grammar school under this system each year (Jefferson proposed twenty grammar schools across the state), the single boy who demonstrated "the best learning and most hopeful genius and disposition" would be sent to the College of William & Mary for three years at the state's expense.[34] Though Jefferson's 1789 plan called for an initial cohort of 153 boys to receive free schooling at the grammar schools each year, a reworked proposal he put forward in 1817 slashed this potential population to just eighteen.[35] So, not only did Jefferson's radical egalitarianism envision that, in the nation's largest state, just one boy per year would merit a publicly supported college education, but—when he revisited this plan more than a quarter-century after first proposing it—he sharply reduced the suggested annual cohort of grammar school students!

An Aristocracy, but of Merit

The democratic revolutionaries Jefferson and Rush accepted the notion of aristocracy, but they sought a different kind of aristocracy that set aside monarchical notions of privilege. A significant portion of those who came to the colonies during the seventeenth century were the second sons of landed gentry in England. Not surprisingly, they cast a skeptical eye on the feudal practice of primogeniture, in which fathers left their entire estate to the first-born son. It was Jefferson who introduced legislation in Virginia in 1776 to eradicate primogeniture,[36] and the practice was formally abolished in all states between 1784 and 1796.[37]

This change marked a radical assault on conventional European notions of aristocracy. In its place, Founders like Jefferson and Rush did not advocate a radical egalitarianism but a new conception of aristocracy—one rooted in merit rather than birth. As Jefferson wrote to John Adams in 1813, "I agree with you that there is a natural aristocracy among men. The grounds of this are virtue and talents."[38] Observing and accepting the hierarchy of merit, both Jefferson and Rush wished to preserve a division between the laboring and the learned.

For Rush, education was a tool for *creating* the two classes. For Jefferson, it was a means by which to *identify* the two classes. Rush sought an aristocracy that would be based upon the education obtained in colleges and universities because, he thought, this was where real learning would be reserved for those students whose families could afford the tuition. The laboring class would be formed by the mass of boys whose families could not afford continued education. Rush's goal in all this was a stable social order. Where he saw stability in the transfer of advantage or disadvantage from one generation to the next, contemporary observers see injustice and potential instability.

Jefferson proposed a very different division of the laboring and learned than did Rush. His "natural aristocracy" (as opposed to the "pseudo-aristocracy" based on wealth and birth) was to reflect individual virtue and talent. For this reason, it was necessary to educate both poor children and rich insofar as it enabled educators to find "worth and genius . . . from every condition of life."[39]

In calling for universal excellence, today's reformers set for themselves a far more ambitious aim than Jefferson or Rush ever contemplated. Indeed, where disparities in wealth and educational opportunity worked in concert for Rush, advantaging the wealthy and restraining the poor, today's reformers seek to counter inherited disadvantage. The modern educational ethos echoes Jefferson's commitment to the equality of opportunity, but with an unshakable faith in the ability of all youth to learn that would have shocked the most radical egalitarians of the Enlightenment.

Early Plans for an "American" System of Schooling

Building upon the thinking of Rush, Jefferson, and their peers would become a cottage industry in the early years of the republic. A window into the most expansive thinking of that era is proffered by participants in an American Philosophical Society contest held shortly after the conclusion of the American Revolution. Contestants were asked to describe "the best system of liberal Education and literary instruction, adapted to the genius of the Government of the United States."[40] In the end, the prize was split between Samuel Knox and Samuel Harrison Smith for essays that offer a revealing peek into the aspirations of that era.

Knox, a former Presbyterian minister and headmaster of Frederick Academy in Fredericktown, Maryland, fretted that the localized system of the colonial period could undermine the new American democracy due to "the precarious uncertainty of casual, partial or local" efforts.[41] He thus called for a system that would be "established uniformly and generally by the united wisdom and exertions of a whole nation." Given that the United States was a product of "citizens blending together almost all the various manners and customs of every country in Europe," he wrote, it was especially important to "harmoniz[e]" the new people via a "uniform system of national education." To do that, Knox championed a uniform national curriculum with uniform textbooks throughout the land.[42]

The question that plagued Knox was to whom such a curriculum ought to be geared. More than two centuries ago, we can see Knox sidestepping the tough questions with precisely the same focus on process and with the same airy sentiments favored today. "The course of education," Knox wrote, should be designed for "youth in general, whether they be intended for civil or commercial life, or for the learned professions."[43] If that wasn't sufficiently vague, Knox elaborated that it would be "narrow and illiberal" for schooling to focus only on "knowledge of mechanical, commercial or lucrative arts; or even a knowledge of the world, as far as it can be attained by literary accomplishments."[44] As for putting this system into practice, Knox advised, "There ought to be a Printer in each State, for the express purpose of supplying the various seminaries, in their respective states, with such school-books and other literary publications, as should be recommended or directed."[45]

Samuel Smith's winning entry also envisioned the need for an ambitious state role, given his limited faith in the ability of parents to educate their own children. Smith was an influential publisher who came to Washington, D.C., at the request of Thomas Jefferson to establish the *National Intelligencer,* the leading daily Washington newspaper at the time.[46] Smith was also a member of the American Philosophical Society, founder of the Washington Library in 1811,[47] and president of the Washington branch of the Bank of the United States.[48]

In his winning proposal, Smith wrote, "It is the duty of a nation to superintend and even to coerce the education of children" and that "high consideration of expediency" required a public education system that would be "independent of, and superior to, parental authority."[49] Echoing Rush, Smith thought it necessary to remind parents "that their children belong to the state" and that a child's schooling should "conform to the rules which it prescribes."[50]

Smith proposed the establishment of a national board charged to "form a system of national education to be observed in the University, the colleges, and the primary schools; to chuse [sic] the professors of the University; to fix the salaries of the several officers; and to superintend the general interests of the institution."[51] He envisioned a board with one representative from each of what he deemed the fourteen major components of the curriculum, including representatives for "manufactures," "military tactics," and "elements of taste, including the principles of . . . gardening."[52]

Finally, Smith was particularly concerned about the impact of misguided parents on the beliefs of new citizens. He explained, "Error is never more dangerous than in the mouth of a parent. . . . Prejudices are as hereditary as titles."[53] The need to gauge the state of schooling, promote national norms, and address the demand for vocational education without compromising academic instruction—these modern aims were evident in the grand designs of would-be reformers more than two centuries ago.

FROM A MEANS TO AN END

Until the past few decades, the dominant educational tension in the United States has been between families leery of being forced to have their child subjected to state-directed education and the desire of the state to mold students in desired ways. As we note in the chapters ahead, these clashes would take the form of arguing over which Bible students should read in school and even whether private schooling ought to be permissible at all. In the modern era, however, the ground beneath this debate has shifted in important ways. In the past half-century, most notably since the U.S. Supreme Court's historic ruling in *Brown v. Board of Education of Topeka,* the demand for a free, quality education has gradually come to displace demands to be left alone.

The notion that every individual has a right to rise as high as their talents might take them is a thoroughly contemporary and peculiarly American ideal, one seemingly implicit in the Founders' vision of an "inalienable right to life, liberty, and the pursuit of happiness," but one that was also alien to the educational system that those Founders contemplated. The expectation that most or all citizens might climb into the aristocracy of merit would have struck America's Founders as naïve, misguided, or even dangerous. Indeed, the only Founder who could envision a world in which all students reach high levels of proficiency was Rush—but the prospect struck him as such a perilous recipe for social disorder that he advocated for a system of schooling that *would not democratize opportunity*. In other words, the only Founder who deemed today's aspirations possible agitated for a system intended to avoid them.

Government-run schools staffed by employees selected and monitored by public authorities may be a sensible way to help construct the "republican machines" that Rush thought necessary for a nascent republic. But that approach seems a poor match for our ambitions in the twenty-first century. Today's reformers, who broadly agree that most students have the ability to succeed at high levels and wish to see schooling trump the effects of class and family, are engaged in a profoundly ambitious social project. Their noble hopes mark a profound break with historic norms. Indeed, the fact that such ambition is, at most, a few decades old would seem to counsel reflection, humility, and the importance of asking whether aged public bureaucracies and schools designed to guard against the perils of runaway democratization are equipped to discharge our modern agenda.

3

The Long View

"We'll persuade nurses and mothers to tell the approved tales to their children and to shape their souls with tales more than their bodies with hands."

—Plato

"Formal instruction should be 'one and the same for all.'"

—Aristotle

Like someone standing too close to an elaborate mural, our proximity to the contemporary education debates can make it difficult to grasp the larger picture. We've stepped back a few paces, seeking a broader perspective on the Founders' approach toward schooling. Let's take just a moment and back up a bit further. Just as a longer view of American history can help in emancipating ourselves from a myopic focus on today's verities, a longer view of the Western educational tradition can put the American experience in a larger frame. To do so, we'll focus on a couple of tensions and developments that pointed the way to the American educational tradition and that foreshadow some of the key challenges we still wrestle with today.

I am not about to attempt even a thumbnail sketch of the relevant history. Such a task is beyond our purposes and would require more time than we have. As I've noted previously, there are many other scholars who have penned such accounts and done so far more expertly than I could here. Rather, my intent is to flag a few key themes that are critical for the purposes of this volume, illustrating how fundamental, long-running, and irreconcilable are some of the central educational debates that we keep hoping to "solve." We'll also get useful insight as to just how hoary and anachronistic were some of the building blocks of American schooling even in the time of the Common School reformers. And finally, we can see how some arrangements that are denounced (or celebrated) today as novel—like paying some teachers more than others or giving families more control over choosing schools and instructors—have claims to legitimacy that stretch back toward the earliest days of Western education.

Surveying the sweep of two millennia, we see that a variety of arrangements that have emerged over time have today been adopted or rejected with little attention to whether the resulting arrangements are well designed to serve today's students. So, let's pause here for a quick time-out and briefly consider the longer backdrop for seven issues that continue to loom large in education debates today.

HOW MUCH UNIFORMITY IS NECESSARY?

No Child Left Behind and the more recent push for "common" (for example, "national") standards have once again brought front and center questions about how uniform expectations for student mastery ought to be. In debates over these questions, essentialists pulling for an explicit content-based core, "twenty-first-century skills" advocates championing a broader and more amorphous mix of knowledge skills, and child-centered pedagogues skeptical of a mandated standard curriculum battle on in the conviction that, if they marshal enough experts and evidence, this time we'll get it right. Absent is the humility implicit in recognizing that there may not be a "right" answer. Indeed, the challenge is as old as Western education.

The conviction that there are certain, essential things that all children need to know can be traced back to Plato's *Republic* and its instructions on raising virtuous citizens. As Plato, the Greek philosopher and one of the Western world's foundational thinkers on education, instructed, "Carefully censored literature and music, selected for its formative influence, would help model the character of the developing child."[1] Plato was particularly adamant that tales and stories, both true and untrue, be selected in order to cultivate the right attitudes and habits of mind. He explained, "We must supervise the makers of tales. . . . We'll persuade nurses and mothers to tell the approved tales to their children and to shape their souls with tales more than their bodies with hands."[2]

Aristotle, Plato's student and intellectual heir, extended his mentor's vision, arguing that uniformity in good citizenship meant that "formal instruction should be 'one and the same for all,'" for those fortunate children who would be citizens and therefore required schooling.[3] For that select population of children, Aristotle proposed that their education should always entail instruction in gymnastics, reading and writing, simple arithmetic, drawing, and music. In essence, the notion of a "standard curriculum," focused on academics and the arts, can be traced back over more than two millennia.

So, does this mean that Plato and Aristotle were essentialists? Well, not necessarily. The story gets a little more complicated. In 383 B.C.E., Plato founded his renowned Academy, a school for academically talented high-achievers. Ironically, given Plato's belief in the value of regimented instruction, historian Edward Power has observed that the Academy was arguably the "first progressive school." Power notes that the Academy was "informal; it counted on students to plan their own programs and to take full responsibility for their own future and relied on them to call upon the teachers for assistance only when they had exhausted their own resources. And then their teachers were not to tell them what to do or to think, but were there to lead them down the road to understanding."[4] The school would have horrified most modern champions of standards, accountability, and best practices. It foreshadowed the most radical of today's constructivist, student-centered schools—except it featured even less by way of lesson plans and explicit objectives.[5] The Academy seemed to represent quite a break with the vision of the ideal school system that Plato had so painstakingly sketched out in *The Republic*.

Was Plato a hypocrite? Power thinks not, explaining, "It was not that Plato rejected system or precision. . . . He believed that system was unnecessary when advanced students with exceptional intellectual acumen were the object of instruction. He knew by intuition what we have since learned: it is no unfamiliar experience to find that what is the best education for the exceptional man is the worst possible education for the rank and file."[6] Plato—perhaps Western civilization's first proponent of a public, standardized education system—believed it appropriate to fundamentally alter the means, ends, and methods of schooling to serve the students who attended his Academy. Yet he also bequeathed a vision of systematic schooling, standardized instruction, and a specified "core curriculum," which he regarded as foundational to a healthy city or state. How did Plato reconcile the tension between the exhortation that all students be trained in set ways and his actual teaching practice? He fudged it. He explained that standardized and prescriptive instruction was the right course for most but not all students—and that the students at the Academy were, due to their age and ability, among the minority who required something more customized and self-directed.

The question of how we might reconcile the needs of individuals with the charge of uniform preparation for adulthood was first asked more than two thousand years ago, with Plato's own conflicted stance seeming to suggest that there is no one pat answer. Yet, in contemporary debates, many would-be reformers casually deny the tension. Some deny that focusing on basic skills may narrow the curriculum, while others simply assert that methods that are effective with gifted or highly motivated students will work equally well for their peers. Failing to acknowledge that this conflict is ancient while overlooking the possibility that different students might benefit more from one or the other approach wastes time and energy in a fierce tug-of-war over a potentially healthy tension.

HOW SHOULD WE BALANCE ACADEMIC AND VOCATIONAL EDUCATION?

Unlike the fierce battles that mark the contemporary curricular debates, discussions of vocational education have suffered a very different fate—an attempt by both sides to insist that their stances aren't in conflict after all. Two truisms run through this debate: one, that every child must be prepared for college or the workforce, and that this means every child needs rigorous academic preparation; and two, that many children do not wish or need to attend college, and that these students will thus find high-quality vocational instruction more useful and engaging than academic instruction. These two sentiments cannot be readily reconciled or simultaneously achieved—not that this stops reformers from trying. The favored response is to duck any seeming conflict by defining high-quality vocational instruction as nothing more than academic instruction with a couple of applied twists, promising to give students the best of both worlds while ignoring limitations due to resources, time, or the vagaries of student interest. The notion that we can avoid these dilemmas if we just get the programs "right" by splitting the difference is tempting, but it willfully ignores the hard truth of the academic-vocational tension, one that is as old as Western schooling.

As they were the trailblazers of Western education, it naturally happened that the Greeks were the first to wrestle with the now-familiar tension between academic learning and practical skills. We have already noted the virtues Plato and Aristotle attributed to instruction in reading, math, and the arts. Historian Gerald Gutek has noted that Athenians embraced a broad curriculum in pursuit of "a cultivated and many-sided person who was both an excellent man and a contributor to the general welfare."[7]

With Athens' prosperity, however, came a growing call from its expanding trading class for a more practical type of education. The Sophists emerged in response to this demand. Deviating from the traditional pedagogy of Socrates and Plato, the Sophists—including such historically recognizable names as Protagoras, Hippias, and Gorgias—catered to the professional, political, and social ambitions of their students. Historian Christopher Lucas has characterized this split as cast between the Sophists' "narrowly conceived vocational kind of training emphasizing oratorical skills" and the "more general and intellectual education as fostered by the founders of philosophical schools."[8] Meanwhile, children of the lower classes were marked for a much more prosaic sort of vocational training, entering apprenticeship programs that could direct their energies toward preparing for a future trade. Even Plato, proponent of academic training that he was, believed, "Any one who would be good at anything must practice that thing from his youth upwards. . . . He who is to be a good builder, should play at building children's houses; he who is to be a good husbandman, at tilling the ground."[9]

In grappling with the tension between academic and practical education, the Greek city-state Sparta adopted a much less equivocal response than did Athens. A centralized, militarized society, Sparta developed a highly disciplined, state-centric system of schooling focused on teaching youth the vocation of war. In a vision that would resonate powerfully with the Founders almost two thousand years later, schooling was regarded primarily as a tool for forging citizens obedient and useful to the state. Plutarch said of Sparta, "The city was a sort of camp in which every man . . . looked upon himself as not born to serve his own ends but the interest of his country."[10]

The zeal with which Spartans prepared their youth for such practical purposes was immediate and unyielding. Spartan children were regarded as the "property of the state, not of their parents."[11] At birth, male infants were inspected, and only the healthy were allowed to live. When their formal education began at the age of seven, boys were sent to the government-run training school, which was directed by a government-appointed leader called the *paedonomos*. Attendance was compulsory, and citizenship was contingent upon completion of training and military service. Students were supervised by men in their early twenties called *eiren*. The physical and intellectual education was militaristic and disciplined; as Lucas notes, it was even "customary for the *eiren* to encourage pupils to steal so they would learn cunning."[12] Isocrates, a Greek rhetorician, reported that the Spartan education was so militarily focused that Spartans often completed schooling without learning to read or write.[13] In many ways, Sparta thus represented the height of vocational preparation, in the narrowest sense.

As far back as the Greeks, then, we see disagreement about whether the purpose of schooling is to provide vocational training or to promote intellectual development and academic mastery. Where Athenian philosophers defined schooling to include music, art, poetry, and physical grace, the Spartans and the Sophists each emphasized different sets of practical skills, or what today we might equate with vocational training. The very antiquity of this tension raises useful questions about our inclination to pursue a uniform understanding of what schooling ought to entail.

Indeed, one frequent solution is that we can merely split the difference. Educator Linda Nathan gave eloquent voice to the "we can have it all" camp a few years ago, arguing that there is no conflict between pursuing "basic academic mastery" and other "preferred social values"—that any such "tradeoff is unnecessary [because] strong academic habits and mastery of literacy are essential and are furthered by an intellectually open and challenging spirit of inquiry."[14] If we really could simply provide every kid with an education featuring the best of both worlds, I'd be on board. But the hard truth may be that such aspirations are far more tractable in theory than in practice.

Enduring disagreements regarding educational priorities, the importance of the arts, and what skills are most useful might commend the virtue of humility to those eager to proclaim this or that approach as the "right" one. In fact, they might do well to recognize that there may be value in diverse approaches when it comes to serving millions of children with varied needs and talents. Of course, drawing upon multiple impulses requires regarding a rich mix of schools, pedagogies, and educational approaches as a strength, not a weakness.

HOW SHOULD EDUCATORS BE PAID?

When it comes to altering the way in which America's teachers are compensated, critics of differentiated pay are eager to depict various proposals as unprecedented, unproven, or a betrayal of our shared values. Proposals for merit pay linked to student achievement, as seen in Washington, D.C., and elsewhere, have been hotly contested and denounced by union leaders as a threat to teacher professionalism, while efforts to support a variety of modest differentiated-pay initiatives in Minnesota and Florida have also engendered fierce criticism from state union officials. National Education Association president Dennis van Roekel has argued, "Merit pay systems force teachers to compete, rather than cooperate. They create a disincentive for teachers to share information and teaching techniques."[15] Such concerns skip past the fact that educational organizations like colleges and tutoring firms routinely pay some employees more than others based on imprecise and uncertain judgments of individual value and performance. More to our point here, however, they also overlook the fact that there is ample historic precedent for doing this in primary and secondary education. Indeed, if we look back far enough, we see that the ancient Romans and Greeks thought it perfectly unexceptional that some teachers would be paid more than others.

In the Greek city-state of Teos, for example, elementary teachers were paid 600 drachmas for the first grade, 550 for the second, and 500 for the third.[16] Equally noteworthy is that the Greeks also paid instructors differentially depending on the subject taught. Teosian archery and javelin teachers were the lowest-paid teachers, at 250 drachmas per year; literature teachers earned 500 to 600 drachmas; and music teachers were the highest-paid teachers, at 700 drachmas.[17] Clearly, the Greeks had few qualms about the effects of basing pay on the perceived difficulty and importance of the subject in question.

In Athens, meanwhile, both the Sophists and the Philosophes charged the tuition they saw fit, with students then choosing who to study with in the same manner that families select private schools today. One of the several Greek Sophists who wrote under the name Philostratus said, in recounting the salary schedules in Athenian schools, "When one paid one hundred drachmae, it was possible for a student to listen to lectures at any time they were given. In addition [the teacher] had a library in his house which he shared with his pupils in order to complement his lectures."[18] The fees paid for listening to these lectures were supplemented by valuable gifts given to the instructors by the student.[19] Allowing students to determine whether to pay for select lectures a la carte or to buy education in bulk permitted them to customize learning to their circumstances and interests.

By the time of the Roman Empire, such practices were systematized. In the fourth century c.e., the Roman emperor Gratian established a salary schedule throughout the empire, with pay routinely differentiated based on judgments regarding the import of various instructional roles. In the city of Treves, pay reflected the level of students taught, with Sophists who taught at the "professor" level receiving an *annona* (an assortment of foodstuffs that functioned as salary) 50 percent greater than that of Latin grammarians or secondary teachers.[20]

The notion that some teachers should be paid more than others is certainly not new and it's puzzling—in a nation that casually accepts paying quarterbacks more than blockers and law professors more than Latin scholars—why it is seen as radical. Nonetheless, much ink and political blood has been spilled debating this rather innocuous point. As one outraged National Education Association (NEA) delegate told Education Secretary Arne Duncan at the NEA's 2009 annual meeting, "Quite frankly, merit pay is union-busting."[21] That teacher was merely echoing the NEA's party line, as argued in the union's official organ, *NEA Today:* "Basing teacher pay on student performance is no answer—it's a thinly disguised assault on us."[22] Even a quick glance backward can remind us how peculiar a statement that really is and how ordinary is the notion that not all teachers must be paid similarly.

DOES REPUBLICAN VIRTUE REQUIRE STATE-RUN SCHOOLS?

As noted in chapter 1, defenders of the familiar K–12 system routinely suggest that educating the citizenry of a well-functioning republic requires a government-operated school system. Questioning that assumption by supporting school-choice plans that allow students to receive public vouchers that can be used to pay tuition at private schools can quickly get one labeled an enemy of public education—or even of democracy itself. The People for the American Way have denounced school vouchers and tuition tax credits as part of a "campaign to discredit the very notion of public education."[23] The National Education Association has charged, "Vouchers are designed to destroy public schools and end education as a public institution."[24] James B. Conant, former president of Harvard University, put a scholarly gloss on this threat, declaring that unity among the citizenry is only possible "if our public schools remain the primary vehicle for the education of our youth." Conant feared that a system reliant upon both public and private schooling could only "threaten the democratic unity provided by our public schools."[25]

Such histrionics would have puzzled the denizens of ancient Rome, the republic that served as the model to which our nation's Founders aspired. There, it was taken for granted that students could learn civic virtue in the home or from private tutors just as readily as from agents of the state. Historian Francesco Cordasco notes that Roman parents each played an active role: the "rearing of the child was in the hands of the mother; the training of the boy, largely reserved to the father."[26] Raising a child in accord with Roman values was a task of utmost seriousness; Plutarch said of Cato that, "as if producing a work of art, [he] moulded his son into a virtuous citizen."[27] Cicero explained, "The Roman Republic stands strongly on a foundation of men and *mos maiorum*."[28] For the Romans, *mos maiorum*—"the way of our ancestors" (or, "tradition," in more contemporary terms)—provided the basis for educators to identify appropriate behavior, lessons, and goals.

Parents sought to provide an education emphasizing basic literacy, Latin literature, and mathematics.[29] Instruction for boys, and for some girls, began at about six or seven years of age in elementary schools with studies in reading, writing, and counting, and then the boys continued on to grammar school around age twelve.[30] Girls, if allowed, continued their studies at home.[31] At about age fifteen or sixteen, boys would become Roman citizens and then typically serve as apprentices to a family member or close family friend for a year before beginning their two-year military training.[32] All in all, a wide range of private and public arrangements was thought equal to the designs of the republic.

Around the second century B.C.E., the Roman system evolved as private tutors became accessible to a fee-paying public for the first time.[33] The highest families of Rome began importing teachers from Greece to tutor their children. Especially after Greece became a province of Rome with the Roman conquest of 146 B.C.E., these tutors were seen as a mark of status. Typically former Greek aristocrats, they were eagerly sought and jealously guarded.[34]

The Romans, like the Athenians, accepted a far murkier distinction between public and private institutions than we tend to presume today. Both, for instance, thought it unremarkable that parents, private tutors, and competing scholars could provide instruction that promoted civic virtue and loyalty to the state. The point is not to suggest that they were "right" or that they should carry any talismanic weight, but merely to note that successful republican cultures have at times embraced arrangements that some today would summarily label illegitimate.

HOW SHOULD WE BALANCE CHURCH AND STATE?

We just considered the general issue of the sanctity of state-run schools. Let's spend another moment on the particular question of the role of religious schooling and its profound influence on the Western education tradition. On the more immediate question of whether vouchers and like proposals violate the First Amendment's "establishment" clause, the U.S. Supreme Court believes they do not. The Court ruled in 2002 that Cleveland's voucher program passed constitutional muster so long as it did not discriminate against par-

ticular faiths or between sectarian and nonsectarian schools. However, the Court's decision did little to assuage skeptics concerned
that there is something dangerous or problematic in allowing public
dollars to fund religious schooling.

Yet, in crucial ways, our vision of even "public" schooling has
been shaped by church schools. After the fall of the Carolingian dy-
nasty in 899, the Roman Catholic Church stood as the only sustained
institution in Western Europe and emerged as the collector, pre-
server, and transmitter of culture. In the long centuries that stretched
from the fall of the Roman Empire until the first blush of the Renaissance in the fourteenth century, church-sponsored education struggled to preserve the knowledge and culture that survived from Greek
and Roman civilization. Historian Thomas Woods has argued that
while the significance of the monastic tradition is widely understood
because "everyone knows that the monks preserved the literary in-
heritance of the ancient world," it is equally important to note that
"one can scarcely find a significant endeavor in the advancement of
civilization during the Middle Ages in which the monks did not play
a major role."[35]

The church-sponsored schools that arose in the centuries that
followed would provide ready models for emulation when the Renaissance brought a new interest in schools and schooling. Two are
deserving of a bit more discussion here: monastic and cathedral
schools.[36] Monasteries were intended to be centers for the devout
study of scripture and theology, not necessarily places of learning.
However, while reading was not the focus of monastic life, it was essential that a prospective monk be able to read and interpret the Bible. Saint Benedict, an early leader of monasticism in the sixth century, had called for monks to complete seven hours of manual labor
and two hours of reading daily.[37]

As general literacy declined through the Dark Ages, many aspirants were unable to read. In response, monasteries began to provide
schooling in reading, writing, and other subjects. (For better or worse,
this probably constituted the first attempt at remedial education.)

The monasteries also set their aspirants and monks to the exhausting task of preserving and copying ancient manuscripts to secure the cultural legacy of Greco-Roman civilization.[38] The result was that, as former Cambridge University professor David Knowles noted, in the century preceding the Norman Conquest the monasteries became the "cultural and educational heart of England."[39]

Christopher Lucas observed that it was only later, "when it became clear prospective monastics would have to be taught to read by the order so as to understand the Bible," that more elaborate provisions were made for their instruction.[40] By 1000, a regular course of studies for novitiates (who typically started at age eleven or twelve) had evolved at monastic schools. It was separated into seven liberal arts subjects: the *trivium* (grammar, dialectic, and rhetoric) and the *quadrivium* (arithmetic, geometry, music, and astronomy). The *trivium,* because it dealt with reading and rhetoric, was deemed the more critical.[41]

The courses of instruction in the *trivium* and *quadrivium,* drawn from the Greek and Roman tradition, should sound more than a little familiar; they went on to provide the basis for the secondary curriculum as we know it today. In the late 1920s, Scott Buchanan, developer of the Great Books curriculum, explained that in his curriculum, for instance, "Modern mathematical content fits into the traditional forms . . . figures, numbers, ratios and proportions, equations and functions, correspond to the *quadrivium.* The poetic content is well revised to fit the *trivium.*"[42] Conversely, George Bugliarello, chancellor of the Polytechnic Institute of New York University, has charged that the heavy hand of these aged curricula is a burden, writing, "The heritage of the medieval *trivium* and *quadrivium* that remains at the core of our humanities education is simply inadequate. . . . There are other questions, from the nature and the implications of an explosively urbanizing world to cloning, that are equally essential to the future of our civilization."[43]

Cathedral schools gradually replaced monastic schools as the predominant source of education in the Middle Ages.[44] They were centers of learning operated by major Gothic cathedrals that "had evolved from an informal *grammar school* for training clergy into an institution for highly advanced studies."[45] The decisions made by church leaders at the Council of Rome in 853 reflect the import and focus of church-sponsored schooling. The Council dictated that each parish (a congregation served by a single priest in a specific geographic area) should provide some form of elementary education for parishioners so that they would know the rituals of religious life and could participate in the celebration of Mass. Only sporadically obeyed, the edict nonetheless reflected both the church's unique role in that era as the bearer of learning and its efforts to provide a basic level of schooling and promote literacy.

During the Protestant Reformation, religion would again play a crucial role in the spread of literacy. German schooling expanded rapidly in response to Martin Luther's conviction that salvation depended on one's ability to read the Bible.[46] For good or ill, modern models of schooling constitute modifications on the several versions of church-run schooling that preserved Western culture through the Dark Ages and that served as convenient models when the dawning Renaissance rekindled interest in schooling.

Where church schools and religious questions once dominated the educational landscape, we are now in a peculiar historical moment where the possibility that public funds will support religious schooling is deemed a mortal threat. Given the long and tangled relationship between religion and schooling, a less visceral response may be appropriate. In a land where right and left have bemoaned the degree to which cities have been stripped of local institutions over the past forty years and where long-standing parochial schools are now threatening to fail en masse, a more inclusive and more tolerant view would seem in order. Such a stance would also help make it easier to address prohibitions and rules that can complicate efforts to provide tutoring, service learning, apprenticeships, and other instructional services.

HOW CAN WE LEVERAGE TECHNOLOGY?

White boards, computer-based distance learning, iPod tutorials, e-books. Even as new technology washes over us, schools and educators have had enormous difficulty finding ways to thoughtfully or cost-effectively leverage these tools as there has been a tendency to cling to the familiar and the comfortable. It is only natural that parents and teachers prefer to see students spending every available moment in classrooms or small groups, rather than learning via a computer simulation or being tutored via the Internet. Thus, our preference for using technology has typically amounted to pouring new computers and software into the same old classrooms, rather than using them to rethink the shape of schooling. The challenge is an old one. The power of new technologies is in their ability to help us conceive of new, smarter solutions—but that frequently requires letting go of familiar routines. Consider, for instance, the disruption introduced by something as seemingly sedate as the printing press. The notion that students could learn by sitting with a book, independent from their instructor, was once a radical notion. Books threatened the ability of teachers to control what their students learned and threatened to shatter the communities created by the daily interaction of instructors and their disciples. But today, it is taken as a truism that education was ultimately enriched, strengthened, and democratized by the printed page. The shift may indeed have weakened those intimate scholarly communities and been deemed unfortunate by a few, but we regard it as a small price to pay. Such perspective can help when assessing today's new technologies.

Let's return to the Greeks for a moment, to note how an instructional practice adopted in one set of circumstances can take on talismanic status even when conditions have changed. Perhaps the best-known legacy of Athenian instruction is the pedagogical technique known as the Socratic method. Socrates argued that genuine knowledge already existed in each child and the teacher's task was to summon it forth through extended and in-depth dialogues with the child.[47] What is too readily forgotten today is that Greek instructors relied heavily upon this method in large part *because they had no choice.* The Socratic method was an innovation that met an existing challenge given the confines of the day, when the printing press was still a thousand years away from being invented. The only convenient tool for communicating knowledge or cultivating understanding was the teacher's voice, so students had to learn through direct interactions with a teacher.

As someone who not infrequently leads college seminars, I'm as big a fan of the Socratic method as anyone. But we've too often elevated this one model of interaction into something of a universal ideal. Today's defenders of the status quo have often romanticized the ideal of the Socratic method—rejecting instructional approaches that don't feature a teacher and student cheek-to-jowl when recent advancements offer new, promising opportunities for instruction that even Socrates himself might well have found alluring.

While the reflexive deference to the Socratic method illustrates the perils of clinging to familiar tools, readers need look no further than the nearest bookshelf to locate examples of a once "new" tool that was fiercely opposed. The single most dramatic advance in educational technology prior to the development of modern communication and computing was the invention of the printing press by Germany's Johann Gutenberg in 1455. Prior to that time, education was limited by the supply of written material. The printing press made books available outside of monasteries, offering an alternative to the Greek model of teacher-student interaction or the traditional apprenticeship. It meant that knowledge need not always be communicated orally by a scholar to a pupil seated in the same room or directly from a master to an apprentice at his elbow.

At that time, most books were the property of monasteries or princely libraries, and university students were required to rent volumes from a university book dealer in order to complete their studies. As University of Rochester professor John Rothwell Slater recounted, "Scribes were not allowed at first to sell their manuscripts, but rented them to the students at rates fixed by university statutes. A folded sheet of eight pages, sixteen columns of sixty-two lines each, was the unit for which rental charges were based. Such a sheet at the beginning of the thirteenth century rented for about twenty cents a term; and since an ordinary textbook of philosophy or theology of canon law contained many sheets, these charges constituted no inconsiderable part of the cost of instruction."[48] Consequently, as printing historian Douglas McMurtrie has noted, "Education beyond the merest rudiments was out of the reach of the masses."[49] However, the emerging Renaissance stimulated interest in learning and reintroduced Europeans to Latin and Greek literature. McMurtrie further observes, "An awakened Europe was calling for books with which to study and learn, and there was an urgent demand for some method of producing books in quantity, rather than one by one, and at a reasonable cost."[50]

The printing press made it possible to meet that demand, but like other revolutionary technologies, its introduction was not without controversy. Those with entrenched interests in the status quo often do not take kindly to new tools that threaten their old way of life with the promise of greater efficiency, and the printing press profoundly unsettled several groups. One of the most strident opponents was the Catholic Church. According to printing historian Elizabeth Eisenstein, "The vernacular translation movement went together with a belief that Gospel truths were so simple that they could be understood by ordinary men.... Once plain texts, plain speaking and open books were associated with Protestant doctrine, Catholic reaction took the contrary path justifying mystification, elitism, and censorship ... to foster lay obedience."[51] Municipal figures also worried about the impact of more available published material, as when seventeenth-century Englishman Sir Roger L'Estrange fretted "whether more mischief than advantage were not occasion'd to the Christian world by the invention of typography."[52]

Despite such concerns, the printing press was an immediate popular success. By the end of the fifteenth century, Gutenberg's invention had been widely adopted, with "1,120 print shops in 260 towns in seventeen European countries."[53] By 1500, roughly 40,000 different texts and more than 10 million books were printed in Europe.[54] The landscape of learning was profoundly changed. Knowledge was no longer the sole province of the instructor, and students no longer needed to be in the physical presence of a teacher to learn. Historian Harvey Graff has observed that there followed a "major shift from the famed humanist printers to the jobbers and printers of more ordinary materials."[55] The rote instructional practices that had predominated in cathedral and monastic schools were no longer the only logical alternatives for teaching reading and conveying information, and old barriers gave way to new systems and new providers. As Elizabeth Eisenstein notes, "The flourishing of the printed book-trade hinged on opportunities to market popular products without confronting the long delays, heavy fines and personal risks that censorship often entailed."[56]

In tracing the rise of literacy in England, Lawrence Stone notes that the printing press increased the appetite for the ability to read, observing, "It would be difficult to over-emphasize the importance in this study of that well-worn subject, the invention of cheap paper and movable type."[57] Much like the revolution that occurred on the heels of the printing press's introduction, modern technological advances summon both celebration and concern. Yet, it's vital to recognize that virtual learning has the ability to radically and interactively expand learning and instruction on a scale that profoundly eclipses that of the printing press. While it makes good sense to tend to reasonable concerns regarding accountability and instructional quality in addressing new technologies, it is equally crucial to recognize the new horizons that are opened and not mistake the way teaching and learning have traditionally been done for the way they should or must be done.

WHAT IS THE PURPOSE OF SCHOOLING, ANYWAY?

Reflexive embrace of slogans like "universal proficiency" and "education is the new civil right" can too readily excuse inattention to the broader purposes of schooling and the challenges those purposes can pose to various reform agendas. If we look back to the Enlightenment era, for instance, it may be useful to consider the thinking of two giants of the Western tradition, Britain's John Locke and France's Jean-Jacques Rousseau, who spent their careers grappling with the aims of education.

Locke and Rousseau were part of a wave of Enlightenment thinkers, emerging from centuries of feudalism, who wrestled with how much control the state could and should assert over its citizenry. Historian Christopher Lucas has noted that whether "the state ha[d] a right (or obligation) to compel parents to send their children to school" was the "major educational question debated everywhere in Europe during the latter part of the eighteenth century. For centuries, education had been a family concern and was conducted according to custom, not law, under private arrangements," but now it was increasingly a public question.[58]

Locke, the philosopher who famously asserted that all men have a natural right to "life, liberty, and property," helped shape the thinking of America's founders but made no allowance for any such universal equality in his two treatises on schooling. His *Some Thoughts Concerning Education,* published in 1684, was intended as an education manual for the sons of the elite, while *On Working Schools,* published in 1697, addressed the education of the children of the poor. For the upper classes, Locke encouraged a focus on cultivating physical health and the qualities of a gentleman, so as to create moral, rational young men—an enterprise that education historian John William Adamson termed the "breeding of children destined to occupy positions of social prominence."[59] For the poor, Locke proposed to promote self-sufficiency by teaching a good work ethic and encouraging them to become useful and God-fearing in designated "working schools" where all pauper children from the ages of three to fourteen were sent daily.[60]

Ben Franklin would later echo Locke's blueprint when he sketched a bold vision for an expansive but unapologetically separate and unequal system of schooling in his "Proposals Relating to the Education of Youth in Pennsylvania."[61] We can also hear the aftershocks of Locke's arguments in the writings of Samuel Knox, an influential Missouri representative from the early nineteenth century. As scholars Erwin Johanningmeier and Theresa Richardson have noted, "Like Jefferson, [Knox] believed schooling could be used to promote a meritocracy.... He did not want compulsory attendance for all students at the public's expense but he did urge that each school enroll 'at least three promising boys, whose parents could not afford to educate them.' "[62]

Jean-Jacques Rousseau, Swiss-born political philosopher of the Enlightenment era whose thinking helped spur the French Revolution, proposed in the 1762 novel *Emile* an education system that would rear independent men by emphasizing experiential education rather than book learning. Rousseau and his compatriots would revisit the same pedagogical and curricular debates that plagued Plato and Aristotle two millennia previously. Because of Rousseau's premise that children were born fundamentally good—as "noble savages"—and that it was society that ultimately corrupted people, it made sense that a child's education should be directed by his intuitions and emotions and that the aim of schooling was to discipline youth to keep them safe from pernicious social influences.

Rousseau believed the state should treat individuals of the same class similarly but did not imagine that it was the state's role to narrow disparities between the nobles and the poor. For all his radical democratic tendencies, he thought that "the poor man has no need of education,"[63] but that nobles of both higher and lower status should be educated, in accord with their status under the constitution of the state.[64] In his *Considerations on the Government of Poland,* Rousseau explained, "It is education that must give souls the national form, and so direct their tastes and opinions that they will be patriotic by inclination, by passion, necessity."[65] Rousseau, a profound influence on Thomas Jefferson and a radical apostle of democracy, urged that youth be schooled so that "this love [of country] is his whole existence; he sees nothing but the fatherland, he lives for it alone; when he is solitary, he is nothing; when he has ceased to have a fatherland, he no longer exists; and if he is not dead, he is worse than dead."[66]

Rousseau further thought that each country, government, and class required a distinctive system of schooling. In the preface to *Emile* he wrote, "One kind of education would be possible for Switzerland and not in France; another would be adapted to the middle classes but not to the nobility."[67] This sentiment that a new republic required a new system of schooling would find much sympathy among America's founders.

These two thinkers, so intent upon investigating man's nature and how it might be tamed, profoundly disagreed on the purposes and nature of schooling. In this, they reflected the same splits that the Athenians and Romans had earlier accommodated by accepting a broad mix of arrangements. In today's America, however, a diverse nation of 300 million, reformers are prone to seek universal solutions that they can impose upon the systems and machinery that the Common Schoolers and Progressives have bequeathed us. If education is ultimately not a matter of one thing, but of many things, then this may be a fruitless and ultimately self-defeating task.

BACK TO THE PRESENT

Please don't misunderstand. I am not for a moment suggesting that we should be emulating or romanticizing educational practices of the Greeks, Romans, or anyone else. And I am certainly not suggesting that because something was done by the Romans or during the Renaissance that it is useful for our purposes. Rather, I am arguing that it is a big, complex world, and that we would be well served if we were more expansive in our thinking, more reluctant to declare ideas out of bounds, and less prone to imagine that this or that new orthodoxy is the singular way forward.

In this light, as noted at the beginning of this time-out, stepping back in this manner can help in three crucial ways. First, as with teacher compensation or the role of religious schooling, it can reassure us that ideas that are sometimes denounced as radical or antithetical to the nature of schooling can be seen as a normal and established part of the Western educational tradition. Second, it can reassure us that some fights, such as those over the relative merits of academic and vocational education, are long-running and not likely to be finally and conclusively settled anytime soon, even by the most well-intentioned programs or most elaborate research. And third, as in the case of technology, it can remind us how deep-seated our routines can be and how wedded we can become to solutions and approaches that may have outlived their initial purpose. With that, it is time to return to the more immediate past.

4

The Common Schoolers and the Push for Uniformity

"The chief end is to make good citizens. Not to make precocious scholars . . . not to impart the secret of acquiring wealth . . . not to qualify directly for professional success . . . but simply to make good citizens."

—Newton Bateman, Illinois Superintendent
of Public Instruction, 1862

"If we do not 'Americanize' our immigrants by luring them to participate in our best civilization . . . they will contribute to the degeneration of our political body and thus de-Americanize and destroy our national life."

—William T. Harris, future U.S. Commissioner
of Education, 1877

The story of American education is often told by enthusiasts as a triumph of expanding opportunity and noblesse oblige. While that rosy vision may indeed characterize the past fifty years, the century from 1830 to 1930, encompassing the Common School and the Progressive eras, may be better described as a bureaucratic conquest pursued by moralistic, bean-counting xenophobes. While their efforts made sense in that place and time, and yielded indisputable benefits, we err when we treat their handiwork as a monument rather than as the improvisation that it was.

The Common School movement launched in the nineteenth century enjoyed some remarkable successes. But it is a mistake to think of those successes as amounting to the laying of a concrete foundation upon which later generations would build. It is more accurate to think of the Common Schoolers as having hastily erected a primitive tenement, which successive generations have augmented, refurbished, and expanded, but which still very much helps to define the shape and nature of schooling. Like looking at a blueprint to see what lies under decades of additions and modifications, considering their efforts can make clear how much their needs and agendas continue to dominate our notions of schooling.

American schooling was not borne of the expectation that all children would be educated, much less that all students would be academically proficient, lifelong learners. As noted earlier, Thomas Jefferson, radical egalitarian that he was, called for identifying one boy each year from all those born in the nation's largest state and providing that one youth with a college scholarship. While such advocacy was sufficient to mark Jefferson as a wild-eyed proponent of public education, even those most skeptical of efforts to boost rates of college attendance today recoil from Jefferson's stance as hopelessly elitist. Such a revolution in aims would inevitably seem to imply an equally bold rethinking of means. Instead, today we consume our energies striving to fine-tune machinery built to provide *universal access* even as our goal has shifted to *universal excellence.*

Beyond this misalignment of means and ends, American schooling also suffers from a fundamental tension between the decentralized nature of American government and the universalist aspirations of reformers. Common Schoolers, Progressives, and rafts of contemporary reformers view the American passion for checks and balances, its suspicions of federal government, and its attachment to localism as plagues to be combated or, at best, tolerated. Reformers sought to impose order through administrative systems, financing, and bureaucracies, but were limited by the nation's federal design and the political clout of communities and school districts. Thus, today's 90,000 schools in 14,000 school districts across fifty states are governed by an interlocking web of federal, state, and local policies. We have created a curious hybrid in which schooling is uniform in appearance and process, but where pursuing reform requires the simultaneous voluntary cooperation of a vast number of independent officials and units of government. Perhaps it's no wonder that our rhetoric changes far more frequently than our schools do.

Reformers of earlier eras did not envision K–12 schooling as a way to rigorously educate all children nor as an essential avenue to personal success. The Founders, and several generations following, regarded schooling primarily as a tool for forging good American citizens. In the course of the next century, Common School champions sought to get children off the streets and out of the workforce, and to inoculate them against baleful influences. Yet, proposals to alter the systems and arrangements we have inherited are frequently denounced as a retreat from pluralism, tolerance, and educational opportunity. Defenders of the status quo impute to the present system virtues that it was never intended to embody, and that it may be poorly configured to promote.

STARTING FROM SCRATCH

Those rushing to reform schools today can forget just how long it took to establish a system of schools in a sprawling, decentralized nation. Arriving at the point where schools could provide seats, teachers, and books for all of the nation's children took long centuries of effort. As noted earlier, Massachusetts adopted the first education statutes in the American colonies, more than four centuries ago, in order to support the "worthy" poor, industrial training, and apprenticeships.[1]

Massachusetts adopted the colonies' first compulsory education law in 1642, requiring "parents and masters to see to the education of the children under their control and levying fines upon all adults who failed to do so."[2] Historian Forest Chester Ensign termed the law "one of the most famous bits of educational legislation in history. It . . . gives directions for dealing with delinquents; and for the first time in English history provides for the literary instruction of every child."[3] The 1642 law required that students be taught to read, be instructed in religious orthodoxy, and be schooled in the capital laws so that they might be good citizens of the state and the church.[4] The law did not establish schools, instead entrusting education to the children's parents.[5] But five years later, in 1647, the Massachusetts General Court started requiring every town of fifty or more households to create a school, with the teacher to be paid by families or through local taxes. Fines were imposed on towns that failed to comply.[6]

The laws were seen as a lever for promoting faith and citizenship. When the first public schools were created in Massachusetts, the Congregationalist journal the *New Englander* cheered, "These [public] schools draw in the children of alien parentage with others, and assimilate them . . . so they grow up with the state, of the state, and for the state."[7] In the 1600s and 1700s, and well into the 1800s, schooling was frequently coordinated by local church elders, who selected teachers and arranged for classes to meet in local church facilities.

In 1785, the American colonies enacted their first joint measure to promote schooling. That year, Congress (operating under the Articles of Confederation) enacted the Land Ordinance of 1785. The measure divided a vast swath of Western territory into townships of six square miles, each subdivided into thirty-six sections, the sale or use of one of which was reserved to support a school. Two years later, the Northwest Ordinance asserted that "schools and the means of education shall forever be encouraged" in order to promote "religion, morality, and knowledge."[8] Together, the two bills marked what is arguably the most significant step forward for national K–12 legislation before the twentieth century.

Compulsory education laws coupled with the legislative push for school construction helped fuel a rise in attendance. No reliable data on enrollment or schooling are available from the early nineteenth century, but schools enrolled youth from the ages of three to seventeen for a total of anywhere from eight to fourteen years—often for sporadic periods that included many interruptions.[9] There was no expectation that a typical child would attend for a set number of years or for their education to lead to college attendance. One estimate places the number of Americans who had ever attended an

American college in the early nineteenth century at seventeen in every ten thousand, or less than one-fifth of 1 percent.[10]

Until the early 1900s, most students entered the workforce directly from elementary school. In 1870, for instance, only about half of the 8 million children enrolled in school actually *attended* on a given day. Students attended school for an average of 78 days a year (out of a 130-day school term).[11] In 1890, barely 5 percent of fourteen- to seventeen-year-olds were enrolled in high school,[12] and just under 12 percent of that small handful were preparing for college.[13]

From 1880 to 1940, in a sixty-year tsunami, enrollment nearly doubled every decade. During that span, enrollment in grades nine through twelve exploded, from 110,000 to over 7 million.[14] Simply managing the flood of new bodies posed a remarkable challenge. K–12 schooling steadily expanded its reach over time, first to working-class boys, then to girls, and eventually to African Americans.

In 1850, 45 percent of girls aged five to nineteen were enrolled in school. By 1900, that figure had inched up only slightly to 51 percent. In the first decades of the new century, however, it climbed steadily, to 60 percent in 1910, 70 percent in 1930, and 78 percent by 1950.[15] Before the Civil War, black enrollment was largely limited to a modest population in the North (at a time when 95 percent of the nation's black population lived in the South).[16] After emancipation, black enrollment climbed to 34 percent in 1880, before plateauing through century's end. It began to grow again after 1900, soaring to 75 percent by 1940, when it approached that of the white population. By 1970, enrollment rates for white and black students were similar.[17]

It took more than three centuries from the time when the first school laws were adopted in colonial Massachusetts, in the 1640s, until 90 percent of children were enrolled in school and most were completing high school. The priorities and ambitions of that long struggle have left indelible marks on the schools and systems that stand today. It was against this backdrop that the nineteenth century Common Schoolers would set out to render schooling more uniform and to extend its reach.

THE COMMON SCHOOL MOVEMENT

In 1830, public primary schools existed in all twenty-four states. Supported with a mix of state and local support and coordinated by community leaders, the system of schooling was highly decentralized and featured dramatic variations in quality and organization. It was against this backdrop that reformers would embark upon what we now call the Common School era, which is typically regarded as running through the latter part of the nineteenth century before giving way to the Progressive era. It was marked by—surprise!—a commitment to making schools "common," or widely open to the public regardless of social class. Horace Mann, who would serve as the first secretary of the Massachusetts State Board of Education from 1837 to 1849, was perhaps the first prominent leader of this push. Other Common School proponents, including James Carter, Henry Barnard, and Catharine Beecher (and her better-known sister, author Harriet Beecher Stowe), believed universal education was instrumental for social stability and sought to extend and systematize schooling across their young nation.

The Common School movement was profoundly shaped by the national debate over slavery and by the westward expansion, with proponents believing Common Schools would be essential in forging a shared sense of destiny and in knitting the growing nation together. Common Schoolers wanted schools to Americanize the millions of non-Anglo immigrants who flooded into the United States starting in the 1830s.[18] In the aftermath of the Civil War, the (mostly abolitionist) Common Schoolers sought schools that could absorb millions of newly freed slaves and help make them into good Americans.

Horace Mann, arguably the movement's most influential champion, touted the Common School (perhaps immodestly) as "the greatest discovery ever made by man."[19] The Common School "movement" in America was a confederation of reformers who emerged first in New York, Pennsylvania, and New England, seeking to expand and then universalize education for every white child.[20] United by this mission, the young network of Common School advocates looked abroad for a model to emulate, as European nations had set an international precedent by enacting compulsory education laws starting in the eighteenth century. In 1763, for example, Prussia, under Frederick the Great, was the first to adopt a compulsory education statute, with Denmark following suit in 1814, the United Kingdom in 1880, France in 1882, and Ireland in 1892.[21] Far less concerned than the Founders about the perils of emulating Europe, the Common Schoolers imported these European traditions and practices which would become the defiantly "American" system decades later.

To see how European traditions helped shape the burgeoning Common School agenda, one need only take stock of Horace Mann's 1843 tour of European schools and their particular model of classroom management. At the time, American schools frequently had teachers working with students of various ages, much like the conventional notion of the one-room schoolhouse filled with local students young and old. While visiting Prussia, however, Mann was especially impressed by the Prussians' strict and orderly age-based classroom grading, and he became an ardent champion of the region's practice upon returning to the United States. "The first element of superiority in a Prussian school," Mann explained, "consists in the proper classification of scholars. In all places where the numbers are sufficiently large to allow it, the children are divided according to ages and attainments; and a single teacher has the charge only of a single class."[22]

While Mann was busy importing age-based arrangements lock, stock, and barrel into American classrooms, it's impossible to know if those school leaders who were adopting the radical new system fully grasped the specific historical context from which these arrangements grew. As we know now, the Prussian model traced its roots to the early nineteenth century after Napoleon's French army had stripped Prussians of half of their land. In an attempt to bolster their countrymen's sense of national pride, the remaining Prussian leaders instituted a highly regimented education system in hopes of instilling a "higher and nobler spirit" in their youth.[23] The notion of an orderly progression of grades, with students assigned in "platoons" to a particular teacher, appealed to the strictly disciplined sensibilities of the early 1800s Common Schoolers, who rallied for the adoption of this system of classroom organization; however, overlaying a nationalist agenda from the other side of the Atlantic onto a very different reality at home did not always have the expected outcomes.

Given the stark difference between the roots of mono-graded classrooms and the conditions in early American education, it's unsurprising that age-based grading did not lend itself to the mixed-age schoolhouses of rural America. Instead, it initially took hold in cities, where greater population density enabled students to be divided by age groups into chronologically homogenous classes. By 1900, however, age grading had become common practice across the country.[24] Along with the mono-grade classroom came the mono-grade teacher who would, without fail, bid adieu to their students at the end of the school year. For those of us who have seen a particular student forge a powerful bond with a given teacher and wondered, at the end of the year, why schools across the land unthinkingly sever those relationships, the answer is our peculiar devotion to a model that defeated Prussian leaders developed in order to salvage the last vestiges of their shattered national pride.

Once the basic structure of their ideal system was in place, the Common Schoolers looked to state legislatures to help fill schools. The previously mentioned 1852 Massachusetts law requiring that children aged eight to fourteen attend school for a minimum of twelve consecutive weeks each year,[25] while not enforced, sounded the starting gun on legislation to mandate compulsory enrollment.[26] After compulsory schooling took hold, reformers began to eagerly track progress in terms that could sound a lot like an account of warehouse management. A rhapsodic 1876 *New York Times* editorial reflects the eager attention accorded to enrollment in that era, gushing, "The Board of Education is to be congratulated. . . . The Superintendent, Mr. Stanton, a careful and efficient officer, reports that the cases of 10,189 'truants and non-attendants' have been looked into; of these 1,690 had no residence that could be found, and some 4,300 were detained at home by poverty or sickness, leaving 4,194 habitual truants residing at home. Of this number, 2,597 were returned to school."[27]

Despite legislatives interventions and earnest early adopters, compulsory education faced stiff opposition from many in school systems and state houses. In 1889, William T. Harris, then U.S. Commissioner of Education, issued a report that chronicled a series of failed efforts to promote compulsory schooling.[28] According to Harris, New Jersey's initial compulsory schooling law of 1875 was not enforced because of a lack of facilities.[29] In California, the 1874 compulsory schooling law had proven ineffective, according to state superintendent Ira G. Hoitt, due partly to a lack of school accommodations and partly to the "indifference and negligence of parents and guardians."[30] New Mexico passed compulsory schooling legislation in 1870 before a public school system had taken root, with the result that "compulsion existed only in name," while an 1877 law was "so defective in wording" that it "did not compel anything or anybody."[31] Access is always easier to secure than excellence, yet even the push for access in this period proved immensely challenging.

Over time, states would gradually move to lower the required entrance age, boost the minimum leaving age, extend the number of weeks a child had to attend school, and strengthen enforcement. By 1890, most states and territories had compulsory education laws. The last to adopt a compulsory education statute was Mississippi, which finally did so in 1918.[32]

Getting Kids Out of the Factories

While the Common Schoolers were busy trying to fill schools with kids to help fulfill their visions of a uniformly developed society, a parallel push for compulsory schooling was being driven by unions and social reformers seeking to get children out of the labor force.

Historian Carl Kaestle has traced those concerns back to as early as 1837, when the Pelz Committee reported on child labor in Philadelphia's cotton mills. According to Kaestle, the committee found, "The working day for children and adults alike ranged from eleven to fourteen hours. One-fifth of the employees were under age twelve, and no provision was made for their education. Of all the employees under eighteen, only one-third could read or write."[33]

By the end of the nineteenth century, the percentage of children in the labor force topped 20 percent, bringing to a head concerns about the impact on children's well-being and on adult employment and wages.[34] While most will be familiar with the heroic tale of child labor opponents gallantly fighting to protect children from the harsh realities of the industrial world, labor unions were increasingly advocating for expanding education as a means to reduce the supply of cheap labor.[35] Understandably enough, unions resented the downward pressure that child labor exerted on wages.[36] In Illinois, for instance, Chicago's labor unions took an active interest in compulsory schooling and explicitly tied it to child labor legislation.[37] Labor unions in Baltimore established their own "Education Committee" intended to promote the enforcement of child labor and compulsory education laws.[38] By 1900, the North's industrial states had all enacted laws limiting child labor in mining and manufacturing. By tying these restrictions to educational legislation intended to address the potential problems posed by unoccupied, unsupervised children, unions became a major driver for the universal schooling vision pushed by their Common School contemporaries.[39]

Making Good Americans

For Common Schoolers, having bodies in seats was a significant victory and necessary prerequisite for their broader goals of shaping the next generation of Americans. As noted earlier, the Common Schoolers shared an overriding concern with the America's founders: instilling all children with "American" values through a uniform schooling system. It's no coincidence that the Common School push took wing in the 1830s and 1840s as unprecedented waves of suspect Irish Catholics migrated to the United States. The pace of immigration was staggering, with nearly 19 million people arriving between 1830 and 1900—in a nation whose 1830 population had numbered only 13 million.[40] Most troubling to those concerned with preserving a homogeneous culture was that more than four out of five new immigrants hailed from lands other than England, Scotland, or Wales—marking a profound shift in the ethnic makeup of the fast-growing nation.[41] Indeed, the 1830s saw the arrival of over 170,000 Irish immigrants, accounting for a third of all immigration in that decade. The numbers grew even larger in the following decade, when 650,000 more Irish arrived, constituting 46 percent of total immigration during the period.[42]

In light of those seismic demographic shifts, Common Schools were seen as the mechanism for turning unwashed and ill-kept immigrant children into productive, law-abiding citizens while preserving the Protestant fabric of America. "How can we expect the fabric of the government to stand," Horace Mann implored, "if vicious materials are daily wrought into its frame work?"[43] Only by socializing poor immigrant children through these schools, he argued, would society be able to protect against sinister forces: "Let the common school be expanded to its capabilities, let it be worked with the efficiency of which it is susceptible, and nine-tenths of the crimes in the penal code would become obsolete; the long catalogue of human ills would be abridged; men would walk more safely by day; [and] every pillow would be more inviolable by night."[44]

The impact of immigrants was a matter of sustained popular concern during this time, and the saving power of the Common Schools was widely accepted. In 1876, the *New York Times* contended, "The great source of our evils is, of course, an ignorant foreign immigration,"[45] while later that same year, another editorial cheered that, "The daily average attendance of the public schools has risen . . . making a total number of 7,614 children who have been taken from the ranks of the ignorant."[46] William T. Harris, who would go on to be U.S. Commissioner of Education, warned in 1877, "If we do not 'Americanize' our immigrants by luring them to participate in our best civilization . . . they will contribute to the degeneration of our political body and thus de-Americanize and destroy our national life."[47]

The shape of the Common Schools was not preordained, but instead the product of nineteenth-century agendas and values, and we should view it with that in mind. As historians Robert Church and Michael Sedlak have observed, what made the Common School "common" was that "it taught the common subjects and common values and it was common because it was to enroll every single child in the United States in order to socialize him."[48] If the nineteenth-century agenda no longer reflects our aims for schooling—and, as I suggested in chapter 1, I think it's fair to say that it does not—then the institutions erected to advance it ought to be regarded with appropriate skepticism.

THE INSTITUTIONAL LEGACY OF ANTI-CATHOLIC SENTIMENT

The Irish and other immigrants from eastern and southern Europe scared the Common School reformers not just because they hailed from suspect lands but also because so many were Catholic. Common Schoolers wanted schools to combat this alien religion and free the children from attachment to papist superstitions. Doing so meant that Protestant teachings needed to be promoted by common schools and that Catholics be required to attend them.

The battle lines for this contentious issue were drawn at the dawn of the Common School movement. By the mid-1800s, public schools routinely started the day with students reciting from the King James Version of the Bible. Such policies unsurprisingly angered Catholics, who demanded that their children be exempted from school prayers or be allowed to engage in prayers of their own faith. As one New Haven Catholic priest explained, "We simply ask

Catholic prayers for our Catholic children, without expressing the least desire to interfere with the children of others. We consider that we have a constitutional right to have our children say their own prayers."[49]

Outnumbered and outflanked, Catholics had little hope in challenging the Common School orthodoxy that reigned in the nation's public schools. But intrepid church leaders changed the terms of the game by establishing their own schools. When the nation's Catholic leaders convened at the 1884 Council of Baltimore to address the matter, they issued a call to arms for parishes across the country: "Wherever parochial schools are possible, they are ordered to be opened . . . [and] when a school is found in which Catholic doctrines or moral principles are attacked, it is the duty of the pastor in its neighborhood to prohibit attendance at it by the children of his flock."[50] The Church went so far as to threaten to remove from their position those priests who failed to follow the council's edict.[51]

In answer to the expansion of Catholic schooling, Protestants sought to ensure that tax dollars could only be used to support state-run schools. By 1876, fourteen states had adopted constitutional amendments specifying that public dollars could not be used to support any sectarian private school. Fourteen years later, twenty-nine states had adopted such amendments.

These measures came to be known as "Blaine Amendments" after James Blaine, speaker of the U.S. House of Representatives from 1869 to 1875. President Ulysses S. Grant, who had pledged in 1875 that he would "encourage free schools, and resolve that not one dollar be apportioned to support any sectarian schools," enlisted Blaine in his effort.[52] Blaine, who was angling for the presidency, hoped that sponsoring a constitutional amendment prohibiting public funding of religious schools would help to lock down the Protestant vote. The bill passed the House but fell four votes short of the necessary two-thirds majority in the U.S. Senate.

Blaine's efforts nonetheless had a sizable effect, filtering down into state constitutions and other legislation. While the constitutional and statutory provisions that resulted are often romanticized today as a principled separation of church and state, the motivations were anything but noble and the spirit anything but tolerant. Legal scholar Joseph Viteritti has observed, "Blaine's history shows that it was borne out of a spirit of religious bigotry and intolerance directed against Catholic immigrants during the nineteenth century. It was not conceived in the spirit of the First Amendment but to impose restrictions."[53]

In an even bolder effort mounted to ensure that all students were exposed only to state-approved instruction, Oregon enacted a compulsory education law in 1922 for children ages eight to sixteen, requiring that they attend public schools and prohibiting enrollment in private schools. The campaign was spearheaded largely by the Scottish Rite Masons and the Ku Klux Klan. Concerned that Catholic schools were promoting papist dogma and undermining good citizenship, the Masons and the Klan sought to ensure that every student would be trained by state-selected educators in a state-selected curriculum. They believed the result would diminish unhealthful parental influences and strengthen the state. The Klan argued, "Compulsory education in state-run schools could avert the risks created by social pluralism." King Kleagle, a Klan leader, explained, "To defend the Common School is the settled policy of the Ku Klux Klan and with its white-robed sentinels keeping eternal watch, it shall for all time . . . cry out the warning when danger appears and take its place in the front rank of defenders of the public schools."[54]

A Catholic teaching order, the Society of Sisters of the Holy Names of Jesus and Mary, brought suit against the Oregon law. In a case that eventually went to the U.S. Supreme Court as *Pierce v. Society of Sisters,* they claimed that the statute "conflict[ed] with the right of parents to choose schools where their children will receive appropriate mental and religious training" and "the right of schools and teachers therein to engage in a useful business or profession."[55]

Ultimately, the U.S. Supreme Court found for the Society of Sisters, ruling, "The fundamental theory of liberty upon which all governments in this Union repose, excludes any general power of the state to standardize children by forcing them to accept instruction from public teachers only. The child is not the mere creature of the state."[56] The Court also took care to stipulate, however, "No question is raised concerning the power of the State reasonably to regulate all schools, to inspect, supervise and examine them, their teachers and pupils; to require that all children of proper age attend some school, that teachers shall be of good moral character and patriotic disposition, that certain studies plainly essential to good citizenship must be taught, and that nothing be taught which is manifestly inimical to the public welfare."[57] This compromise, with the Court's emphasis on public supervision rather than on the necessity of direct public provision, supplies a useful foundation for emancipatory inquiry. How this authority should be employed is the critical question.

Today, discomfort with public support for church-linked schools has become a convention, even as hundreds of parochial schools are folding in cities where the availability of safe, orderly, and reputable schools is sparse, at best. Indeed, we now see efforts in Washington, D.C., and elsewhere to convert established parochial schools into secular charter schools because their low-income families cannot afford even the minimum tuition at these schools. Tapping into the per-pupil funding that charters enjoy is the only way to keep these community anchors in existence. What's remarkable is how little we wonder at the justification for our bias, which, after all, marks a profound shift in a nation where most educational provision once involved church leaders disbursing public dollars, often for schools housed in church facilities.[58]

DIVERSITY AS THE NEW STANDARD

Whereas the Common Schoolers sought, above all else, to curb the cultural heterogeneity they saw threatening their young republic's unity, contemporary education leaders and educational school professors frequently and unequivocally demand that schools expose children to peers of varied ethnicities and backgrounds. There are two obstacles to this goal. The first, which we will address later, is that today's schools and districts do not do a particularly good job of creating diverse environments. The second, which we address here, is that it is not clear that existing schools and systems are equipped for the challenge.

Advocates for increased diversity are prone to celebrate familiar schools and school districts as central to the great "melting pot," a phrase first applied to American society in 1907 when a New York rabbi delivered a Passover sermon depicting America as "the melting pot of nationalities."[59] The term was popularized in the 1908 play *The Melting Pot,* when the main character proclaimed, "There she lies, the great Melting-Pot—listen! Can't you hear the roaring and the bubbling? There gapes her mouth—the harbor where a thousand mammoth feeders come from the ends of the world to pour in their human freight. Ah, what a stirring and a seething! Celt and Latin, Slav and Teuton, Greek and Syrian,—black and yellow—Jew and Gentile . . . how the great Alchemist melts and fuses them with his purging flame!"[60]

If the aim of schooling is not to smelt American youth of various cultures, religions, and ethnicities into a uniform mass but to celebrate diversity and promote "tolerance," then the Common School formula is problematic. As we've covered, Common Schools were intended to defend "American" norms, English language, and Protestant values, an agenda now deemed morally dubious by those who carry the Common School banner. Indeed, calls for assimilation are today widely decried as racist and even xenophobic by the rising number of those within the professional education community who believe that schools should actively "celebrate diversity."

In fact, when it comes to promoting a respect for democratic values, Princeton University scholar Steven Macedo has noted that the Common School suffers from serious handicaps in terms of fulfilling some of our ambitions. Macedo has observed,

It is hardly surprising that schools serving more cohesive communities may have an easier time generating trust among students, teachers, and indeed parents. After all, in common schools—schools containing students from diverse religious, racial, ethnic, and class backgrounds—a certain amount of energy will have to be expended to build the trust and mutual understanding that more homogenous schools can (to a greater degree) take for granted.[61]

The Common School legacy itself may leave schools ill equipped to forge cultures that can combat anomie or apathy, to foster curricular and faculty coherence, or to support disciplined, consistent instruction.

The Lingering Effects of "Uniformity"

In 2006, the Florida Supreme Court was asked to weigh in on a school voucher program that allowed Florida students at some persistently low-performing schools to transfer to participating private schools at state expense. The Florida Supreme Court struck down the program based on a constitutional provision calling for "uniform public schooling."

The Florida constitution, and the constitutions of thirteen other states, includes clauses that call for a "uniform" system of public schools. Florida's "uniformity clause" reads, "The education of children is a fundamental value of the people" and therefore "adequate provision shall be made by law for a uniform, efficient, safe, secure, and high quality system of free public schools that allows students to obtain a high quality education."[62] Of course, this language is more a wish list than a constitutional framework, as many Florida children attend traditional district schools that fail to fulfill those assurances. At the time and still to this day, Florida—like every state—offered a markedly uneven system of public schooling, with some schools offering Advanced Placement courses, International Baccalaureate programs, sophisticated computers, arts programs, terrific faculty, or foreign language instruction, while other schools lack such programs.

This violation of uniformity seemed not to concern the court, making clear that it interpreted uniformity to mean fidelity to the bureaucratic apparatus envisioned by Common Schoolers over a century ago rather than educational opportunities available today.[63]

The thorny question is whether and when the pursuit of a "uniform" system might actually make it more difficult to deliver a "high quality" education. After all, many of the best school options for disadvantaged youth today, from magnet programs to recognized charter schools, are anything but paeans of "uniformity." Some of today's most effective recruiters of teachers, tutoring providers, purveyors of learning software, and community programs for at-risk youth are neither uniform nor even obviously identifiable as elements of a "public school system." The high ideals cited by the court have been used to dig a moat around a swaying edifice that may not be equal to its burdens.

Today, public educators are encouraged to respect differences, not eradicate them. The irony of using uniformity to squelch creative problem solving is increasingly clear. After all, a 2009 *Washington Post* story noted regretfully that in recent decades, "The government forced native peoples to abandon their languages through vehicles such as boarding schools that punished youth for speaking a traditional tongue. Many Native American . . . languages never recovered."[64] When the concern shifts from stamping students with similar experiences to preserving diversity, the architecture of the Common School is of uncertain utility. Yet, the Common School legacy continues to fuel an attachment to standardization and even "uniformity"—an odd aspiration in a nation where schools are asked to serve 50 million students with widely divergent needs in a variety of contexts.

THE TROUBLE WITH COUNTING

Since the early 1980s, American schooling has seen the emergence of a standards-based reform movement focused on specifying what it is that students are expected to learn. Boosted by 1983's *A Nation at Risk,* standards proceeded in concert with the creation of tests to measure whether students mastered the indicated knowledge and skills. This emphasis on *content* marked a profound shift from the historic emphasis on *time* spent in the classroom, or the more recent fascination with the *number of students* in a given classroom. More recent developments, particularly the rise of virtual schooling, challenge the notion that seat time or class size constitutes a useful proxy for learning or for school quality.

Shifting from a focus on process to content may sometimes seem like a recent insight, but it is actually a venerable one. In the nineteenth century, libertarian icon John Stuart Mill called for defining schooling in terms of content rather than time, believing it would promote state oversight of education without requiring the bureaucracy of a uniform state-run school system. Mill explained,

> An age might be fixed at which every child must be examined, to ascertain if he (or she) is able to read. If a child proves unable, the father, unless he has some sufficient ground of excuse, might be subjected to a moderate fine, to be worked out, if necessary, by his labour, and the child might be put to school at his expense. Once in every year the examination should be renewed, with a gradually extending range of subjects, so as to make the universal acquisition, and what is more, retention, of a certain minimum of general knowledge virtually compulsory. Beyond that minimum there should be voluntary examinations on all subjects, at which all who come up to a certain standard of proficiency might claim a certificate.[65]

The Millsian approach did not prevail, however. Allegiance to seat time rather than learning has meant that efforts to educate children in new environments must traverse a gauntlet of political opposition. When alternative arrangements are approved based on their ability to prove that students are spending requisite time in schools, they then typically unfold with little assurance that students are mastering essential skills and content. The cases of home schooling and virtual schooling illustrate the perils of holding fast to old habits in a new era. In each case, the reliance on time spent in a classroom has created stiff headwinds for new forms of provision that are tied to student outcomes rather than the passage of hours.

Nowhere has the emphasis on counting bodies bequeathed by the Common Schoolers been more evident than in our infatuation with class-size reduction—with its mantra of hiring more and more teachers to do the exact same job. The United States has adopted the peculiar policy of compensating for declining teacher quality by hiring ever more teachers, and then asking them to each do the same job in the same way. Since the early 1970s, growth in the teaching force has outstripped growth in student enrollment by 50 percent.[66] If policy makers had maintained the same overall teacher-to-student ratio over that period, we would need 1 million fewer teachers, and hiring could be far more selective.[67] As Chester Finn Jr. wryly observed just a few years ago, the United States instead opted to "invest in many more teachers rather than abler ones. . . . No wonder teaching salaries have barely kept pace with inflation, despite escalating education budgets."[68]

There are alternatives. Several nations that perform impressively on international assessments, including South Korea and Japan, boast average middle-school class sizes of more than thirty-five students per teacher—reducing the need for teachers and making it possible to invest more heavily in training and compensating each teacher.[69] As economist Dan Goldhaber has pointed out, those nations that invest more heavily in teacher quality than in teacher quantity make the profession more prestigious and attract a larger pool of talented candidates, even as they position themselves to be more selective. Whereas most U.S. teacher preparation programs accept just about every candidate that applies, in Singapore only about one-fifth of those applying to teacher training are admitted.[70] The legacy of gauging our educational success by measuring inputs like class size or school spending has made it even more difficult for us to successfully use new tools or technologies, and it has reinforced our inclination to cling to the familiar by merely layering new resources atop old. The result has pulled us away from asking what reforms are intended to accomplish and impelled us to focus on how cleanly they fit within or atop existing inputs.

Squeezing New Wine into Old Bottles

The challenges posed by our attachment to the orthodoxies of seat time and small classes are especially evident in the case of virtual schooling, which is a fancy label for efforts to rethink what schools should be like and how instruction should be delivered in the age of the Internet. Critics of virtual and distance learning have persistently leaned on old laws, often enacted at the behest of Common School or Progressive reformers for reasons addressed above, to stifle new arrangements:

- In Wisconsin, a union lawsuit charged that "Under the charter school law, children are required to be physically present in the charter school they transfer to, which rules out virtual schools."[71]
- In Oregon, the Oregon Education Association and its legislative allies enacted a bill that required any virtual school to enroll at least half of its students from the district in which it is based, limiting the ability of schools to serve students outside district boundaries or to expand.[72]
- In California, state rules limit cyber schools to serving students in a small geographic area, specify how schools will expend funds, and mandate a student-teacher ratio no larger than that of the largest local school district.

As political scientists John Chubb and Terry Moe have noted, "The rules . . . go a long way towards eliminating the very features that are distinctive and advantageous about cyberschools."[73]

Students enrolled in virtual courses or schools pose intriguing challenges to the Common School legacy. Measuring whether students are mastering skills and knowledge, rather than seat time and class size, presents new obstacles. Virtual arrangements rest uneasily alongside funding systems based on full-time enrollment and staffing arrangements based on "full-time equivalents." New forms of schooling raise the same questions that the Supreme Court wrestled with nearly a century ago in *Pierce v. Society of Sisters*. How aggressively should the state restrict or regulate the alternatives to state-run schools? How much should the state care about where children are schooled, how they are schooled, or how much time they spend being schooled—rather than whether they master the knowledge and skills the state has deemed essential?

Showing Up, but Tuning Out

While the counting tendency has squelched new provision attempts like virtual schooling, it has also contributed to stale classrooms in existing schools. Today, for instance, every state requires children to attend school until at least age sixteen, while seventeen states require attendance until age eighteen.[74] Enrollment rates have remained over 90 percent since they first crossed that threshold in 1960.[75] The problem is no longer getting children to attend school; a much larger concern is that vast numbers of teens are utterly disengaged while in school. The national High School Survey of Student Engagement reports that 17 percent of teens are bored in "every class" in high school, and another 50 percent say they are bored "every day."[76] More than seven in ten teachers agree that their students "only do enough work to do as well as they need to get by."[77]

Ohio State University education professor Helen Marks has noted that it has been more than a quarter century since researchers first presented a "troubling picture of . . . dispirited teachers and disengaged students 'putting in their time' while negotiating a sprawling and fragmented curriculum."[78] That pattern has not changed noticeably over time. As of 2000, 40–60 percent of students are regarded as chronically disengaged, and this is a figure that *excludes* absentees and dropouts.[79]

The very premise of state-imposed education is occasionally critiqued for the way in which its Common School rhythms produce the kind of lassitude and placid mediocrity that Theodore Sizer so famously evoked in his 1984 book, *Horace's Compromise*.[80] Murray Rothbard, author of *For a New Liberty*, inveighed in 1974, "The New Left tactic of breaking into high schools shouting 'Jailbreak!' may have been absurd and ineffective, but it certainly expressed a great truth about the school system. For if we are to dragoon the entire youth population into vast prisons in the guise of 'education,' with teachers and administrators serving as surrogate wardens and guards, why should we not expect vast unhappiness, discontent, alienation, and rebellion on the part of the nation's youth?"[81]

Would-be reformers focus on tweaking the traditional high school by shrinking its size, promoting dual enrollment with local colleges, making vocational education more rigorous and relevant, and raising graduation requirements. The larger problem may be that high schools as designed—with their instructional routines, subjects, age configuration, and the rest—may be ill suited for millions. Addressing that challenge may require, rather than tinkering with course requirements or teaching styles, a wholesale rethinking of how to educate and engage teens in the twenty-first century.

CONCLUSION

Common Schooling constituted not a vague commitment to "democracy" or the public good, but an attempt to promote a particular, now disdained view of what it meant to be a good American. Calvin Stowe, a nineteenth-century Common School reformer, warned, "Unless we educate our immigrants, they will be our ruin" and that American prosperity required "a *national* feeling, a national assimilation."[82] Compulsory education was not a strategy to ensure widespread academic excellence but a way to ensure that kids were kept out of the workforce and were being subjected to the homogenizing influence of the Common School. Reformers pursued this agenda with the tools of their day, relying upon new bureaucracies and the tenets of "best practice" factory management. As we note in the next chapter, making the machinery of schooling more expansive entailed compromising curriculum, expectations, and norms.

A commitment to serving students whose native tongue is not English and to respecting native cultures has displaced the stern push for wholesale assimilation that once predominated, but this balancing act is still fraught with difficulty. Teaching in accord with these twin pressures is tricky enough, but addressing it in bureaucratic institutions with extensive regulations and standardized procedures, and in a manner responsive to a wide array of families and students, may well make for an insuperable challenge. Now, it is certainly possible that institutions built to serve certain ends can be repurposed. Schools built to promote homogeneity may be reprogrammed to foster diversity; compulsory attendance systems designed to get students into school could provide the backbone for monitoring virtual instruction. But that's probably not the way to bet.

"Common" schools may find it more difficult to establish strong norms than schools free to define their mission and to focus on serving those students for whom their academic program is a good fit. The need to forge consensus among a diverse mix of families and students can make it more difficult to promote strong norms when it comes to behavior, homework, self-discipline, or respect. This is particularly relevant for at-risk students who benefit most from a disciplined, focused, and affirming culture. The irony is that the Common School model, with its focus on standardization and public governance, makes it more difficult to establish clear norms or a strong culture. School systems striving to emulate the powerful cultures of the most admired charter schools, for instance, often find themselves stumbling over statutes, established disciplinary policies, concerns from this or that constituency, and the conflicts inherent in trying to serve a huge swath of children with varied needs.[83]

If we stipulate that the goal is to help every student master an identifiable body of knowledge, skills, and familiarity with duties and rights of citizenship, but not more than that, we may find substantially more room for new forms of delivery. Such a stance may give rise to second thoughts about the weight accorded to the dream of uniformity, with the attendant conviction that we can identify with precision an optimal way to engineer schools, content, and pedagogy. This struggle for standardization has yielded balky bureaucracies that transform every disagreement into a policy debate and every effort at creative problem solving into an assault on the status quo.

5

The Progressives and the Quest for Universality

"We must stand as educators, shoulder to shoulder, an unbroken phalanx, in maintaining the incomparable superiority of the thorough knowledge of the classics for the attainment of that broad, intellectual discipline, which the higher interest of science, religion, education, and politics will always demand."

—Chicago school superintendent A. F. Nightengale, 1887

"I am fundamentally a complete skeptic as to the necessity of any subject whatever as an element in the education of a gentleman and a scholar."

—Charles W. Eliot, president of Harvard and chairman
of the Committee of Ten, 1897

One needs only surf the Web for a few minutes to find complaints that our schools are falling short when it comes to basic skills, science and advanced math, combating childhood obesity, closing racial achievement gaps, promoting community service, teaching the arts, and much else. Yet we rarely stop and take the time to note that a century of success in universalizing education has meant that every district and school is asked to take on more and more responsibilities for more and more students. It should not be a surprise that schools encouraged to be everything for everybody have found it difficult to be exceptionally good at anything.

Competing schools of thought on content, instruction, and expectations have flourished over the centuries and can be traced back to the disputes between the Greek philosophers and Sophists. As noted in chapter 3, the ancients also debated instructional methods and the centrality of athletics and the arts. But the relevance and asperity of these fights have increased hand in hand with our very success in universalizing schooling, as the attendant pressures of compulsory attendance and a standardized curriculum forced entire communities to decide or compromise on these long-contested issues.[1]

The twentieth century yielded decades of fierce conflict among the champions of competing curricula and pedagogies. Disputants have grimly settled into myriad "math wars" and "reading wars." The ensuing debates have rarely addressed how the assumptions of the Common School aggravate natural tensions and force instructional, philosophical, and cultural disagreements to be battled out through the machinery of public policy and school governance, leaving educators stuck in the cross fire. This tension reflects the same clash of interests that political scientists John Chubb and Terry Moe described in 1990, when they pointed out that the democratic control of schools has fueled bureaucratization and heavy-handed regulation while "discourag[ing] the emergence of coherent, strongly led, academically ambitious" organizations.[2]

The result has been a procession of would-be reformers leaping from one fad to the next, in which new reforms are embraced, eventually discarded in disappointment, and then sometimes resurrected later on in a modified form—all without our ever learning much in the way of humility, the importance of design, or the perils of universality.[3] Thus, in the 1950s, the Life Adjustment Movement, initiated by vocational teacher Charles Prosser and adopted by the U.S. Office of Education, pushed to dramatically restructure high school curriculum for the 60 percent of students deemed to lack the intelligence to attend college.[4] In the 1960s, the National Council of Teachers of Mathematics (NCTM) pushed its "new math," emphasizing abstract concepts and real-world examples rather than rote computation skills. This was followed in the 1970s by the "new, new math," advocated by those who thought the NCTM's "fuzzy math" belittled right answers, as Diane Ravitch notes, "in a field where right answers not only exist but are absolutely necessary."[5] The 1980s brought the rise of phonics-eschewing "whole-language" literacy with its founder, Frank Smith, asserting that "the effort to read through decoding is largely futile and unnecessary."[6] And so on.

Unable to resolve the destructive cycle of faddism, to establish and stay focused on a set of priorities, or to concede that some debates cannot and perhaps need not be resolved, we have now increasingly turned to science in the hope that it will settle the issue with definitive evidence on best practices. Best-practice proponents, like the New Progressives, hope that test designers can help put an end to millennia-spanning debates by designing tests so meticulously that they can finally render conclusive verdicts on what skills and habits of mind are desirable, how students will best master them, what "works" . . . and what doesn't. The problem, of course, is that deciding what is important, what should be measured, or even what it means to "work" are almost inevitably subjective decisions. Wrongheaded assessments can provide misguided direction or present a misleading façade to those unaware of the problems lurking behind the numbers.[7]

A more fruitful course may be possible if we accept that not every dispute need be resolved. The conviction that some skills or habits of mind are critical need not mean that each and every student needs to master them, only that enough students master them so that the full tapestry suffices to meet the needs of the community or nation. The trick is to set the bar as to what constitutes the range of the permissible; here's where our modern search for standards can be enormously constructive, if pursued out of reflection and not reflex.

A NEED, AND TASTE, FOR BUREAUCRACY

By the dawn of the twentieth century, the Common Schoolers had given way to the Progressive reformers. The Progressive movement encompassed a broad push to rationalize and improve American life through the expert application of data and measurement. Celebrating scientific inquiry and teeming with boundless faith in new management techniques and the promise of apolitical, professionalized government, Progressives sought to bring order to the political and economic spheres. Progressive triumphs included the creation of the

Interstate Commerce Commission, the Federal Trade Commission, and the Food and Drug Administration as well as breaking up the cartels and monopolies that dominated the landscape of the early twentieth century. Underlying many of these reform efforts was an innate belief in human progress, the power of the state to foster equality, and the ability of science to direct these endeavors. The Progressive impulse broke up monopolies and checked their power in the private sector, where the power of government was limited. In the world of schooling, however, where competition and private property imposed no similar limitations, Progressive energies would produce large, factory-style monopolies that could serve a vastly larger student population.

And what better model for such operations than Henry Ford's tightly managed, carefully quantified assembly line? Progressives latched onto a rote notion of early-twentieth-century "scientific management" as the optimal way to manage schools and school systems. Made famous by Frederick Taylor, scientific management concerned itself with boosting efficiency by minimizing waste and maximizing output via precise measurement, as articulated in Taylor's 1911 monograph entitled *The Principles of Scientific Management*.[8] The new orthodoxy of its day, Taylor's approach marked the triumphant and conclusive application of science to the task of organizing vast, burgeoning enterprises in the industrial age.

Enamored by "efficiency," reformers, superintendents, and educational psychologists eagerly sought to apply the insights of scientific management to schooling.[9] As historian David Tyack has noted, scientific management arose "mainly to meet pressing internal problems of sheer numbers and chaotic conditions in the schools of swollen villages and booming cities. They struggled with the daily tasks of housing, classifying, teaching, promoting, and keeping records on the thousands of children crowding the classrooms."[10] Preaching a faith in science and technical expertise while rejecting the messy business of politics, the apostles of this movement sought to build orderly, apolitical, and expert management structures through increasingly bureaucratic systems. The machinery they erected, for good and ill, has defined how we think about school management and data to the present day.

The cult of efficiency had become widespread after the first decade of the twentieth century and its adherents freely borrowed from the industrial era handbook. In 1905, at the annual meeting of the National Education Association (NEA), George Martin of the Massachusetts State Board of Education said, "The contrast between modern business methods and the most modern methods in education is so great as to suggest some searching questions."[11] George Herbert Betts, professor at Cornell College in Iowa, explained in his 1912 book *Social Principles of Education,* "Our schools may be looked upon as a great system of education factories in which the children are both the raw material and the workers. . . . The problem in the school, as in any other factory, is to secure the largest output with the least waste of material and labor."[12] The next year, Paul Hanus, a professor of education at Harvard University, would tell the NEA that the promise of school improvement lay in the application of technical information, asserting that "We are no longer disputing whether education has a scientific basis; we are trying to find that basis."[13]

The crush of numbers and the desire to emulate the leading organizational models of the day led the Progressives to their faith in the power of statistics, data, and precision—at least for the things they could readily count. They enthusiastically tracked how many students attended school, how many courses they completed, and how many truants were disciplined. Their innovations included attendance counts, Carnegie Units, and labor agreements that carefully stipulated the number of instructional minutes per day. Tyack relates: "Well into the twentieth century superintendents continued to report attendance and tardiness statistics down to the second and third decimal point. 'A school with an enrollment of fifty, daily attendance fifty and none tardy,' wrote a lyrical superintendent, 'is a grand sight to behold in the morning and afternoon.'"[14]

Reformers counted not just bodies, but dollars, too. In 1898, William T. Harris, then U.S. commissioner of education, reported on the accomplishments of American schooling since 1870, noting enrollment had more than doubled, from 7 million to 15 million, and that spending had grown from about nine dollars per pupil in 1870 to more than thirteen dollars per pupil in 1898.[15] As state aid became tied to average daily attendance, districts focused their administrative machinery on counting carefully and getting children in the seats. Official data tracked the percentage of pupils in attendance, the number of parents and children prosecuted for truancy, the number of convictions obtained, and the number of children sent to correctional institutions.

In the early twentieth century, reformers seized upon that orthodoxy of scientific management and bureaucracy and used it to expand and systematize schooling, just as their private-sector counterparts did. There was nothing wrong with any of this. Given the tools of the day—especially a new but labor-intensive ability to monitor process and a limited ability to coordinate across distances—large all-purpose organizations that micromanaged employees made a certain amount of sense. In the early years of the twentieth century, the bureaucratic model worked very successfully for giants like the American Tobacco Company, the American Sugar Company, the U.S. Leather Company, and the imposingly named North American Company (an electric utility holding company). In the fullness of time, as the challenges and available tools evolved, these heavy-footed behemoths were broken up, displaced by more agile competitors, or acquired by new ventures that imposed new management. In schooling, however, the bureaucratic legacy has remained.

DEBATING INSTRUCTION, AGAIN AND AGAIN

The fierce debates about what children should learn, which children should learn it, and how it should be taught that have raged since the days of Plato were still being fought by Progressive reformers at the dawn of the twentieth century. We saw this earlier in the split be-tween the distinctive curriculum of Athens—with its emphasis on reading, writing, arithmetic, and music—and Sparta—with its focus on physicality and military preparation.

Plato is credited with the aphorism, "Knowledge which is ac-quired under compulsion has no hold on the mind."[16] But even Plato also called for requiring students to learn "the works of great poets . . . by heart, in order that he may imitate or emulate them."[17] Plato's conflicted thoughts on discipline and enthusiasm have hardened over the millennia into two competing camps. Today, that quarrel plays out between two clashing camps: those who embrace "teacher-centered" instruction focused on teaching a core body of content and those who champion a "child-centered" vision which is more focused on engaging the student and less concerned with content.

In the United States, notions of curricular standards have shifted over time. Even Thomas Jefferson, remembered for his commitment to education, thought the nation's largest state need only produce ten students per year "of superior genius, well taught in Greek, Latin, geography, and the higher branches of arithmetic" and another ten "of still superior parts, who, to those branches of learning, shall have added such of the sciences as their genius shall" dictate.[18]

WHAT MUST GRADUATES KNOW?

These curricular debates have perhaps shown up most clearly in dis-putes about what high school students must know. The latter nine-teenth century saw much experimentation when it came to high school courses of study. When it came to such matters, no two high schools were alike. Historians David Angus and Jeffrey Mirel noted that curricular decisions "were made by locally elected boards of education, not by career educators" and that they were influenced by parental pressures, ethnic voting blocks, and fiscal crises.[19] These pressures produced significant variation in curricula and school provision.

During this time, decisions governing content and curricula were left primarily to tens of thousands of local school boards. This fragmentation left Progressive reformers concerned about inconsistent standards, and in their characteristic fashion, they sought out a solution to render schooling more orderly and efficient. One response was increasing the use of standardized textbooks. Such texts were also thought to help address concerns about teacher capability. "The poorer the teacher," explained education professor H. L. Donovan in the 1920s, "the better the textbooks need to be."[20] In the early 1900s, twenty-four states featured boards of education that mandated the adoption of certain textbooks, while New York State imposed fines of $50 to $100 for not using preapproved books.[21]

While legislators and school boards mandated specific texts, policy makers ducked explicit decisions about how or what should be taught by directing teachers to do a little of everything. Witness the 1915 Massachusetts law that called for students to study "orthography, reading, writing, the English language and grammar, geography, arithmetic, drawing, the history of the United States, physiology and hygiene, and good behavior, bookkeeping, algebra, geometry, one or more foreign languages, agriculture, sewing, cooking, vocal music, physical training, civil government, ethics, thrift, and such other subjects as the school committee may determine may be taught in the public schools."[22]

Progressive reformers deemed this inconsistency untenable and were determined to bring order. Speaking to the Harvard Teachers Association in 1901, influential educator and education philosopher John Dewey outlined his preferred structure of secondary education, arguing for "proper economy of instruction, and harmonious organization instead of blind confusion in the curriculum."[23] During the 1880s and 1890s, the National Council of Education of the National Education Association produced reports on topics including "Harmonizing of Higher, Secondary, and Elementary Schools" and "The Relation of High Schools to Colleges."[24]

In 1894, the influential Committee of Ten on Secondary School Studies, convened by the National Education Association, issued a landmark report addressing "the teaching of the subjects of the secondary school, the need for uniformity in content, standardization of requirements, time allotment, and admission to college."[25] Though many of the smaller reports prepared by subcommittees detailed specific best practices within the subject or on the range of course requirements across schools, the overarching focus of the report was the need to improve secondary school curriculum in order to facilitate easier access to higher education. As noted earlier, the committee acknowledged that in any national secondary school system, "the preparation of a few pupils for college or scientific school should in the ordinary secondary school be the incidental, and not the principal object."[26] However, the committee's report also sought to open schooling to more students by recommending a more standardized curriculum that could allow students from public high schools to earn admission to colleges and advised that all courses "be taught consecutively and thoroughly, and . . . [that] all be used for training the powers of observation, memory, expression, and reasoning."[27] Historians Freeman Butts and Lawrence Cremin have concluded, "By and large, [the committee] determined the course of American secondary education for a generation following its publication."[28]

Aside from the report's noteworthy content, the committee evinced the budding Progressive era's fascination with measurement. Theodore Sizer, former dean of Harvard's Graduate School of Education, has noted that after being asked to "consider the proper limits of its subject," the committee focused on "hours per year, not knowledge, skills, and values. . . . The questions they asked were mechanical—how long, when, how—never what and why."[29] The ensuing recommendations would quickly become norms.[30] Sizer lamented that the committee opted to ignore "the problem of the student who was not academically inclined. Although few such students were attending secondary schools at all in 1894, the figures available to the Ten suggested that an increasing number would be doing so. . . . But they ignored the future and prescribed for the schools of the present."[31]

The incipient expansion of secondary schooling was not addressed until the NEA convened the Commission on the Reorganization of Secondary Education in 1913 to contemplate "a comprehensive program of reorganization" of the nation's secondary schools.[32] Unlike the Committee of Ten, which sought to establish rigorous standards for a limited population, the commission's report on the Cardinal Principles of Secondary Education contemplated a curriculum suitable for a much broader population. The Cardinal Principles established what Lawrence Cremin has deemed a "pedagogical revolution" that ushered in "a whole new age in American secondary education."[33]

Seeking to devise a course of studies for an expanding school population, the Cardinal Principles sketched a vision of secondary education guided by health, command of fundamental processes, worthy home membership, vocation, citizenship, and ethical character. The commission recommended that, "Education should equip the individual to secure from his leisure the re-creation of body, mind, and spirit, and the enrichment and enlargement of his personality," and rebuked schools for failing "to organize and direct the social activities of young people as [they] should."[34] The Cardinal Principles reflected the universalizing impulse to provide an education useful to everyone, the academically inclined and disinclined alike.

The Cardinal Principles report tasked schools to cultivate an array of skills, including both preparing students to "become effective in the various vocations" and ensuring that they "obtain those common ideas, common ideals, and common modes of thought . . . that make for cooperation, social cohesion, and social solidarity."[35] The Cardinal Principles would come to be seen as the antithesis of the content-centric Committee of Ten report. Historian Diane Ravitch has observed that the report was a "milestone in the history of American education," with its seven principles exerting a profound influence on how Americans viewed the defining aims of schooling. Ravitch regarded this as anything but a happy outcome, lamenting, "Its conclusions showed the influence of a generation of education reformers who opposed teaching any subject matter as an end in itself and who preferred that schools adopt functional objectives such as vocation, health, and citizenship."[36]

The contrast between the two watershed reports, a quarter century apart, illustrates the tensions that emerged in the wake of universalization. The Committee of Ten offered a commitment to focused academic excellence, while the Cardinal Principles sounded a strategic retreat, deliberately abandoning pretensions of rigor in favor of a more diffuse notion of utility. This unpalatable trade-off may be inescapable, and it poses hard choices, choices that a generation of reformers have ducked with bland paeans to "excellence for all."

Many European and Asian nations deal with this dilemma by unflinchingly sorting students into distinctive tracks: they test students at particular ages and then sort them based on those results (without much fretting about whether those results may be biased or the product of familial advantages). Other nations, mostly in the developing world, avoid this dilemma because the system of education is informal and piecemeal. The United States, however, built out a formalized system of schools charged with serving every child but without any clear notion of what educators, schools, or systems were supposed to do well. Instead, educators were vaguely instructed to do many things, and they naturally wound up prioritizing on the basis of administrative convenience, parental demands, and constituent pressure. The result was an incoherent system of incoherent parts.

THE ESSENTIALIST-CONSTRUCTIVIST DIVIDE

American schooling continues to be the site of bitter, ongoing clashes between essentialist proponents of the Western canon and advocates of child-centered, constructivist learning—reflecting, in many ways, the disputes surrounding the merits of the recommendations proffered by the Committee of Ten and in the Cardinal Principles. Both camps can point to models that have enjoyed success, but both have also had difficulty ensuring that their approaches are adopted with fidelity and used effectively.

One of today's most celebrated student-centered school models is Providence, Rhode Island's "The Met," an alternative charter high school that became the model for the Uncommon Schools network. At The Met, there are no classes, no tests, and no grades. Students spend two days a week in internships that they help to select, and rather than take tests, students give public exhibitions. Dennis Littky, Met co-founder and a freethinker with little tolerance for hierarchies, believes that schools should teach students how to learn rather than dictate what students learn. Says Littky, "What we need is not just smaller schools and realistic education goals, but authentic relationships between educators and kids. What we need are truly personalized schools. . . . In a personalized school, the teachers' primary concern is educating their students, not getting through a certain body of subject matter. And in doing this, their primary concern becomes the individual students themselves."[37]

Child-centered constructivists like Littky believe that children are natural learners—and that great schooling is about engaging their interest and giving them the freedom to ask big questions. The constructivist rationale is appealing and its intellectual lineage can be traced all the way back to Rousseau's *Emile*. In *Emile,* as noted in chapter 3, Rousseau argued that man is born naturally free and good and can stay in that state unless corrupted by society: "Let us lay down as an incontestable maxim that the first movements of nature are always right: there is no original wickedness in the human heart."[38] Thus, for Rousseau, and other naturalistic educators of the eighteenth and nineteenth centuries like Johann Pestalozzi and Friedrich Froebel, education's mission was to help children find their natural selves and stave off corruption, not to impose society's deadening discipline.[39]

In the United States, constructivism was championed most influentially by John Dewey, particularly in his role as founder and director of the Laboratory School at the University of Chicago at the turn of the century. Dewey embraced what he termed "experimental logic," as students first "engage[ed] in activity to try out ideas" and then experienced "the consequences of that activity."[40] In the 1930s, the Deweyan vision was preached by leading scholars at Columbia University's Teachers College, including George S. Counts, who held that schools should be "agencies of active social reform,"[41] and William H. Kilpatrick, who wanted students, as much as possible, to "plan, direct, and execute their own learning."[42] Today, child-centered educators are particularly concerned about the prevalence of standardized testing and No Child Left Behind–style accountability. As George Wood, executive at the constructivist Alliance for Excellent Education, has charged, "The skills needed to do well on these tests at best reflect a shallow kind of learning and at worst indicate only a better ability to take tests."[43]

The complication is that, despite its intrinsic appeal, constructivism has proven poorly suited to bureaucratized delivery, requires an exhausting degree of precision and commitment to be executed properly, and consequently flounders when attempted on more than a boutique scale. From the Dewey Lab School in Chicago to Deborah Meier's famed Central Park East Secondary School in New York City to the hundreds of schools in the Coalition of Essential Schools network that Meier and Theodore Sizer formed in the 1980s, inspiring models have lapsed into disappointment as the energy, talent, and focus that marked their initial success proved difficult to sustain or deliver more broadly. Central Park East, for instance, lost momentum when Meier left as Meier's handpicked staff drifted off and the school's distinctive approach was diluted. Eventually, Meier sadly noted, "I stopped visiting. It was too painful."[44]

The constructivist disdain for a canon of content knowledge is anathema to those essentialists who believe in the importance of what former University of Virginia professor E. D. Hirsch Jr. has termed "core knowledge." In Charlottesville, Virginia, just off the grounds of the University of Virginia sits the Core Knowledge Foundation that Hirsch founded in 1986.[45] The Foundation works to promote the curriculum that Hirsch and two colleagues sketched in 1988 in the seminal *Cultural Literacy: What Every American Needs to Know*. Arguing that children require a grasp of essential facts, dates, events, and concepts if they are to be academically successful, Hirsch advocates a "core curriculum" that ensures all children have mastered a prescribed body of essential historic, literary, and scientific content. Hirsch believes that a mastery of basic curriculum should be the first priority, and that "the how-to elements of creativity, problem solving, language comprehension, and critical thinking are far, far less important than domain-specific knowledge."[46]

Essentialists, like Hirsch, worry that constructivism fails to acknowledge that children need to master key facts and ideas before tackling higher-order skills.[47] Hirsch ally Diane Ravitch, professor of education at New York University, has argued that progressive pedagogy fails in its most basic goal—developing a sound body of knowledge that can serve as a springboard for future intellectual pursuits. Ravitch has argued, "Whenever the academic curriculum was diluted or minimized, large numbers of children were pushed through the school system without benefit of a genuine education. As the academic curriculum lost its importance as the central focus of the public school system, the schools lost their anchor, their sense of mission."[48] The Hirsch-Ravitch stance has much to recommend it, except the frustrating reality that the push for clear, rigorous, specific standards has repeatedly gotten waylaid by the familiar politics and compromises of universalism, while state bureaucracies and local districts have typically implemented the resulting directives clumsily and without much conviction. The result is that the core-knowledge curriculum, which Hirsch has touted as a model for vast state and district systems, has been most widely and enthusiastically adopted primarily by charter schools.

Recent decades have seen constructivists and essentialists clash repeatedly over the merits of phonics versus whole language, arithmetic versus problem solving, and standardized testing versus "portfolio" assessment. In the 1990s, Congress waded into the reading debate by approving funding "to convene a national panel to assess the status of research-based knowledge, including the effectiveness of various approaches to teaching children to read."[49] From its inception, the National Reading Panel (NRP) aggravated the conflict between advocates of phonics and champions of "whole language" instruction.[50] In the end, the NRP's final report "suggests that teaching a combination of reading comprehension techniques is the most effective. . . . When used in combination, these techniques can improve results in standardized comprehension tests."[51]

In 2006, a companion National Mathematics Advisory Panel (NMAP) was charged with using the "best available scientific evidence . . . to foster greater knowledge of and improved performance in mathematics."[52] Assessing American math education, NMAP unanimously concluded that "the delivery system in mathematics education . . . is broken and must be fixed."[53] Like the NRP, NMAP found merit in both sides of the clash between essentialists and Progressives, asserting, "Debates regarding the relative importance of these aspects of mathematical knowledge are misguided."[54] Dr. Larry Faulkner, chairman of NMAP, threw cold water on the long-running debate, concluding, "There is no basis in research for favoring teacher-based or student-centered instruction. . . . People may retain their strongly held philosophical inclinations, but the research does not show that either is better than the other."[55]

The battles are ceaseless, sapping energy and fueling efforts by victorious parties to wedge their favored outcomes as deeply into rules and regulations as possible. Rendering all this a particularly dubious exercise is that it remains unclear whether favored approaches can consistently confer meaningful benefits. For instance, even as U.S. Secretary of Education Arne Duncan traveled the country in 2009 avidly championing the importance of states' adopting common curricular standards, an influential study that year by former U.S. Institute of Education Sciences commissioner Grover

Whitehurst reported that there does not appear to be any systematic relationship between standards and student outcomes. The finding implied it may well be impossible to settle upon the "right" curriculum.[56]

Despite decades of fervent efforts and stacks of studies, the evidence on the merits of child-centered and essentialist pedagogy remains muddled. Constructivist instruction may well benefit children who have already mastered essential content and skills or those fortunate enough to benefit from the expertise and support evident at The Met, but it may be ineffective, or even destructive, when adopted more universally. It is equally easy to envision essentialist approaches better serving students who lack the building blocks, basic skills, or habits of mind needed for child-centered learning to work as intended. Lisa Delpit of Georgia State University has offered the wise if obvious caution that students learn differently in different educational settings for any number of reasons, including culture, background, socioeconomic status, interest, and natural gifts. Thus, argues Delpit, when it comes to instruction, what matters is what works, not the pursuit of uniformity.[57]

Today, loose networks such as Core Knowledge and Uncommon Schools link together scattered member schools. The limitation is that these confederations reside in the interstices, between and atop the pre-existing systems. The result is watery and half-baked execution. An emancipatory approach seeks room for essentialists and constructivists of various stripes to demonstrate their mettle while teaching as many children as effectively as they are able. That requires not just accepting but encouraging systems of schools that disagree about philosophy and pedagogy.

VOCATIONAL EDUCATION

The trick with universalization is that it asks schools to serve more and more students, ensuring that schools will be asked to educate students with varying needs, talent, and dreams. Consequently, all fights about content, of course, are not about academic subjects. Vocational education was crafted to provide "relevant" instruction to less affluent children in an era when manufacturing jobs were plentiful and offered a relatively substantial wage. It is little wonder that we have repeatedly had difficulty retooling such instruction for an era in which we seek universal academic proficiency and worry that a high school diploma and practical skills are unlikely to deliver a comfortable, middle-class life.

As noted earlier, the first hints of vocational education can be seen in ancient Sparta. The earliest *formal* vocational education can be found during the Renaissance, when the trades organized guilds and when apprenticeships provided training and entry into specialized, exclusive fields. The apprenticeship system was perpetuated in the American colonies and through the Civil War, but declined in the face of mass education for mass production during the Industrial Revolution.

During the middle and late nineteenth century, early vestiges of vocational schools emerged from the apprenticeship system in the industrial Northeast. In Philadelphia, the combined interests of industrial managers and educational reformers gave birth to one of the first systems of industrial training, the Spring Garden Institute developed by Baldwin Locomotive Works. University of Greenwich professor Andrew Dawson has explained that Spring Garden made the city "into a leading center of the manual training movement by the end of the century.... Philadelphia's educational reformers explicitly linked their curriculum to the requirements of local machine builders. Spring Garden led directly to the foundation of the city's vocational high schools."[58]

Labor unions were deeply involved in efforts to marry vocational education, child labor laws, and compulsory education. The National Association of Manufacturers (NAM) pioneered some of the earliest programs while "investigat[ing] how education might provide a more effective means to help American manufacturers compete in expanding international markets."[59] In 1898, Theodore

Search, president of NAM, allowed that "classical and literary studies . . . have their place in all educational systems, but it is unfair to the great material interests of the land to leave out of account the obvious demands of industry and commerce."[60]

The first several decades of the twentieth century were marked by a surge in popular support for more vocation-based schooling. Educational philosophers like David Snedden, a staunch Darwinist who believed in the propriety of natural social stratification, thought vocational education's primary purpose was to identify and prepare students of limited intellect for industrial employment in order to meet the needs of the labor force.[61] As John Gray, head of the economics department at the University of Minnesota, bluntly opined in 1914: "Men [must] be trained for their work. That training cannot be obtained outside of the schools. The mass of the people cannot be held in the schools to get any kind of an education unless the public schools are vocationalized."[62] Amidst growing support for the expansion of vocational education, in 1917 Congress enacted the Smith-Hughes Act. The act provided funds for education in "trade, industrial, and agricultural subjects" in secondary schools and an assortment of specialized and evening schools.[63]

Whereas contemporary reformers worry that vocational education frequently segregates minority and low-income youth into dead-end tracks, a century ago vocational education was lauded by black leaders such as Booker T. Washington as an avenue to advancement. Washington, who founded the Tuskegee Normal and Industrial Institute in Tennessee in 1881, was criticized for his faith in vocational schooling, which was perceived by his critics as a retreat from equality. As he argued in a speech at Fisk University, African Americans needed to learn to do things: "to put brains into the common occupations of life" and "to dignify common labor."[64] Washington saw vocational education as an opportunity for blacks to exploit a void within southern industry and believed that occupations regarded as menial could be dignified by the application of intelligence and education.[65]

Intentionally or not, vocational education today has reinforced social divisions along racial lines, as black students have been far more likely to be enrolled in vocational education than are white students.[66] Echoing the fears of many in the field, the 1994 National Assessment of Vocational Education warned that vocational education was quickly becoming "an educational backwater, a dumping ground for the economically disadvantaged and the disabled."[67] This does not have to be the case. If school systems designed courses in nonacademic subjects, recruited instructors in the applied trades, focused on serving students who have often been marginalized, and found ways to collaborate with local employers, vocational education could be a valuable addition to the more academic offerings. Not surprisingly, however, districts and schools have tended to neglect this potential boon or have pursued it without the requisite thoughtfulness.

ACADEMIC TRACKING

The debate over vocational education mirrors that over the academic "tracking" of students into classes based on their academic achievement. Critics of tracking have shifted in recent decades from attacking systems that explicitly sorted students by race and class to mounting a broader assault on efforts to organize students based on prior performance. In an influential declaration, the Carnegie Council on Adolescent Development's 1989 *Turning Points* report condemned tracking as "one of the most divisive and damaging school practices in existence."[68] But as Tom Loveless, a scholar at the Brookings Institution, has noted, "For most of this century, schools used IQ tests to sort students . . . into classes of vastly different curricula that predetermined their fates. But today's tracking systems function differently . . . [and] are guided by successful completion of prerequisite courses, prior achievement, and teacher recommendations, not IQ tests."[69]

The reasonable response to vulgarized tracking has morphed into a conviction that attempts to organize students for instruction in a manner that reflects achievement or knowledge is problematic. Rather than arranging students to facilitate disciplined and skilled instruction, the proponents of expansive detracking expect each individual educator to find ways to accommodate students with vastly different knowledge and interests in the same classroom. Educators, tasked with this difficult duty, have increasingly turned to workaround solutions like "differentiated instruction," a technique peddled by a cottage industry of researchers, consultants, and charlatans that supposedly allows teachers to simultaneously instruct all these students. The evidence that this "best of both worlds" solution works consistently is as thin as readers might expect.

There are particular concerns that the search for a happy medium shortchanges high achievers. University of Wisconsin researcher Adam Gamoran has pointed out, "We also know that when tracking is eliminated, students at high levels don't gain as much as they do in high-level or [Advanced Placement] classes."[70] In 2007, Steve Farkas and Ann Duffett's National Teacher Survey documented the concerns of Advanced Placement (AP) teachers about how their gifted students were faring. Over two-thirds of teachers responded that struggling students were most likely to be the focus of their school's efforts to raise test scores as a result of mandated tracking of achievement data.[71] While advocates of detracking have long insisted that it benefits high achievers as well as students who are less proficient, the teachers suggested otherwise—with 84 percent reporting that implementing differentiated instruction on a daily basis was "difficult."[72] Seventy-seven percent of teachers agreed that "getting underachieving students to reach 'proficiency' has become so important that the needs of advanced students take a back seat."[73] We have increased the number of tasks a given teacher is expected to do and asked her to simultaneously do them all, and better.

As disinclined as we are to acknowledge the implications, there is no dispute that at any age some children are more knowledgeable and advanced than others. This is due partly to home and family circumstances, partly to natural gifts, partly to the quality of schooling that students have previously received, as well as to a variety of other possible influences.

A student with a 500-word vocabulary and another with a 5,000-word vocabulary have distinctive needs. It should not surprise anyone that students who lack a basic mastery of phonics, language, or arithmetic are ill served by child-centered instruction that fails to help them master those skills. At the same time, the emphasis on ensuring that lagging students master essential skills has stifled and shortchanged more advanced students who are eager for something more. Efforts to sort students for purposes of instruction were historically hierarchical and designed in ways that reinforced class-based inequities.

Other possibilities exist, however. For instance, a feature that characterizes acclaimed schools ranging from the much-admired Thomas Jefferson High School for Science and Technology in Alexandria, Virginia, to the seventy-odd KIPP (Knowledge is Power Program) Academies that operate across the nation is an ability to focus on serving a particular kind of student as best they can. This focus allows leaders, teachers, and staff to relentlessly concentrate on perfecting particular pedagogies and a particular vision of success. Thomas Jefferson is a district school operated by Fairfax County but admits students based on test performance and seeks students of "high ability, aptitude, and interest in math, science, and technology." Its mission statement flatly explains that it aims to provide "a specialized education for selected students."[74] The KIPP mission, and that of similarly inclined charter schools such as Achievement First, is to focus on serving disadvantaged students and to help them master core academic skills, develop self-discipline, learn the "code" of mainstream success, and graduate high school prepared for college.

With sufficient thought and care, students can be sorted in productive ways without reinforcing social hierarchies. The challenge is to sort for instructional purposes in a fashion that is nimble enough to allow groupings to vary by subject, skill, and interest, and to shift over time. Ultimately, the "antitracking" dogma—if stretched to mean that any form of sorting or self-selection is problematic—means that each and every teacher must be equipped to effectively instruct children with wildly divergent needs, skills, and interests. That is a recipe for futility. Of course, some fret that allowing students to self-select into distinctive schools or organizing them by instructional need may crimp social interaction among students of different races, incomes, or backgrounds. Schools today don't do a particularly good job at this, as we'll discuss a little later, but it is a valid concern that can and should be addressed through more conscientious program design.

THE CHALLENGE OF UNIVERSALIZING HIGH ACHIEVEMENT

Just as their Progressive forbearers sought to universalize schooling, today's New Progressives seek to universalize excellence. This is a laudable goal, but one that invites the same kinds of diluted expectations that plague any other attempt at universalization. A 2007 report from the National Assessment Governing Board (NAGB) found that high school seniors were faring worse overall on key national assessments than in the previous decade, even while receiving significantly higher grades and taking what seemed to be more rigorous courses. About 35 percent of twelfth graders tested in 2005 were proficient in reading—their worst performance since the test was launched in 1992. At the same time, the average high school grade-point average rose from 2.68 in 1990 to 2.98 in 2005, the percentage of graduating seniors who completed a standard course of study rose from 35 to 58 percent, and the percentage who took the highest-level curriculum doubled.[75] This gap between transcripts and test scores has struck many, including Darvin Winick, chairman of the National Assessment Governing Board, as "very suspicious."[76] Daria Hall, director of K–12 policy development for the advocacy group Education Trust, has noted, "What it suggests is that we are telling students that they're being successful in these courses when, in fact, we're not teaching them any more than they were learning in the past . . . we are, in effect, lying to these students."[77] Education Trust's president, Kati Haycock, lamented, "The core problem is that course titles don't really signal what is taught in the course and grades don't signal what a kid has learned."[78]

Former National Center for Education Statistics commissioner Mark Schneider has documented this same dubious trend when it comes to high school math. The average number of math credits completed by a high school graduate rose from 3.2 to 3.8 between 1990 and 2005, even as average math GPAs rose from 2.2 to 2.6. On top of that, there has been a dramatic increase in the highest level of math that students have taken. Whereas only one-third of students completed algebra II in 1978, over half did so in 2008. All of this should clearly signal that students are learning more, shouldn't it? Unfortunately, what we see is the same watering-down trend noted in the case of transcripts. The National Assessment of Educational Progress shows that those students enrolled in algebra I, geometry, and algebra II in 1978 scored higher than their 2008 counterparts in those same classes. The result, explains Schneider, is a "delusion of rigor" in which we celebrate success at getting students into classes with more impressive course titles even though "what American high school students know and what they can do in math" are static.[79]

We see similar downward trends in the contemporary push to "democratize" AP, a well-intentioned policy effort that nonetheless arouses fear in many who worry that the program's rigor is being compromised. The decade-long initiative to boost AP enrollment—and subsequent fears of diluted curriculum—led the College Board in 2007 to stage a nationwide assessment of 130,000 teachers, asking them to furnish written proof that their courses were sufficiently rigorous and insisting for the first time on the right to reject syllabi. The *Washington Post* reported, "An explosion in AP study . . . has bred worry, particularly among college leaders, of a decline in the rigor for which the courses are known. Once the exclusive province of elite students at select high schools, AP study or its equivalent is now more or less expected of any student who aspires to attend even a marginally selective college."[80]

Andrew Flagel, dean of admissions at George Mason University, commented, "What we're hearing from people is that . . . the push to get so many people into [them] has led to a tendency or a temptation to lower the rigor of the course," and AP officials discussed concerns that some schools "simply make up courses and call them AP."[81] As mentioned before, pollsters Duffett and Farkas reported in 2009 that 39 percent of AP teachers think the quality of their students has declined over the past five years and many are concerned that "too many pupils may be in over their heads."[82] These concerns are the predictable fruits of successful efforts to enroll more students in advanced classes. The disheartening result is that, at least as schools operate today, steering more students into more-demanding classes risks adversely impacting rigor and the caliber of instruction.

AN IMPERFECT SCIENCE

When frustrated by seemingly endless debates over curriculum or tracking and the difficulty of settling on a strategy that seems to work universally, there is a natural impulse to turn to research as a way to fairly and finally settle the question. This is the mantra of to-day's "data-driven" reformers, including the New Progressives, who, like the original Progressives a century ago, rely on scientific metrics to free them from these tendentious debates and point the way forward. Before leaning too heavily on the tantalizing promise of research, however, it is useful to recall that science and measure have been asked to provide conclusive answers before, sometimes with discomfiting results.

Perhaps the most prominent early effort of this kind got started in 1911, when the National Education Association created the Committee on the Economy of Time, to investigate how classroom time was allocated among the various subjects so as to identify optimal instructional materials, grade placement, and school organization, and to flag unnecessary or wasteful subject matter.[83] The committee marked the launch of the "fact-finding era" in K–12 education, as termed by Progressive educator and Teachers College professor Harold Rugg, and resulted in a raft of related, if not damning, inquiries.[84]

Many similar examples followed shortly. In 1916, Teachers College professor W. C. Bagley examined the twenty-five most frequently used U.S. history textbooks in order to determine the relative importance of historical topics; importance, Bagley thought, could be gauged by comparing the average percentage of page space devoted to each topic.[85] University of Iowa professor B. B. Bassett's 1919 study of civics curricula gauged each topic's importance based upon the linear inches of textbook space it received. Bassett explained that the metric that he and his colleagues employed had the virtue of being "entirely impartial" and was "justified upon the assumption that, given a sufficiently long period of time, the topics most discussed are most important."[86] Walter Monroe, former director of the Bureau of Educational Management, wrote in 1917 that the "minimal essentials" of arithmetic should be determined by measuring the number of questions pertaining to various industries relative to the portion of the U.S. population employed in each industry (for example, the number of people employed in "farming" was charted against the number of questions featuring "farming" examples to determine if the curriculum was sound).[87]

Increasing enrollment and expanding bureaucracy bred a pursuit of more uniform measurement systems, focused first on quantifying time usage and native ability, and later on achievement. While the Progressives were introducing input metrics like enrollment and the Carnegie Unit, they also eagerly sought to devise evaluation tools that would track outcomes. One such tool was the standardized test, the modern form of which can be traced to the late nineteenth century. In 1897, Joseph Meyer Rice made the then-novel claim that the amount of spelling children learned was not proportionate to the time they spent studying the subject, and urged the adoption of spelling tests.[88] This notion likely strikes the modern reader as commonsensical, but Rice's contemporaries were more than a little skeptical. Progressive icon Ellwood Cubberley observed that Rice had "startled the country" with his claim that "the results of teaching spelling could be measured by means of a spelling test" and that the "proposal was greeted with ridicule by many."[89] But Cubberley, unlike his peers, would cheer such efforts, asserting, "We can now measure an unknown class and say, rather definitely, that, for example, the class not only spells poorly but is 12 percent below standard; that the class is 8 percent ahead of its place in speed of writing, but 15 percent below on quality."[90]

More than a decade later, Frederick Kelly of the State Normal School in Emporia, Kansas, created the first modern multiple-choice test (the 1914 to 1915 Kansas Silent Reading Test) while seeking to devise a test that had one valid answer for each question and that could be administered and graded efficiently.[91] Others followed suit. In the first decades of the twentieth century, Edward Lee Thorndike and Charles Judd investigated every phase of the school curriculum, devising achievement tests in spelling, handwriting, arithmetic, composition, and other areas.[92] By 1923, the *Guide to Educational Measurements* estimated that more than 300 standardized scales were available.[93] These instruments meant it was possible, for the first time, for scientists to measure which individuals and populations were above and below a selected average.

For Progressives worried about the corrupting influence of politics on education, Cubberley explained the new protections offered by standardized exams: "Standardized tests have meant nothing less than the ultimate changing of school administration from guess work to scientific accuracy. The mere personal opinion of school board members and the lay public . . . have been in large part eliminated."[94] Leaning on the familiar appeal of scientific management, he enthused, "Teaching without a measuring stick of standardized length, and without definite standards . . . is much like the old time luck-and-chance farming, and there is no reason to think that the introduction of well-tested standards for accomplishment in school work will not do for education what has been done for agriculture."[95]

Measuring Intelligence

In addition to subject tests, the Progressive era was marked by extensive efforts to develop intelligence tests. Great energy and expertise were poured into efforts to develop an accurate intelligence test that could be used uniformly to sort students and organize them for instruction and work, though the assessment's roots lie elsewhere. The IQ test was created in response to the advent of World War I, when mobilization meant that a large number of recruits had to be sorted rapidly for training and assignment. In response, the U.S. government gathered elite psychology professors, who proceeded to develop a measurement system that would reveal a person's "mental age" and "actual age," reflecting their innate intelligence. In hindsight, of course, some of the results appear less than reliable.

In one such analysis, testing expert H. H. Goddard "identified as 'feeble-minded' 83 percent of Jews, 80 percent of Hungarians, 79 percent of Italians and 87 percent of Russians among a small group of immigrants assessed at Ellis Island."[96] Similarly, Robert Yerkes, a Harvard researcher involved in developing the IQ test, analyzed intelligence for military recruiting and concluded in 1921 that "37 percent of whites and 89 percent of negroes" could fairly be classified as "morons."[97] Yerkes had few concerns that tests that labeled perhaps all of his fellow citizens might be providing misleading results. He explained that the tests were "constructed and administered" to address biases due to English proficiency or other factors and "are now definitely known to measure native intellectual ability."[98]

Harvard University historian Patricia Albjerg Graham notes that concerns about the tests soon emerged. One part of an August 16, 1918, test asked "whether Yale was in New Haven, Annapolis, Ithaca, or Cambridge"—using knowledge of Yale's location as a metric for gauging innate intelligence.[99] As more than a few observers would later point out, only a Yalie would manage to miss the problem there. In 1922, observing the growing fascination with this new science, journalist Walter Lippman complained, "The danger of the intelligence tests is that in a wholesale system of education, the less sophisticated or the more prejudiced will stop when they have classified and forget that their duty is to educate."[100]

Today's school reformers can take important lessons from innovations like the IQ test. Too often, we forget that research is a tool—and that the answers it provides depend on the quality of the instrument and the deftness with which it is wielded. On this score, I'll offer one last example, just as a reminder of how our enthusiasm for science can get away from us. In 1914, Bird Baldwin of Swarthmore College suggested that grade placement could be more efficient and orderly if based strictly on a student's height, weight, and lung capacity. Baldwin judged these to be indicators of physical (and presumably mental) maturity. He wanted "tall, healthy children of accelerated physiological development" to "proceed through school as rapidly as possible within the limits of thoroughness" while "small, light children of retarded physiological development [would] be kept below or in the normal grade, doing supplementary work."[101] Admirers of William Brennan, Milton Friedman, or Woody Allen can only give thanks that Baldwin's research-based strategy didn't harden into orthodoxy, or those influential figures would have been shunted aside.

While excited claims on behalf of "best practices" and "scientifically based research" sometimes imply that they are new ideas in education, the truth is that the sector has been long plagued by attempts to apply scientific techniques in wrongheaded, inappropriate, or problematic ways, and we must learn from these missteps. The reality, of course, is that testing is unlikely to *ever* provide a perfect and timeless solution. Science is always an awkward, lurching process—although the search for new orthodoxies and the accompanying faith in the power of their new tests, assessments, and measurements has repeatedly led would-be reformers down the path of hubris.

CONCLUSION

Fundamental disputes about what students should read, which skills are most valuable, or whether vocational education is important may well be unsolvable in a standardized, bureaucratic system committed to universal excellence. Our present course—with its insistence on districts and systems that will simultaneously address bulky standards, serve all children, and address an array of needs—ensures that educators and educational leaders will be constantly bombarded by a multitude of competing demands and constituent claims, making it difficult to focus on doing anything particularly well.

Indeed, educational leaders, the U.S. Supreme Court, and corporate leaders have argued that we all benefit when communities encompass heterogeneous experiences, perspectives, knowledge, and skills. Scholarship on leadership studies has made the case that diverse perspectives will lead to better decisions.[102] Absent sufficient diversity in knowledge and thought, public and private organizations are susceptible to what psychologist Irving Janis famously termed "groupthink," in which shared knowledge and assumptions among members of a group can "override their motivation to realistically appraise alternative courses of action."[103]

Instead of expending more and more time seeking the one best way to educate all children, the path out of this tangled thicket lies in defining an essential *minimalist* body of skills and knowledge for all students and then taking care to avoid prescriptions about methods or content beyond that floor. The minimalist core recognizes that there are building blocks that students need to master, while restraint in defining that core is critical if we are not to unduly impede teaching that serves different needs or reflects important differences regarding pedagogies and philosophies of learning. As we shift from a focus on educational inputs to one more occupied with outcomes, we have witnessed the temptation to imagine that new metrics can precisely gauge school or teacher effectiveness. It can be easy to forget that testing is merely a tool; it can be wielded foolishly or well.

We would do well to heed those limitations, so that our frenetic efforts to impose new orthodoxies via test-defined excellence don't look as naïve a century hence as the efforts of Progressive-era measurement enthusiasts do today.

We dismiss the stumbles of the past and insist that we can make the same machinery and strategies work, *this* time. It is useful to recall, however, that our fascination with standards and assessment—a mantra of today's would-be reformers—is not a new phenomenon. For a century, reformers have proudly declared that they finally got it right, only to be regarded by each successive generation as misguided bumblers. The thing is, this same cycle plays out with disconcerting regularity. It's true that everyone before us just keeps getting it wrong. But it may be that the problem is less with inept reformers than with a philosophy of school improvement and a system of schooling that renders success impossible.

6 Teachers and Teaching

"Women teachers are often preferred by superintendents because they are more willing to comply with established regulations and less likely to ride headstrong hobbies."

—*Harper's Magazine,* 1878

"Not a ship arrives with either redemptioners or convicts, in which schoolmasters are not regularly advertised for sale, as weavers, tailors, or other trade: with little other difference that I can hear of except perhaps that the former do not usually fetch so good a price as the latter."

—Jonathan Boucher, rector at Annapolis, 1678

We've talked in broad strokes about schooling. Let us now turn to the question of teaching. In chapter 1, we discussed the tendency to conflate "schools" with "schooling" and how that reflex impedes creative problem solving and stunts transformation. The problem also bedevils us when it comes to teaching—we have taken to conflating "teacher" and "teaching." The act becomes reduced to the person who inhabits the job, and the Common School became a holding tank for dozens of isolated individuals doing the same job in classroom after classroom.[1] The result is that our vision of how to provide quality education to 50 million students is guided by the assumption that we must recruit and retain 3.3 million terrific full-time, careerist teachers in our schools.[2] And those 3.3 million teachers only represent a little more than half the 6 million adults who work in public schools and school systems.

For perspective, that 3.3 million figure is more than twice the total number of practicing attorneys and physicians, combined, in the United States.[3] Given that current staffing requires hiring more than 280,000 new teachers a year,[4] and that U.S. colleges issue perhaps 1.5 million four-year diplomas a year,[5] schools are seeking to hire nearly one in five new graduates. Given that only about one in five graduates emerge from a selective college or university, the severity of the challenge is clear. No wonder that shortages are endemic and that quality remains a persistent concern.

So long as we retain the shape and scope of the familiar classroom-teaching job, we are not going to recruit or retain our way to a workforce of 3.3 million high-quality teachers. It is not going to happen. Not in 2014, not in 2024, and not in 2124. No matter how much training, respect, support, or additional pay we offer, those 3.3 million teachers represent more than 10 percent of employed Americans with a college degree. Trying to retrofit a twentieth-century teaching profession without revisiting its basic assumptions may well be a futile task.

That does not mean we're in a hopeless situation. It does, however, mean that we're in a hopeless situation *if* we continue to define the job of teaching in the same manner we did a century ago, when our expectations were dramatically lower, we could draw on a pool of captive talent, and we had few tools for leveraging high-quality instructors beyond their classroom. The challenge is to revisit existing assumptions governing what it means to teach, who should teach, and how the teaching profession might be ordered.

A PROFESSION BUILT FOR THE NINETEENTH CENTURY

Today's teaching profession is the product of a mid-twentieth-century labor model that relied on a captive pool of female labor, presumed educators to be largely interchangeable, and counted on male principals and superintendents to micromanage a female teaching workforce. Teaching has clung to these industrial rhythms while recruitment, professional norms, and the larger labor market have shifted underfoot.

Before Teaching Was a "Profession"

The expectation that every teacher should be a full-time careerist was a makeshift Common School solution to a nineteenth-century challenge that hardened into orthodoxy. Before that time, teaching typically served as a short-term occupation for men working toward another career (or, in a pinch, women before they were married). In Renaissance Europe, grammar school teaching was viewed as a second-choice profession, with teachers often viewed with pity or contempt. Medieval historian Martin Kintzinger writes, "Doubtless it was generally accepted that notaries could be of great use in disputes [and] doctors in the event of sickness. . . . However, what about those who had studied the Arts Faculty? A satire about the career prospects of 'Artists' dating from 1489 [portrayed them as scholars] who begged for a living and, on the side, taught small children." During the Middle Ages, Kintzinger notes, the term "artist" referred to an individual "of low social status" and "school teachers in particular."[6]

In the early American colonies, men often regarded teaching as temporary employment, as historian Gerald Gutek notes, while they "prepared for a higher-status career as a minister or lawyer."[7] Some teachers were college or academy students on vacation, and others were indentured servants.[8] In 1678, Jonathan Boucher, rector at Annapolis, wryly observed, "Not a ship arrives with either redemptioners or convicts, in which schoolmasters are not regularly advertised for sale, as weavers, tailors, or other trade: with little other difference that I can hear of except perhaps that the former do not usually fetch so good a price as the latter."[9] Centuries later, sociologist George Counts observed that in even the most progressive states in the mid-1800s, most teachers were younger than twenty-one and taught only a few years. "Those who remained longer were often looked upon as a 'little queer,'" he observed, and regarded "as women who failed to find husbands or as men who feared to compete with their peers in the economic struggle.'"[10] Teaching was not imagined to be a career. Instead, it was typically a brief stepping-stone on the way to another career.[11]

Upon this boggy ground, the Common Schoolers and subsequent reformers like the Progressives sought to fashion a more systematic model of teaching. Understandably they responded to concerns about charlatans or incompetence by standardizing training, duties, and licensure. Their preference for routinization rather than professionalization also reflected a widespread belief of the time that the growing numbers of female teachers were frail and of limited ability, needing strict guidelines and oversight.

The Feminization of Teaching

The overwhelmingly female teaching force in the twentieth century was the product of a captive female labor force that had few other professional options and increasing rates of postsecondary schooling. The result was a bubble of cheap, plentiful talent that the Progressives leveraged to staff a rapidly growing school system and that lasted the better part of three generations. This cheap labor pool resulted from changes in culture and practice that feminized the teaching force during the first half of the nineteenth century. The teaching force in America was almost entirely male until the early 1800s; just one in ten teachers was a woman.[12] Women taught occasionally, but mostly in "dame" schools that they hosted in their homes. By 1870, however, six in ten teachers were women.[13] The rapidity of the shift meant that by the time of the Civil War, the American norm was for teachers to be female.[14]

This shift was accompanied by cultural changes that redefined the "domestic sphere" so as to make teaching a socially acceptable task for women. Previously, it had been thought inappropriate for women to work outside of the home in that fashion. During the nineteenth century, notions of "domestic feminism" meant there were few occupations to which young middle-class women might aspire, and as the notions were expanded, teaching became popular largely because it was one of the very few kinds of work thought appropriate for young women to undertake.[15]

By 1892, eight in ten teaching school students were women, even though women constituted just 19 percent of university and college undergraduates.[16] By 1920, more than eight in ten teachers were women.[17] As late as 1940, less than 4 percent of women aged twenty-five or older had graduated from college.[18] Since there were just over 37 million women older than twenty-five in 1940, that amounted to about 1.4 million women college graduates.[19] Yet, those women constituted more than 770,000 of the nation's 1 million K–12 teachers.[20] In other words, about 55 percent of all women college graduates were teachers.

The era of captive female talent meant that districts could afford to reject teachers for any number of reasons. For instance, during the 1930s, it was still common practice for boards of education to refuse to hire married women or to void teaching contracts if a woman married.[21] In 1931, seventy of the nation's ninety-three largest cities terminated women teachers upon marriage. Even in New York City, where the marriage ban was repealed in 1920, a female teacher who married was still required to report her marriage and her husband's name to the superintendent.[22]

The available female labor worked to the advantage of the Common Schoolers, for whom the feminization of teaching was a matter of simple math. Female teachers were cheaper and helped make the great Common School push affordable. The broad effort to expand schooling required a vast number of new teachers (the number of teachers doubled from 200,000 in 1870 to more than 430,000 by 1900), and there weren't enough men willing to take those positions at the going rate.[23] As school terms became longer and more demanding, school districts were unwilling or unable to pay the increased salaries needed to attract or retain male teachers.[24] Instead, women were hired to fill the growing number of Common School classrooms, while supervision was entrusted to male principals and superintendents. Historian Carl Kaestle has explained that Common Schoolers turned to the "introduction of inexpensive female teachers" as a money-saving innovation. Kaestle quotes a Samuel Lewis of Ohio, observing that counties that employed women as teachers "are able to do twice as much with the same money as is done in the counties where female teachers are almost excluded."[25]

Indeed, many concluded that women were ideal teachers, as the Boston school committee approvingly observed in 1841, precisely because they were thought to be "less intent on scheming for future honors or emoluments [than men]. As a class, they never look forward, as young men almost invariably do, to a period of legal emancipation from parental control."[26] The Littleton, Massachusetts, School Committee concluded in 1849 that, "God seems to have made woman peculiarly suited to guide and develop the infant mind, and it seems . . . very poor policy to pay a man 20 or 22 dollars a month, for teaching children the ABCs, when a female could do the work more successfully at one third of the price."[27]

The discount-rack feminization of teaching would dictate the staffing strategy, job description, and approach to preparation that became the foundation upon which twentieth-century reformers would build.

The New Labor Market

A century ago, or even a half century ago, K–12 leaders did not worry about market competition for teachers. That situation changed markedly in the 1970s, as women flooded into the professions and new careers. Since that time, the salaries of women entering teaching have lagged those of female college graduates who enter other fields.[28] In the 1960s, when only about one-tenth of young women had college degrees, over half of working college-educated women were teachers. By the 1990s, when nearly three times as many women were completing college, just one-sixth of working, college-educated women were teachers.[29]

These trends have continued to accelerate. In 2007, women accounted for just over half of all workers in "the high-paying management, professional, and related occupations" such as public relations managers, financial managers, medical and health services managers, accountants and auditors, budget analysts, biological scientists, and writers and authors.[30] Despite the radical change in labor market circumstances during the twentieth century, the teaching profession today looks much like it did a century ago.

Indeed, an aggressive push to boost hiring and reduce class sizes launched the most recent drive to triple the teacher workforce, from 1.1 million in the 1950s to 3.3 million in the early 2000s. In the 1950s and 1960s, as this enormous expansion was getting under way, the K–12 monopoly on women graduates was ending, meaning the mass expansion in hiring was accompanied by a steady dilution of talent. Economist Susanna Loeb has noted that while "almost 25 percent of new female teachers in the 1960s scored in the top 10 percent of their high school graduating class," by 1992 the number had dropped to 10 percent.[31]

The legacy of the nineteenth-century teaching model has shaped key elements of the profession down to the present—including our approach to teacher licensure, teacher pay, and teacher tenure— trapping today's educators and policy makers in a doomed effort to nurture a world-class twenty-first-century teaching force within the bounds of outmoded policies and practices. It is to those policies and practices that we now turn.

LICENSED TO INSTRUCT

Given their interaction with impressionable youth, it is easy to understand why we have always sought some way to screen the quality of instructors. However, while the intention of licensure is to ensure quality, the machinery of licensure fails to provide much quality control and can too readily serve to insulate mediocrity or advance ideological agendas.

There is real reason to doubt whether licensure provides useful quality control. In a study of 120 teacher preparation programs, those at the graduate level reported admitting nearly eight in ten applicants, and all programs reported weeding out only about *2 percent* of all teacher candidates during their student teaching.[32] Meanwhile, though defenders of licensure claim it does not deter promising teachers, the evidence suggests otherwise. In fact, in 2009, Teach For America (TFA) received 35,000 applications for about 4,000 slots—suggesting that many individuals who are interested in teaching are steering clear of traditional preparation programs.

In 2009, the absurdity of how licensure can too often play out in practice drew public notice in the case of Jonathan Keiler. The only faculty member at his Maryland high school with National Board certification and a law degree, the teacher of a popular Advanced Placement class, and the coach of a recognized Mock Trial Team, Keiler was told by district officials just weeks before school started that he would have to produce three extra credits by September or lose his teaching license. Keiler responded that district staff had mis-read his file and that "they are essentially firing me because they do not understand their own rules and procedures, which of course are idiotic in the first instance, but at least they should know them." Keiler's situation was only resolved when a reporter's intervention prompted the district to determine that the problem was an administrative error.[33] The larger question was what possible benefit was being gained by alienating Keiler, entwining educators in a thicket of confusing rules, or signaling that paperwork trumps performance.

Proponents of licensure point to medicine and law, arguing that the prestigious licensure exams in those fields ought to be the model for education. Skeptics reject the analogy. Even in professions with clear knowledge- or performance-based benchmarks for certification, like law or medicine, a license is not imagined to ensure competence in ambiguous, subtle skills like comforting a patient or swaying a jury. The skills that teacher educators consistently suggest are most important, such as listening, caring, and motivating, are not susceptible to standardized quality control. Nor is it clear that teacher preparation develops such skills. Economist Daniel Goldhaber, for instance, has estimated that no more than 3 percent of the contribution teachers made to student achievement in math and reading can be linked to measurable characteristics, including teacher certification, experience, and education. The other 97 percent, Goldhaber explains, is "associated with qualities or behaviors that could not be isolated and identified."[34]

Now, some form of teacher licensure has existed since early Roman times, but it has inevitably been geared to policing teacher dispositions rather than ensuring quality instruction. Early European licensure typically sought to ensure that teachers conformed to the states' dominant religious theories and beliefs. In Charles the Great's ninth-century empire, for instance, the equivalent of a public primary school teacher might have been asked by the licensing authority, "On what day of the month did they say that Christ was crucified?" or "With regard to the lunar cycle, why does it not begin with the paschal terms?"[35] Renaissance historian Paul Grendler has observed that in that era, "Control of the schools guaranteed orthodoxy; it won the next generation to the true faith, whichever it was. . . . [Thus], Mary Tudor began to license teachers in the 1550s in order to enforce religious obedience."[36] In seventeenth- and eighteenth-century Europe, the primary criterion for licensure was religiosity, with the local minister and board of trustees often questioning applicants about the orthodoxy of their religious beliefs.[37]

In colonial America, too, teachers were typically hired with a careful eye to their religious beliefs and were "certified" by local community leaders on that basis.[38] As early as 1647, Massachusetts required that a schoolmaster be of "discreet conversation" and "well versed in tongues." By 1712, the state required that a teacher be approved by at least three local ministers and, by 1789, that he was a college graduate (although what we today call "alternative certification" was available for candidates deemed proficient by an educated minister).[39] However, in an era when the problem was simply finding enough willing teachers, enforcement of such exacting standards was half-hearted.

In the 1800s, teacher licensure focused on assessing a candidate's subject knowledge, usually by means of an examination. The state-regulated licensure apparatus that emerged from the Common School movement relied upon a batch-processing system that focused on tallying requisite course credits. James Carter, an early advocate of teacher training and a founder of the Massachusetts Board of Education, wrote of the need for an institutionalized approach to teacher education in 1825, charging, "Let us . . . establish an institution for the exclusive purpose of preparing instructors."[40] The result was the "normal" school, intended to ensure that new teachers were trained to desired standards ("norms").

Teacher Education

The Reverend Samuel Hall established the nation's first teacher-training school in 1823. Privately operated, it provided three years of instruction: the first two built upon the Common School curriculum; the final year was dedicated to the practice of teaching.[41] James Carter followed suit, opening the first state-regulated normal school in Lexington, Massachusetts, in 1839—the institution still operates today as Framingham State College. Carter's program served as a national model for state-run institutions, and other Massachusetts normal schools quickly sprang up in Barre and in Bridgewater. These two-year programs focused solely on "observation and practice teaching."[42] The irrepressible and seldom understated Horace Mann declared, "I believe Normal Schools to be a new instrumentality in the advancement of the race."[43]

Normal schools proliferated even as state universities started to establish chairs of education; these university positions would later evolve into colleges of education within the universities.[44] By the Civil War, twelve normal schools had been established in eight states. By the end of the nineteenth century, over half of the nation's 430 postsecondary institutions offered courses in teacher education, and normal schools were operating in every state.[45] These modest institutions, with their local, vocational emphasis, would become the gatekeepers to the teaching profession.

Those efforts remained intensely localized through the nineteenth century, with just three states controlling their licensure systems in 1898. Rapid bureaucratization during the Progressive era meant, however, that by 1937, forty-one states had systems in which all teacher certificates were state issued. The move from local certification to more standardized requirements was fueled in part by concerns that local corruption would otherwise trump qualifications in hiring decisions. David Tyack notes the case of an aspiring San Francisco teacher asked "to name all the major bodies of water, cities, and countries on earth—in one hour."[46] Given such abuses, Tyack notes that to "harassed superintendents, beset by political pressures to hire unqualified instructors, and to teachers, victims of capricious certification and employment, such civil service safeguards" were welcome.[47] During the Progressive era, states eliminated exams in favor of professional coursework, making college or university teacher preparation the only route to licensure.[48]

The licensure system relied on paper credentials and vast bureaucracies to monitor teacher quality. This was a crude but reasonable strategy in an era of expansive hiring and had much in common with other aforementioned Progressive efforts to promote civil service reform and "good government." In the early twentieth century, it very likely marked an improvement over the favoritism, political machinations, nepotism, and capricious dealings that had reigned.

Today, the challenges are very different. Schools struggle to recruit an ethnically diverse workforce with subject expertise and essential interpersonal and organizational skills. But candidates must still negotiate licensure arrangements that assume new teacher entrants will be twenty-two years old, female, and lack viable alternative career options.

Alternative Licensure

While hundreds of alternative licensure programs exist throughout the country, a 2007 National Council on Teacher Quality (NCTQ) report found that most alternate-route teachers "have had to jump through

many of the same hoops—meeting the same 'traditional' academic requirements and undergoing much the same training—as typical education school graduates."[49] Alternative licensure provides only a slightly
more accessible on-ramp for those willing to abandon other employment and become full-time classroom teachers. This is especially limiting because the defining characteristic of today's most promising new
teacher recruiting ventures—like TFA, The New Teacher Project
(TNTP), or Troops to Teachers—is that they pursue teachers who
bring fundamentally different profiles and skill sets to the classroom.

There is good reason to fear that a wealth of nontraditional
teaching candidates may be repelled by the expectations they would
face in the traditional licensure track: completing an education degree (or enrolling full-time to obtain a graduate degree in education); spending a dozen weeks in a student teaching practicum under
a mentor of uncertain skill or utility; negotiating the required state
licensure paperwork (no small task if not currently enrolled in a formal training program); and enduring the related costs and head-
aches of pursuing a license to teach. However, even alternative programs like TFA are intentionally designed to capture only a narrow
slice of the untapped teaching pool. TFA targets only new college
graduates, employs an extensive screening process, sends new corps
members to an intensive six-week training camp the summer before
they start to teach, and then requires them to move to a new city. The
model has proven highly effective for its purposes, but is hardly a
recipe for helping to fill 3 million teaching jobs—or serving individuals, of various ages and circumstances, who desire to teach but are
not inclined to abandon other pursuits to be a full-time "teacher."

While it is appropriate to require that all would-be teachers pos-
sess an undergraduate degree and competency in the knowledge
or skills essential to what the candidate hopes to teach, we would do
well to exercise caution against erecting additional regulatory hur-
dles. Rethinking licensure implies a complementary need to expand
our thinking when it comes to professional development. One alternative is some version of the system employed in medicine or law,

where entering doctors or lawyers begin their career with a developmental trial period rather than the presumption that they are "qualified" professionals ready to take on duties identical to those of their veteran peers. The Teach For America model, for instance, provides new teachers with six weeks of intensive training the summer before school commences. Using that as a touchstone, districts might then have new teachers assume half the standard course load and arrange for mentoring and support to guide these new employees through their first couple of years. New-hires would be paid only half of what they now earn, but they would be compensated by free professional development and the savings from not having to pay for a teaching credential. The savings could be put into additional compensation for accomplished veterans who would mentor, evaluate, and monitor the new-hires.

Exploring such avenues raises the question of why colleges and universities should remain central to the teacher preparation process. Housing teacher training at institutions of higher education made sense when travel and communication made it sensible to gather aspiring teachers in one place so that they could be lectured by the faculty and use the college library. But faculty expertise can now be easily shared, and collegiate resources can be accessed from anywhere. The notion that the normal schools would raise the bar of teaching expertise has given way to a concern that they dissuade talented applicants while providing suspect instruction. Meanwhile, the leading concern in teacher preparation is that teachers require more practical, "clinical" experience. Rather than base training programs at universities, in accord with the old normal school model, they might be based at K–12 schools—with university expertise imported, virtually or in person, as needed.

This is just what High Tech High School in San Diego has done, operating a school-based teacher preparation program that has been approved by the California Board of Education and that can certify teachers just like any other state-approved program. The High Tech

High model opens the doors to improved mentoring, smooths the integration of student teachers into the school, and creates a healthy need for academics in schools of education to demonstrate the value of their contribution. Such an innovation could channel some of the billions spent on professional development from teacher colleges and into schools. Cultivating alternative routes is a valuable, incremental step to rethinking the licensure systems assembled over time. But the larger challenge is to rethink the assumptions and the design of licensure more fully.

REGULATING TEACHER DISPOSITIONS

Throughout history, teachers have been expected to display an appropriate disposition. But the "proper" disposition has changed greatly over time. As we've covered, teachers were initially expected to be of a certain religion or display a high degree of morality; today we have imbued licensure criteria with the demand that teachers embrace particular notions of "tolerance" or "multiculturalism." Licensure systems have been used over time to screen teacher obeisance to ideological or religious norms and have been wedded to a restrictive system of training and hiring.

Yet, some reformers continue to regard the regulation of dispositions and habits of mind as a desirable strategy. The National Board for Professional Teaching Standards (NBPTS)—which does not license teachers but does issue a widely recognized credential—has asserted that, among their many other virtues, proficient teachers exemplify "curiosity and a love of learning; tolerance and open-mindedness; fairness and justice; appreciation for our cultural and intellectual heritages; [and] respect for human diversity and dignity."[50] These admirable standards are echoed in language adopted by the National Council for the Accreditation of Teacher Education and by state and local education authorities. The notion of teacher disposition as a qualification is hardly new, though over time the notion of what makes for a good teacher has evolved markedly. The standards heralded by the NBPTS and schools of education are diametrically opposed to those that once held sway, suggesting that humility may be advisable when deciding who should be allowed to teach and what the "correct" teaching dispositions might be.

In colonial America, doctrinal conformity rather than educational competency was the key qualification for teachers. Early Massachusetts law, for instance, mandated that none should be given a role "teaching, educating, or instructing of youth" if "unsound in the faith or scandalous in their lives" or if they had failed to give "due satisfaction according to the rules of Christ."[51]

The Progressives took teacher disposition in a more "scientific" direction. Professor Henry Curtis opined in the 1890s that a healthy teacher would be "a more wholesome model to set before children.... Her health and vitality will be a large element in her success in teaching arithmetic, geography and every other subject; for without health she cannot have enthusiasm or buoyancy or attractive ways."[52] In the 1920s, the National Committee for Mental Hygiene began the campaign "to make personality development the guiding principle of American education."[53]

Consider the tale of New York teacher Rose Freistater, a five-year veteran, who was denied her teaching license in 1931 because, at five feet two inches tall and 182 pounds, she weighed more than the maximum permissible weight. Given six months to lose thirty pounds, she lost only twenty and was fired. Of the many overweight and underweight teachers removed in the decade that the standards had existed, Freistrater was the first to appeal to the state, but was rejected by the State Commissioner of Education in 1935. The Board explained, "Other things being normal, a person of abnormal weight is likely to ... be less efficient as a teacher than a person of average weight."[54]

In the 1930s, reformers sought to build on earlier efforts by addressing the social adjustment of teachers. Professor of educational sociology Harvey Zorbaugh said, "There are many teachers ... whose personalities are so conflicted or inadequate that they are potential sources of infection to the children."[55] *Newsweek* published the "startling" results of a 1935 study in which 33 percent of a group of 100 teachers enrolled in summer courses at the University of Texas "proved emotionally maladjusted, with 12 percent of these 'in need of psychiatric advice.'"[56]

Newsweek again reported the latest research on teacher personality in a 1943 story, "Analyzing the Schoolmarm." It recounted the findings of Columbia University psychologist Percival Symonds, who had determined that "in every instance the teachers' classroom actions were tied directly to their own childhood experiences."[57] Since many of the women had stunted emotional growth, Symonds explained, they were unable to differentiate their roles as adult instructors from their childhood traumas, resulting in "teacher-children."[58] Symonds also opined that "the vast majority of women teachers" were unmarried due "to a family background of prudishness so extreme as to fill the teacher-child with warping, narrowing inhibitions."[59] Symonds, however, rejected the conventional wisdom that "only normal, well-adjusted persons should be teachers," given that "some of the most successful teachers observed were definitely neurotic."[60] It can impart some useful humility, especially to those eager to establish scientifically based practices and routines, how widely accepted in some previous eras were research findings that we now dismiss as nonsensical, or worse.

Concerns about teacher maladjustment fueled efforts to link "good" traits to good teaching and to identify "bad" teachers. In the 1940s, there were concerns that the "unhappy or worried or insecure teacher 'hurts' the children"—prompting calls to help teachers adjust their personality.[61] A 1952 survey reported that 42 out of 237 teacher-training institutions examined had "systematized, regularly used plans" for selecting teacher candidates based on "character 'traits.'"[62] A more expansive 1953 study surveyed 785 accredited teacher training schools and found that 45 percent assessed students' emotional stability.[63] Reformers called for teachers to be issued a "mental health certification."[64]

Researchers would go on to develop and utilize a raft of tests drawing on this work, including the Rorschach test, James Cattell's

16 Personality Factor Test, the Guilford-Zimmerman Temperament Survey, the Minnesota Teacher Attitude Inventory (MTAI), the Minnesota Multiphasic Personality Inventory (MMPI), and the Thurstone Temperament Schedule. Have we learned a sensible caution from these centuries of sometimes ludicrous efforts to identify and then impart the optimal disposition? Well, Dr. Carroll Helm, director of teacher education at the University of Cumberlands in Williamsburg, Kentucky, has written that "great teachers are the ones with . . . big, beautiful, caring hearts"[65] and explains that the "key issue" in teacher education is "to teach particular virtues . . . [by] mak[ing] the students aware of the key dispositions, and then model[ing] them."[66] Patricia Phelps, professor at the University of Central Arkansas, explains, "For twenty years, I have helped to prepare teachers. . . . Although I still teach essential pedagogical knowledge and skills . . . recently, I have made a more conscious effort to shape teacher candidates' dispositions."[67]

A few years ago, the Washington State College of Education triggered a controversy when it flunked a teaching candidate and a faculty member explained that the candidate, a conservative Christian and father of four Mexican American children, had "revealed opinions that have caused me great concern in the areas of race, gender, sexual orientation and privilege."[68] Under the press of public inquiry, the university reversed course and reinstated the candidate. Such instances are not isolated occurrences, however.

Graduate schools of education promote particular social beliefs and political values as part of their responsibility to ensure that aspiring teachers have the right dispositions. In many ways, this is another version of the old "mental hygiene" standard. In 2009, the University of Minnesota came under fire when its College of Education and Human Development announced plans to incorporate a "cultural competence" plank in its admissions standards. The plan listed a series of desired outcomes for prospective teachers, including that they be able to "discuss their own histories and current thinking drawing on notions of white privilege, hegemonic masculinity, heteronormativity, and internalized oppression." They were also to "construct and articulate a sophisticated and nuanced critical analysis" of the American Dream, including the "myth of meritocracy in the United States" and "history of demands for assimilation to white, middle-class, Christian meanings and values."[69] In the words of the Foundation for Individual Rights in Education (FIRE), a civil rights organization that challenged the policy, teachers with incorrect views "were to receive remedial re-education, be weeded out, or be denied admission altogether."[70]

Similar examples are disturbingly prevalent. In 2005, the Brooklyn College School of Education tried to subject history professor K. C. Johnson to an "Integrity Committee" after Johnson criticized what he perceived as viewpoint discrimination from amongst the faculty.[71] In 2008, Stanford's Teacher Education Program (STEP) tried to revoke a binding admission to forty-six-year-old Michele Kerr after she expressed opinions differing with STEP's philosophical orientation. When, with FIRE's assistance, Kerr pushed her way into the program and then had the temerity to blog critical thoughts about iconic education school thinkers such as Paulo Freire and John Dewey, school officials tried to force Kerr to surrender the password to her private blog and threatened expulsion for her teaching philosophy.[72]

This latest strand of mental hygiene orthodoxy is seen in language such as the National Council for Accreditation of Teacher Education (NCATE) requirement that teachers "develop knowledge of diversity in the United States and the world, professional dispositions that respect and value differences, and skills for working with diverse populations" and that programs train teachers "who can reflect multicultural and global perspectives." Innocuous enough in theory, but what this means in practice all depends on who is deciding what good mental hygiene looks like.[73] As FIRE has argued,

> NCATE's recommendation that education schools evaluate teacher candidates using amorphous, malleable criteria—such as the candidate's commitment to "diversity" or "social justice"—raises serious

constitutional concerns. Because no objective consensus on the "correct" meaning of such politically charged terminology can reasonably exist in a diverse democratic society, these vague evaluative criteria too often become vehicles for pressuring teacher candidates to alter or abandon their core political, philosophical, or moral beliefs.[74]

Seeking to enforce ideological orthodoxy excludes teachers who are phenomenal educators but, for myriad personal reasons, don't embrace the prevailing teacher education dogmas. And, if one believes that there may be more than one desirable way to instruct, then screening teachers for their obeisance to the orthodoxy of the moment is both pointless and destructive.

As noted earlier, researchers cannot identify the teacher characteristics that explain 97 percent of the variation in student achievement gains.[75] Effective teachers may share certain instructional practices or habits, but there is no evidence that these vary in predictable ways with particular personality traits or philosophical beliefs. Given that both kindhearted and callous doctors may be effective professionals, it is not clear why we should expect good teachers to be uniform in disposition. In fact, with the array of students that schools serve, it may be useful to hire teachers with diverse views and values.

Time and again, attempts to scientifically identify the "right" teacher or pedagogy can stifle problem solving and yield troubling consequences. The dominant orthodoxy evolves with time. We can either embrace that intellectual diversity or seek to enshrine the orthodoxy of the moment. The bitter irony, of course, is that the orthodoxy of the moment is defended in the *name* of diversity.

MAKING MONEY COUNT

President Barack Obama has declared, "It's time to start rewarding good teachers."[76] While there is little or no scientific proof that paying valuable, hard-working, or effective employees more than their colleagues draws and retains better teachers, that's probably the way to bet. Today, however, even relatively modest measures to rethink pay are fiercely resisted by the teacher unions. The rationale for this resistance is simple enough—veteran members entered the profession with a particular understanding of how they would be paid and are naturally resistant to alterations that jeopardize the perks of seniority. What has resulted, though, is a continued reliance upon an industrial-era pay system poorly suited for today's labor market and ill equipped to attract talented professionals. Private-sector firms that used the same model—like automakers and steel producers—have since gone out of business or been forced to rethink their pay schemes.

Nearly all school systems rely almost entirely on a crude "step-and-lane" pay scale in which teachers are compensated based on the numbers of years they have taught and the amount of postsecondary education they have completed. This approach was a sensible enough way to administer a growing bureaucracy when talent was plentiful, concerns about favoritism and corruption were widespread, an absence of performance measures made it difficult to assess the fairness of individual compensation, and the uniform Common School model did little to note particular skill or expertise. In the new labor market, however, where performance measures are available and it is no longer necessary or advisable to treat teachers as interchangeable, the justification for the existing pay model no longer stands. Its flaws were already visible over a century ago, as when Aaron Sheeley, superintendent of Adams County, Pennsylvania, asserted in 1867 that giving all teachers the same wages "offers a premium to mediocrity if not to positive ignorance and incompetency. Inducements should always be held out to teachers to duly qualify themselves for their work."[77]

Well into the Common School era, the dominant form of teacher compensation was the system known as "boarding round."[78] The local community provided teachers with room and board, though the teacher's role often extended beyond classroom instruction. Teachers frequently performed household chores in addition to their educational duties. Because educational patrons thought teaching to be pretty undemanding work, they would expect teachers to undertake duties that might include "cleaning out the church, ringing the bell, providing a baptismal basin, running errands, serving as messenger, and digging graves, as well as assisting the pastor in reading the Scriptures and leading the singing at church services, keeping records, issuing invitations, writing letters, visiting the sick, and generally making himself useful."[79] Given this history, the Common School push to elevate teaching by standardizing the role was sensible and constructive.

In the late 1800s, grade-based salary schedules emerged. Seeking to standardize pay in rapidly expanding systems, Progressive reformers latched onto the bureaucratic, hierarchical norms favored by scientific management. Districts adopted pay guidelines and states minimum salary levels.[80] By 1900, teacher pay was dictated by salary schedules that reflected years of experience but, as noted earlier, also gender and race. Women and minorities received significantly less pay. In 1876, for example, the salaries of male grammar school teachers in Boston ranged from $1,700 to $3,200, while female grammar teachers earned less than half as much—$600 to $1,200.[81] School administrators were able to take into account subjective judgments of merit, yielding concerns that such determinations were influenced by personal and political considerations.[82] The systematic inequities were thought acceptable. In 1928, sociologist Herbert Tonne explained that "men usually will require a higher economic stipend because they normally have or at any rate will have a family to support."[83] The National Education Association rightfully objected that "a differential based solely upon sex destroys the single salary feature of the schedule as well as the principle of justice and democracy which it is designed to establish in the schools."[84] In that era, an emancipatory thinker might well have embraced the need for a unified pay scale as these blatant inequities fueled calls for reform.

In 1921, seeking to make pay scales more objective and equitable, school districts in Lincoln, Nebraska; Denver, Colorado; and Sioux City, Iowa, were the first to adopt the single-salary schedule.[85] Under the new schedule, pay was determined solely by a teacher's years of experience and of academic preparation. The single-salary schedule brought equity and objectivity where discrimination and capriciousness had reigned.[86] At the time, Cora Morrison, a teacher from Denver, enthused that the new schedule "permits better business methods; it eliminates class consciousness among teachers and defeats unionism . . . [and] it emphasizes high standards of professional attainment and encourages professional study and growth."[87] By 1950, single-salary schedules were used in 97 percent of school districts.[88] It remains omnipresent, due to its administrative ease and millions of veteran teachers who understandably regard proposals to reduce their security and the rewards for seniority as attempts to renege on past promises.[89]

Today, however, the dominant concern with teacher pay is not its capriciousness but its rigidity. The old fights for fairness to all teachers have given way to new and different fights for fairness to children, and especially the need in the new labor market to better reward teachers with critical skills who take on the toughest challenges or who do the best work. While it makes good sense to create a profession with various roles and specializations, differential compensation does not require ossifying those differences into finely graded hierarchies. The key is to devise a system that uses contemporary tools to configure a pay system that rewards the right things. The objective is not to merely revise the existing salary schedule or to link pay to reading scores but to create professional opportunities, allocate dollars to teachers with critical skills or expertise, and reward excellence and extraordinary effort.

As with base compensation, teacher pensions also require rethinking. Today's defined-benefit retirement systems limit portability, penalizing teachers who move across state lines. This was standard in public and private plans during the industrial era but is poorly suited for today's more mobile workforce. Most private retirement plans, especially for professional workers, have now shifted toward defined-contribution models that allow employees to shift their money with them when they move or change jobs. This marks a sensible evolution in pension plans that first originated in the mid-to-late nineteenth century, initially to serve police officers and firefighters.[90] Pensions would go on to be adopted by other public employers, like school districts, and the private sector. Standard Oil of New Jersey adopted a plan in 1903, General Electric in 1912, and Kodak in 1929.[91] By the late 1920s, twenty-three states had pension plans for their teachers.[92]

In 2007, an employee had to work approximately six years to become fully vested in the typical public pension fund; seven of the nation's largest funds required ten years of service or more.[93] This careerist tilt penalizes educators who move or change jobs. Economists Robert Costrell and Michael Podgursky have observed that, because teachers' pensions accrue limited benefits early on before getting much more generous once teachers reach age fifty, "The system therefore pulls teachers to 'put in their time' until then, whether or not they are well-suited to the profession. Beyond that point, the pension system quickly begins to punish teachers for staying on the job too long, pushing them out the door at a relatively young age, often in their mid-fifties, even if they are still effective."[94] The status quo dissuades potential entrants, including talented mid-career applicants and those who might not be inclined to commit to a decades-long career in a single job or locale, from becoming teachers. Contemplating more flexible and portable benefit models, such as those prevalent in the private sector today, could ease exit from and reentry into the profession and equip schooling to more effectively compete for college-educated talent.

FROM PROTECTION TO PRIVILEGE

Today, every state has a teacher tenure statute that evaluates teachers for tenure after two to four years of probationary employment with the district. While teachers can be removed with relative ease during these initial years, those who are granted tenure secure due process rights that permit firing only in the case of financial necessity or just cause. This has amounted to a guarantee of lifetime employment in most districts. There is increasing agreement that this arrangement doesn't work for students or schools. Lily Eskelsen, vice president of the National Education Association—which has long rejected any notion that tenure could be bad for students—declared in 2010, "The purpose of a public school is not to give me a job that I love [but] . . . to prepare each and every individual blessed child . . . to succeed in their lives."[95]

As journalist Steven Brill asked in a 2009 article on New York City's so-called "rubber rooms," "Should a thousand bad teachers stay put so that one innocent teacher is protected?" According to Brill, due process protections for teachers that once seemed essential have grown so onerous that they deserve a fresh look. New York City elementary school principal Anthony Lombardi explained to Brill, "By making it so hard to get even the obvious freaks and crazies that are there off the payroll, you insure that the teachers who are simply incompetent or mediocre are never incented to improve and are never removable."[96]

Such concerns are not new, and they are certainly not merely the result of teacher tenure. In 1893, before teacher tenure laws had ever been adopted, education researcher and Progressive pioneer Joseph Rice opined, "Superintendents should naturally be held responsible for poor teaching, but justly they cannot be so held for the reason that it is almost impossible for them to have incompetents discharged. Indeed, the superintendent has said that he has given up, as a hopeless task, attempting to have incompetent principals and teachers discharged."[97] That said, the issue of tenure has long been recognized as a significant barrier to boosting teacher quality. In 1972, the *Wall Street Journal* reported that a member of the Maryland board of education believed that the state's tenure law had "prevent[ed] school boards from weeding out incompetent teachers during the past 25 years."[98] In 1972, education reporter Fred Hechinger explained in the *New York Times*, "The perennial problem with teachers' tenure is that it protects the incompetent and freezes them into a system."[99]

Where did teacher tenure come from, anyway? New Jersey was the first state to institute a statewide law, in 1909, but the idea had surfaced many years earlier. The National Education Association's

1921 Committee on Tenure noted, "The question of the tenure of public school officials was discussed as far back as the year 1885." The committee explained that, "At that time, tenure was interpreted to mean the application of the principles of civil service to the teaching profession. The chief argument presented was that 'the public-school system should be independent of personal or partisan influence and free from the malignant power of patronage and spoils.'"[100]

In that earlier era, it was easy to identify cases where teachers might need protection from biases linked to religion, politics, and personal beliefs. Laurie Moses Hines, a historian at Kent State, has noted, "School officials and boards also scrutinized teachers' political views. During World War I, the superintendent of the Cleveland public schools suggested firing those teachers sympathetic to Germany."[101] In the 1920s and 1930s, during the Red Scare that followed the Communist revolution in Russia, more than a dozen states required teachers to take loyalty oaths and fired those teachers who would not do so.[102] In the 1950s and early 1960s, in an effort to purge gay and lesbian teachers from Florida's schools, the Florida legislature investigated and discharged dozens of teachers based on their sexuality.[103]

Tenure laws were justified by the need to assure teachers that they would be secure from capricious treatment. The Committee on Tenure argued, "It is only when our teachers feel reasonably secure in the continuity and dignity of their service in a given locality that they will become a constructive power in the economic and social life of that community."[104] In 1947, the NEA platform on the subject of "tenure of service" explained, "The interests of the child and of the profession require . . . teachers who are protected from discharge for political, religious, personal, or other unjust reasons by effective tenure laws."[105] A reasonable case could be made that stronger protections were then needed to protect teachers from being dismissed for reasons unrelated to their performance.

Indeed, the unions fought to prevent a perception of tenure as undeserved lifetime job security. In 1947, when thirteen states had statewide tenure policies, the NEA Committee on Tenure and Academic Freedom issued a report emphasizing that the "purpose and justification of tenure are the betterment of teaching," that tenure was never intended to protect all teachers, and that tenure could help police quality by providing defined procedures for dismissing incompetent teachers.[106] One year later, in 1948, the committee wrote that "a good tenure law . . . protects the qualified teacher," but that it also "provides, at the same time, for the elimination of teachers who because of incompetence, or for other good reason, should be removed."[107]

Twenty years later, American Federation of Teachers vice president Ray Howe had left the NEA's carefully parsed justification behind, terming tenure a "basic civil right" and declaring, "To do away with tenure is to undermine due process of law . . . for if tenure goes [teachers] have no other right—they have only sufferance."[108] Tenure laws were widespread by the 1960s, with thirty-seven states and the District of Columbia having full-fledged tenure policies and a number of other states employing various forms of continuing contracts.[109] By 1974, just nine states lacked tenure laws.[110]

More recently, however, tenure has morphed from a sensible protection against dismissal based on political, religious, or personal grounds into an extraordinary, costly blanket of protection against termination—even when the grounds are as prosaic as incompetence, malfeasance, or the pursuit of cost efficiencies. Ray Howe's "orderly means" have morphed into an extraordinarily expensive, time-consuming process that deters or defeats most efforts to remove the incompetent and the irresponsible.

Tenure policies, job protection acts, discrimination laws, and contract provisions intended to protect against wrongful termination now too often serve mostly to protect ineffective, low-performing teachers. Tenure makes removing even toxic teachers enormously difficult and expensive. In New York City, for example, the cost to fire one incompetent tenured teacher has been estimated at about $250,000.[111] The extreme cost of removing incompetent teachers leads many districts to simply turn a blind eye to even the most egregious offenses. In 2002, a tenured teacher from the Newark Public School System received nine months of pay plus the value of her unused vacation and sick days even after substantial evidence indicated she had used foul language against an elementary-aged student; had "punch(ed)" the student "using a closed fist"; and had exhibited "speech [that] was slurred," "an unsteady gait," and "behavior [that] was inappropriate and unprofessional."[112]

Administrators and state education leaders have reacted by adopting the rational but unfortunate response of simply leaving mediocre teachers in the classroom. For example, in the fifteen years following the 1986 passage of an Illinois education reform package to increase teacher accountability, an average of only two tenured teachers per year were terminated for poor performance—this in a state with 95,000 tenured teachers.[113] A 2009 study by The New Teacher Project (TNTP) examined twelve large and mid-sized districts in four states and found that over half had not fired even one tenured teacher for poor performance in the past five years. Of those that had removed even one teacher, none had dismissed more than a handful.[114] This same study also reported that 86 percent of administrators admitted that they did not always pursue termination even when warranted, since tenure has resulted in "lengthy and burdensome requirements, coupled with the low likelihood of successful removals," and has left "principals . . . reluctant to pursue dismissals."[115]

Tenure may have made good sense given the patronage and politicized hiring that characterized late-nineteenth and early-twentieth-century America in schooling and other municipal services. It has become less essential as civil service and employment law measures have put in place safeguards that did not exist forty or fifty years ago. The result is that tenure's legitimate benefits have shrunk dramatically, while its costs are now large and omnipresent. We are now at a point where the balance of rights ought to be reassessed.

REWRITING THE JOB DESCRIPTION

Most attempts to boost teacher quality focus on trying to find enough teachers to fill existing vacancies or to find professional development that can turn mediocre teachers into great ones. The trouble with this strategy is that it is trying to find more and more people to excel in a job description that may not be well suited for the contemporary workforce. While it was routine through much of the twentieth century for educated workers to placidly accept long-term employment with large organizations, that is less and less the norm. The new challenge is not to determine how to find 3.3 million teachers for yesterday's role but how to configure careers and positions that will attract talented employees in the twenty-first century.

Prior to the Industrial Revolution, most Americans worked for themselves—as farmers, artisans, and shopkeepers. It was only with the Industrial Revolution that workers became tied to large employers, and jobs—like teaching—took on the full-time, careerist cast that we now regard as normal. MIT research scientists Robert Laubacher and Thomas Malone have explained that the nineteenth century saw a transformational change in the meaning of the word "job." Before industrialization, the term had referred to a "specific task" but "in the industrial era, 'job' began to be used to describe a worker's ongoing relationship with a particular employer."[116] Along with new arrangements came the time clock, the salary schedule, and all else that followed from careerist, full-time employment as the norm.

Today, for better or worse, that paradigm is undergoing massive change. While the paternalistic role worked well for big corporations through the 1950s and 1960s, Laubacher and Malone observe, it "is no longer a tenable personnel strategy."[117] The result is a vast number of mostly well-educated workers seizing the opportunity to free themselves from the traditional role of long-serving employee in a large organization. By 2005, there were 10.3 million independent contractors in the United States,[118] representing 6.7 percent of the workforce.[119] New communications technologies and evolving worker preferences are prompting public and private organizations to rethink how to take advantage of the changing workforce and this new environment.

Schooling, however, is an exception. The old rules and norms have kept the traditional framework locked firmly in place, and the teaching job itself has remained remarkably undifferentiated over the last century. Across the land, from Syracuse to Seattle, a visitor can stroll into a school and be confident that all fourth-grade teachers in that district will be expected to cover the same subjects, instruct about the same number of students, and take on roughly the same number of ancillary duties. This may have made sense when little data was available with which to track teacher strengths or student needs, but under modern conditions it represents a careless waste of skill and expertise.

Is it possible to rethink the traditional boundaries of the teaching role, to alter responsibilities, or to tap educators who spend much of their time outside of K–12 schooling? Is it possible to rethink the teaching role and to use new tools to attract talent and allow educators to do more of what they do best? Let's take up three illustrative examples of what these ideas might look like once we have emancipated ourselves from our current system.

For one thing, rather than continuing to accept the notion that one either is a "teacher" or is not, schools might embrace hybrid positions to allow talented educators to grow by leveraging their skills in new ways, even as they continue teaching. A district might ask talented veterans to take on half-time teaching loads and spend the other half of their time on professional development, curriculum development, or parent outreach. In addition, schools could employ community members as instructors to augment the capacities of school staff. Boston-based Citizen Schools, for example, provides highly regarded after-school instruction and career-based learning by arranging for local volunteers to work with students on a regular basis. Rather than simply mentoring or tutoring students, participants teach weekly modules that tackle complex projects with interested students. When an engineer steps off the fast track to start a family, she might consult, freelance, or find some other part-time role with her old employer or a savvy nonprofit. Yet, of those schools that might desire to scoop up such professionals by the bushel, they have no mechanism for recruiting, incorporating, or compensating them.

Second, we need to think very differently about the opportunities offered by specialization, in which elementary reading instruction might be recognized as a role distinct from other tasks, for example, and be buttressed with specialized training programs that help teachers diagnose, instruct, and support early readers. Other professions use precisely this model to ensure that they are squeezing maximum value out of their most talented and most highly trained professionals. In medicine, for example, the American Medical Association now recognizes 199 specialties. While there are 7 million medical professionals in the United States, only 500,000 are physicians.[120] The remainder are trained practitioners with talents that complement those of doctors. In a well-run medical practice, surgeons do not spend time filling out patient charts or negotiating with insurance companies; these responsibilities are left to nurses or support staff. Schools might find more thoughtful ways to employ lead instructors who have had more intensive training and complementary staff who have had less, and then apportion instructional or administrative roles accordingly.

And third, technology offers another menu of options to change the way some education services are delivered. Today's staffing model assumes enough talented teachers that every community will be able to fill all of its classrooms with effective teachers. This expensive "people-everywhere" strategy limits the available talent pool, as some potentially effective educators may be unwilling to relocate to the communities in need. Technology may make it possible to pipe in expertise to complement and compensate for the limitations of any local teaching force. Perhaps the most significant impact of education technology is its potential to eliminate obstacles posed by geography. Web-based delivery systems can take advantage of the wealth of highly educated, English-speaking people in nations like India willing to tutor children at relatively inexpensive rates. For example,

Washington, D.C.–based SMARTHINKING Inc. uses American and international tutors to provide intensive instruction to students. Students can log on to the company's website twenty-four hours a day, seven days a week, and work in real time with experts in various academic subjects.

Such efforts to fully utilize talent and expertise have been largely absent in schooling. The key is to stop thinking of teaching as an "all-or-nothing" job and to contemplate models that include the support and opportunity for steady part-timers who also have other obligations or complementary jobs. Such a "consultant" approach could reflect the way other sectors have tapped into particular expertise or retain the service of talented professionals despite changing life circumstances or fluctuating labor markets. Too often, however, discussions about staffing or technology do not envision the full range of potential problem solving but instead get caught up in negotiating the bonds of existing policy, school organization, and the familiar teaching role.

CONCLUSION

Today, we worry that we do not attract teachers of the caliber that our aspirations require. We worry about the rate of teacher turnover, the quality of professional development, the efficacy of teacher preparation, the level of teacher pay, and the quality of instruction. Each of these concerns merits attention. Meanwhile, larger efforts to remake the profession so it is possible to address these concerns— by addressing policies and practices governing salaries, tenure, and licensure—are routinely attacked by unions and education officials as distractions or as attacks on teachers. There is nothing innately wrong with step-and-lane salary schedules, tenure, or licensure; these have their appropriate uses. Today, however, these impose severe costs, deliver few benefits, and make it more difficult to recruit and retain quality teachers in the modern labor market. There is no magic to these proposals and no reason to think they are solutions in and of themselves. Rather, they are essential tools in making it possible to find, cultivate, and retain excellent instructors.

The contemporary teaching profession was built to rely on a captive pool of female labor that would be micromanaged by male principals and superintendents. Preparation programs trace their roots to a time when one could reasonably expect that most aspiring teachers had chosen that course before entering college. Later, salary ladders that reward continuous service, collective bargaining agreements, defined-benefit pension plans, and more expansive licensure systems were layered atop these foundations. All of these once sensible innovations now hinder efforts to attract scarce talent in the new workforce. A changed workforce suggests the need for the job description and recruiting strategy to change accordingly.

Even many of today's cutting-edge efforts to reform school staffing, teacher recruitment, and teacher preparation represent nothing more than repackaging outmoded assumptions in the hopes of seeing dramatically different results. Such proposals simply ignore the possibility that hiring twenty-two-year-olds as careerists may no longer be a viable model, that licensure might be a poor mechanism for promoting excellent teaching, or that it may be time to rethink the very nature of the teaching job. Addressing the twenty-first-century teaching challenge will have to begin by unshackling ourselves from the legacy of once reasonable arrangements that no longer serve.

7

Some Reassembly Required

> "All national educational systems are embarrassed by what they have inherited, and they have often inherited a system quite different in its implications from what they are now trying to work out."
>
> —Abraham Flexner, Carnegie Foundation, 1911

The notion that there are "right" ways to govern, operate, and organize K–12 institutions is one that has long been with us. In *The One Best System,* historian David Tyack provided the classic account of how Progressive reformers worked diligently to bureaucratize and systematize schooling.[1] In the century since, would-be reformers have responded to lingering problems by seeking new orthodoxies they can apply across fifty states and 14,000 districts.

Upon reflection, it seems remarkable to imagine that there should be any one sacrosanct arrangement for providing education in a free nation. Not only have other free societies organized schooling in a variety of ways over time, but the Athenian democracy, the Roman republic, and our nation's Founders, among others, had no difficulty imagining that a vast array of arrangements working simultaneously could effectively serve public ends. Yet, even seemingly modest proposals to rethink the governance or organization of school systems are routinely portrayed as a retreat from public schooling. Meanwhile, attempts to rethink high schools or the school calendar are met by suggestions that their efficacy be "proven" before new solutions are contemplated.

The last chapter focused on why we might want to imagine the shape of teaching differently. In this chapter, I focus on the ways in which we might reimagine some of the building blocks that shape schools and school systems. I suggest that an array of sometimes controversial proposals—including embracing school vouchers, re-imagining the shape of the high school, redesigning the school calendar, forsaking school boards for mayoral control, or finding alternatives to geographically based school districts—are deserving of serious consideration. I do not suggest that any of these are essential or universal solutions, nor do I try to muster evidence demonstrating that particular changes will boost test scores, increase efficiency, or yield other quantifiable benefits. Rather, I argue that "radical" proposals such as these may offer valuable opportunities to more effectively address our aims in a manner consistent with our values.

THE STATE MONOPOLY ON SCHOOL DELIVERY

Nearly 90 percent of American students today attend traditional district schools that are operated by state officials and staffed by public employees.[2] In these schools, state and local officials not only fund a child's education and set expectations and standards, but they also hire the educators, set policies, manage payroll, dictate the curriculum, and decide how many minutes to set aside for lunch. There is an assumption that this ordering of duties is the natural state of affairs. Alternative arrangements in which families might send their children to other kinds of schools are regarded as a threat to American values.

Debates about alternative ways to provide publicly funded schooling, most especially those proposals that seek to provide families with school vouchers, are frequently bitter and intense. The rhetoric speaks for itself. Scholars Bruce Biddle and David Berliner saw such measures as evidence of a "political agenda designed to weaken the nation's public schools, redistribute support for those schools so that privileged students are favored over needy students, or even abolish those schools altogether."[3] Berliner, a former president of the American Education Research Association, has warned, "Voucher programs would allow for splintering along ethnic and racial lines. . . . Our primary concern is that voucher programs could end up resembling the ethnic cleansing now occurring in Kosovo."[4]

Beyond the fierce battles over vouchers lies a deeper tension over the provision of public schooling and the state's role therein. Political theorist Benjamin Barber has declared, "Public schools are not merely schools for the public, but schools of publicness: institutions where we learn what it means to be a public and start down the road towards common national and civic identity."[5] The rationale for state-based provision of education can be traced all the way back to Plato's call for a uniform state-run system. However, if we recall that democratic Athens and the Roman republic relied upon private arrangements with instructors to serve the public interest, it is evident that the democratic tradition encompasses two competing visions of how to serve the public purposes of schooling. One vision, consistent with Jean-Jacques Rousseau's "general will," suggests that a state-operated school system is needed to universally promote the right values and serve the common interest by their uniform application. A second, more pluralistic vision reflects James Madison's understanding of the public interest as the sum of the interests of individual citizens coalescing in a messy cacophony. Such a view implies that a variety of state-run and nonstate arrangements can serve to foster heterogeneous thinking and balance out one another, thereby best serving the public interest.

While neither perspective is necessarily correct, American traditions in other sectors generally draw more heavily upon the more modest dictates of Madison than the sweeping dictates of Rousseau. The irony of our current debates is that those who ardently champion the state's retention of a tight grip on school operations are also typically among the most hostile to the Rousseauian claim that schools ought to be training Benjamin Rush's "republican machines." Rather, today's proponents of muscular state-operated schools assert the need for schooling that prepares students to be free-thinking, informed, and equipped for life after high school. This is a bit of fancy footwork. They are defending the Common School and Progressive apparatus as inviolable on grounds antithetical to those that motivated its architects.

Today's system of state-run schools was not the handiwork of the Founders but of Common School and Progressive crusaders disdainful of the tenets of pluralism and diversity that we celebrate today. Progressive icon Ellwood Cubberley taught generations of educators that the extent of government control of schooling was the measure of a nation's democratic character."[6] Cubberley, explains historian Diane Ravitch, thought the most evolved nations were those "in which the state, acting through its expert professional staff, exercised complete control over schools" and could thereby "promote the intellectual and moral and social progress along lines useful to the state."[7]

Given contemporary aims, it is not clear why anyone would necessarily presume that educators employed by the state are uniquely suited for this task—or why state-operated facilities and services should necessarily be preferred to alternative arrangements. As John Stuart Mill argued in *On Liberty,* "An education established and controlled by the State should only exist, if it exists at all, as one among many competing experiments, carried on for the purpose of example and stimulus, to keep the others up to a certain standard."[8] Indeed it is not clear that state-operated schools are the best-equipped institutions to teach democratic values. To do anything at all, state-operated schools must negotiate multiple layers of government and public bureaucracy, contend with competing constituencies, abide by extensive public sector regulations and process requirements, and negotiate the tendency to find least-common-denominator solutions to public disputes. The result: state-run schools tend toward a process-based, watery standardization which makes it difficult to establish strong values or disciplinary norms.

In fact, international comparisons suggest both that democratic nations can comfortably embrace a diversity of school operations and that publicly operated schools are not necessarily more effective in promoting "public" values than are autonomous schools. While American schooling is far more decentralized than school systems of other nations, it is also far more restrictive about the ability of non-state entities to operate schools. Countries whose education systems are usually regarded as less free-wheeling than that of the United States—including Canada, New Zealand, Australia—regularly subsidize private, nonstate schools so long as they operate in accord with public standards.

In a study of twenty-six national schooling systems, Boston University professor Charles Glenn reported, "Government provides funding for all or most of the cost of nongovernment schools to ensure that the ability of parents to make decisions about the education of their children is not limited by lack of resources."[9] In France, 20 percent of students are enrolled in private (mostly Catholic) schools whose costs are 80 percent publicly subsidized.[10] German law stipulates that "private schools serve to complete and enhance the state system."[11] Of course, the flip side of that arrangement is that private schools are subject to state supervision.[12] In other words, many nations allow public funds to fully or partially defray the cost of students' attending nonstate schools, under a variety of rules and oversight mechanisms, and all without the rancor that accompanies proposals for similar programs in the United States.

Despite the overheated rhetoric about public education's exclusive ability to impart those virtues we deem valuable in our students, the scant research exploring the impact of public and private schooling on student attitudes tells a different story. In a 2005 Brookings Institution volume, University of Arkansas scholar Patrick Wolf examined the existing body of quantitative studies regarding the consequences of school choice and private schooling on seven "civic values": political tolerance, voluntarism, political knowledge, social capital, political participation, civic skills, and patriotism.[13] Wolf reported that, across forty-eight analyses in twenty studies, "The general effect of private schooling or school choice on civic values trends toward neutral-to-positive." He found three findings of negative effects due to private schooling or school choice and twenty-nine that trended positive. Wolf summarized, "As a whole, these forty-eight findings suggest that the effects of school choice on civic values tend, in almost all cases, to be positive or nil."[14]

Similarly, Wolf's University of Arkansas colleague Jay Greene has noted that private schools typically have positive effects, or at worst, no ill effects, in areas like racial and ethnic integration, racial and ethnic conflict, political and civic participation, and political tolerance. Greene reported that private school students were almost twice as likely as public school students to be friends with students of other racial and ethnic groups in their school and were "better able to form cross-racial friendships and avoid racial conflicts than [were students in] public schools." On the question of volunteerism, Greene found, "Private school students are more likely to volunteer, more likely to volunteer often, and more likely to believe that volunteering and helping others are very important things."[15] Such evidence raises important questions about whether traditional district schools are configured in a manner that enables them to effectively promote democratic values, and, at a minimum, it complicates simple claims that only traditional public schools can advance them.

Ultimately, narrow consequentialist debates about test scores or the rate of volunteerism in schools of choice are peripheral to the larger question—whether providers other than state-operated schools may be able to more effectively serve some students and, if so, what that suggests for the redesign of financing, regulation, and oversight. As Columbia University scholar Jeffrey Henig noted nearly two decades ago, "Some advocates of public-school choice invest the line separating public and private schools with almost mystical significance. . . . [In fact,] it is possible to keep authority and responsibility for debate, deliberation, and decision making in the public sector without treating the line between public and private schools as inviolable."[16]

Pursuing a greater uniformity via state-operated schools was a sensible course for a sprawling and highly decentralized young nation seeking to forge a common culture. Absent national media or communications, and in an era when a trip from Boston to Chicago was an arduous journey, the costs of public bureaucracy may have seemed a modest price in order to more tightly knit the nation

together. Today, however, it is not clear that those earlier justifica-
tions still apply.

ELECTION OF THE BODY SNATCHERS

The school boards governing the nation's 14,000 school districts
have long been the subject of abuse. In one of the more famous quips
directed at American education, Mark Twain drily wrote in 1887,
"In the first place God made idiots. This was for practice. Then He
made school boards."[17] More recently, Lisa Graham Keegan, former
Arizona commissioner of education and advisor to Senator John
McCain's 2008 presidential campaign, offered a take that was only
slightly less acerbic, declaring, "In my experience, those who join
district boards, even those who start out reform-minded, eerily become co-opted and wind up defending the system tooth and nail. It's
just like watching *Invasion of the Body Snatchers.*"[18] Such criticism is
symptomatic of the popular frustration that has fueled calls for the
abolition of school boards and has prevailing enthusiasm for shifting
control of school systems over to mayors.

As a stopgap solution, mayoral control makes good sense in
large, rudderless school systems where an accountable leader can
lend coherence and energy. But the urgent demands sometimes seem
curiously divorced from history. After all, the modern school board
was created by the Progressive reformers precisely for the purpose of
insulating schools from political machinations. Merely leaping from
frying pan to fire and back again hardly constitutes a winning strategy. Mayoral control may be too narrow a response to the challenge
at hand. After all, even this "radical" call for reforming school governance does not question the assumption that schools should be governed by a series of contiguous bureaucratic monopolies.

School boards have existed, in some form, throughout American history. In colonial America, the fledgling education system was
largely run by local communities with little to no oversight from
state government. Meshing cleanly with the nation's commitment to

decentralized control, early boards were local organizations run informally by school committeemen who were charged with such tasks as visiting schools, supervising administrative details, and handling fiscal decisions.[19] This local autonomy allowed school boards, in the words of political scientist William Howell, to focus "on a single objective—providing educational services to the community," which made them well suited to serve as "the engine that drove the most rapid expansion in educational opportunity the world had ever seen."[20]

The number of local boards exploded in the nineteenth century just as schooling did. But by the end of the century and into the next, Progressives pushed to streamline school boards, and later to consolidate school districts in the name of administrative efficiency. In 1893, there was an average of 21.5 board members per city of 100,000 or more, in addition to hundreds of ward board members in the nation's twenty-eight largest cities; Boston had more than 190 school trustees[21]; and in Philadelphia, power was vested in twenty-four local boards.[22] However, by 1913, school board membership had dropped to half the 1893 level, and ward board members had become all but extinct. Boards continued to scale down, and by 1923, the average board had seven members.[23] Many in favor of this consolidation argued that it was time to clean out school boards, which were plagued by patronage and politics. Boston schoolman John Philbrick complained in 1885 that board members were "unexceptionable in respect to character, ability, and faithful devotion to the interests of the schools," and that "everywhere there are unscrupulous politicians who do not hesitate to improve every opportunity to sacrifice the interests of the schools to the purposes of the political machine."[24]

In their efforts to squash mere politics and professionalize schooling, early-twentieth-century Progressives successfully championed reforms that made school board elections nonpartisan and moved the elections off-cycle. The hope in shifting these races so that they were no longer held at the same time as major state or national elections was, in the words of scholar Joseph Viteritti, to "insulate schools from [partisan] politics."[25] In a time of patronage-driven politics and flagrant corruption, and in an era when schooling had not yet acquired much institutional independence or importance, such ambitions were sensible and pragmatic. The Progressives achieved their dream of shielding board members from political accountability and of separating from municipal power centers, while unknowingly costing future schools the price of factionalism, high turnover, and weakened accountability.

Given the evolution in board responsibilities and a more ambitious mission for schooling, the constraints of Progressive reforms have often resulted in stunted boards that may no longer be well suited to their charge. Indeed, frustration with rudderless governance, board micromanagement, and the ability of teacher unions to dominate sparsely attended elections has fueled a series of energetic calls for turning school governance over to mayors. Even U.S. Secretary of Education Arne Duncan has declared, "I absolutely, fundamentally believe that mayoral control is extraordinarily important."[26]

To be sure, mayoral control can offer a heightened opportunity for coherent, accountable leadership—but reformers would be wise to note that this approach's success depends mightily on how it is configured and whether the mayor is willing and able to invest political capital in schooling. Moreover, benefits may depend on the staying power of the current crop of mayors committed to education reform and whether their successors will feel similarly. Touting universal remedies based on the experience of a handful of exceptionally strong and long-serving mayors in locales like Boston, Chicago, and New York City exposes today's reformers to the same perils as their Progressive predecessors, who were blindly invested in a bureaucratic solution that worked in some cases for some boards some of the time.

Moving power from boards to mayors could actually unearth dangers that the Progressives sought to bury as well as unleashing new threats. As one example, Viteritti cautions, mayors "are not beyond the reach of the same organized interests that have retarded reform on local school boards."[27] Mayors, too, can be susceptible to the influence of teacher unions and aggrieved neighborhoods. Indeed, while their broader constituency may dilute the impact of narrow interests, it is also the case that mayors' acute political antennae and professional ambitions may render some of them more sensitive to the concerns of such groups. A second potential problem with handing power over to mayors is the potential loss of transparency. In recent years, malfeasance and irresponsible behavior at firms like AIG, Fannie Mae, or Bear Stearns has shown how an overly cozy culture can enable management to take shortcuts or adopt questionable practices. Corporate accounting and governance reforms have sought to increase the presence of independent voices and ensure that boards keep an eye on headstrong executives, but the development of such safeguards will take time. A third cause for caution is that some voices are likely to be silenced or marginalized under an appointed board; after all, one reason for the chaotic state of elected boards is that board members, for good as well as ill, are inclined to tend to neighborhood or constituent concerns. Vesting mayors with the power to silence or exclude such voices would be a poor trade-off if they acted contrary to reformers' intentions. And finally there's some concern that mayoral control may be too narrow a response to this challenge. After all, even this "radical" call for reforming school governance does not question the assumption that schools should be governed by a series of contiguous bureaucratic monopolies.

Pushing past competing claims regarding the merits of mayoral control raises the question of whether the structure of school districts themselves continues to make sense. Localized control and provision was the only option for school governance in the first century of America, and the Progressive's bureaucratic regime fit well for the needs and concerns of their day. However, the governance challenges that plague both mayors and school boards may be due in substantial part to our clinging to an organizational model that has lived past its expiration date.

THE DISTRICT AS LOCAL MONOPOLY

As we've struggled to find the best district governance style over the last century, there has been a parallel struggle to find the best district configuration. In the early twentieth century, schools typically acted as their own districts, since far-removed management arrangements like those we see today were utterly infeasible with the period's available technology. The Progressives' taste for centralization and hierarchy drove an effort to consolidate these autonomous schools into mega-districts. Between 1930 and 1970, for instance, the number of school districts dropped by 90 percent (from 130,000 to 16,000) as reformers folded many schools into a single district.[28] The number of one-room schoolhouses—the mythological icon of American education—plummeted from 200,000 to 20,000 between 1910 and 1960,[29] while the size of the average school district (as measured in enrollment) increased more than tenfold from 1930 to 1970.[30] Today's districts range in size from the 1 million students of New York City alone to thousands of districts that enroll less than 500 students yet span huge tracts of rural America.

Though their size has grown, districts have consistently played an organizing role in the provision of American schooling. As Chief Justice Warren Burger wrote for the U.S. Supreme Court in the 1974 case *Milliken v. Bradley*—when the court ruled that suburban Michigan districts could not be required to engage in busing with the Detroit schools—"School district lines may not be casually ignored or treated as a mere administrative convenience."[31] The inviolability of district autonomy and the ongoing push toward consolidation had the unfortunate effect of aggravating socioeconomic stratification, as districts became a barrier to more economically and racially diverse schooling. Whereas the rich and poor tended to live closer to one another in the nineteenth century when cities were smaller, transport became a bigger concern with the post–World War II rise of commuter suburbs and the new living conditions increasingly led to economically segregated communities.[32]

As new demographic migration patterns developed in the mid-twentieth century, the once-effective district model not only aggravated divisions, but in fact accelerated them. Schooling organized by districts reinforces the self-perpetuating cycle between community affluence and school quality, as the affluent drive up home prices in communities with good schools, making those communities more exclusive and less accessible to low-income families. Harvard University professor of government Jennifer Hochschild has explained, "Racial and economic separation across geographically based local school districts . . . exacerbate[s] unequal outcomes of schooling."[33] When families can select a school without regard to residence, they are free to select a home based on other criteria. School enrollment policies that allow families to select schools without regard to residential location have been found to equalize housing prices. They result in a decline in class-based residential stratification, which can in turn lead to more socioeconomically diverse schools.[34]

Despite seemingly good cause for taking another look at the school district, we have clung reflexively to the notion of district governance. But why? School districts were institutionalized in the early twentieth century, a time when travel and communication technologies that we take for granted did not yet exist. In 1837, the same year that Horace Mann became president of the Massachusetts School Board, President Andrew Jackson's trip from Washington, D.C., back to the Hermitage in Nashville, Tennessee, took eighteen days. In 1849, during Mann's last year in office, traveling from Washington to California was still a six-month ordeal. Fifty-one years later, just 8,000 automobiles were registered nationwide,[35] and only seventeen out of every one thousand Americans had access to a telephone.[36] School leaders at the turn of the century were hamstrung by the day's travel and communication conditions, when coordinating and overseeing teaching and learning from a distance of even fifty miles would have been an immense challenge and when anything other than geographic monopolies would have been prohibitive in terms of cost, logistics, and coordination.

Having all-purpose operations focus on serving a given geo-graphic community was common in the early twentieth century and hardly unique to schooling. In fact, it was pretty much the state of the art up until a few decades ago, when it was thought natural for a given store to meet all your shopping needs—stocking washers and shoes and dresses and tires. A glance at catalogues from the early 1900s shows the one-stop-shop business mentality of the era. The Sears, Roebuck and Co. catalogue, for instance, features firearms, baby carriages, jewelry, saddles, and even eyeglasses with a self-test for "old sight, near sight and astigmatism."[37]

That's no longer the way providers in most sectors are orga-nized. Today, the world is dotted with providers that specialize in doing a few things—or just one thing—well. Organizing school-ing around a sea-to-sea chain of local monopolies made good sense when the cost of travel and communication was high and communi-ties were composed of residents who routinely lived in one place for decades or even a lifetime. Advances in communications, transporta-tion, and data management technology now make it possible, though, for one provider to oversee outlets in thousands of locations—and to offer the same specialized service in each of them. Yet school dis-tricts are not permitted to operate in this fashion. Delivering a new reading program or replacing a problematic human resources de-partment requires sending a handful of administrators to visit an acclaimed district for a few days, and then asking them to mimic it locally with existing staff and some consulting support. Districts thus inadvertently become chokepoints in the delivery of new ser-vices and an important reason why promising models seem so in-credibly hard to duplicate successfully. Once a provider has devel-oped a way to effectively serve a population or solve a problem, why wouldn't we opt for arrangements that allow them to do so in more and more locales? Why on earth do we continue to imagine that a better course is to have thousands of districts and tens of thousands of schools scrambling to adopt someone else's new "best practices"? A more sensible configuration would allow providers to deliver their services (with their own staffs) directly to a growing population of students or across a range of schools and geographies. Today we push thousands of districts to embrace and implement unwanted programs. If the private sector operated in this fashion, Amazon.com would have restricted its clientele to residents of Washington state, while would-be imitators from across the country flocked in to learn its secrets and then return home to emulate them. These best-practice imitators would frequently have fumbled the execution of the business, and a cottage industry of consultants would pad their pockets claiming to explain Amazon's secrets. We'd regard the whole experience as another failed effort to leverage technology or take a boutique provider to scale. Instead of encouraging school districts to emulate the KIPP Academies model, for instance, policy makers and reformers might focus on enabling and encouraging KIPP to more readily open schools to satisfy local demand. The provider would be focused on serving its target population with staff it has selected and trained, rather than hoping that districts will faithfully deliver its model—without the personal commitment, handpicked staff, or specialized expertise.

Rather than school boards enjoying a local monopoly, multiple boards might operate in any given locale—with some presumably operating across a wealth of locales. Competing boards could vie to serve schools, giving teachers, principals, and communities a variety of choices with whom they partner. Competing boards might operate like today's charter school authorizers, with each responsible for approving and monitoring the schools that it authorizes. Such an arrangement could allow authorizers to focus on serving a particular swath of students or schools, enabling an expertise, focus, and coherence that is so often lacking in all-purpose bureaucracies.[38]

Today, every school district is asked to devise ways to meet every need of every single child in a given area. Since they can't tailor their service to focus on certain student needs, districts are forced to try to build expertise in a vast number of specialties and services. Transforming any sprawling, underachieving organization is enormously challenging under even the best circumstances; it may well be impossible under such conditions. This arrangement demands that districts juggle a vast array of demands and requires them to necessarily become the employers of nearly all educators in a given community. This makes it enormously difficult to selectively hire educators who agree on mission, focus, or pedagogy, and the resulting grab-bag of faculty and leaders must then strive to forge coherent cultures. This is a needlessly exhausting strategy and one unlikely to lead to wide-scale excellence. Once again, the point is not to advocate for some rush to disband geographic districts but that we would do well to cease assuming the district as an inviolable fact and to explore the merits of other ways to coordinate, manage, and deliver services.

THE ANYTHING AND EVERYTHING HIGH SCHOOL

Everybody agrees that the American high school isn't working like we want it to. That should come as no surprise, as high schools are today asked to accomplish ends they were never designed to tackle. As we noted in chapter 1, at a 2005 National Governors Association meeting, Bill Gates delivered a window-rattling speech to the nation's assembled governors. Gates termed the American high school "obsolete," saying, "I don't just mean that our high schools are broken, flawed, and under-funded—though a case could be made for every one of those points. By obsolete, I mean that our high schools—even when they're working exactly as designed—cannot teach our kids what they need to know today."[39] Unfortunately, the response to this challenge has been successive, energetic efforts to tinker with the size, shape, and organization of a convoluted institution. Even bold efforts at reform have tended to leave the underlying regularities of the high school intact.

Modeled first on New England's Latin schools, and later on the then private academies that would soon after emerge, the modern American high school was never designed to serve the range of student demands now thrust upon today's secondary schools. Latin schools were modeled on London's reformed Latin Grammar School, which had been founded in 1510. In the United States, Latin schools would then give way to private academies focused on practical subject matter and intended to prepare high school–aged children from wealthy families for college.[40] Both models charged tuition and educated an exclusive minority for the sole purpose of college preparation, leaving a legacy of limited access well into the nineteenth century.

A little over a century ago, in 1890, just 5.6 percent of America's 5.4 million fourteen- to seventeen-year-olds were enrolled in high school. A decade later, in 1900, still just 6 percent of seventeen-year-olds graduated from high school.[41] Many schoolmen felt that post-elementary schooling was necessary only for a select few students, who would be better served by entering collegiate preparatory schools.[42] Of the students who were enrolled in high school, just two-thirds were in public schools.[43] However, at the same time the high school landscape was beginning to shift. The five hundred high schools in the United States in 1870 had grown to over 10,000 by 1910.[44] In the first decades of the twentieth century, public high school enrollment first started to dramatically eclipse that of the private academies. In 1890, 32 percent of total pupils were enrolled in private high schools. By 1929, almost 92 percent graduated from public high school.[45]

It wasn't until 1930 that half of America's fourteen- to seventeen-year-olds were even *enrolled* in a public or private high school,[46] and it wasn't until 1940 that half of American seventeen-year-olds first *completed* high school.[47] In other words, the expectation of a high school education is only a few generations old and was the product of rapid and often haphazard development that gave scant attention to universal quality control.

Much of this growth was facilitated by an infusion of public dollars. The door for public funding of high schools opened in 1876 when the Supreme Court of Michigan ruled that public funds could be expended for high schools and not just Common Schools (which had been understood to mean grade K–8 elementary schools). That decision gave the Common School reformers substantial opportunity to extend their efforts to erect a hierarchical, graded, and coordinated system of schooling. Historian Carl Kaestle has observed, "In New York City, educators spoke of the need for a high school 'as a part of a perfect system,' and . . . called it 'the splendid crown of our Common School system.'"[48] College presidents also saw expanding and strengthening high schools in their states as a way to attract students and broaden public support. The new state universities in Michigan and Wisconsin, for instance, encouraged the development of local public high schools. The graduates from those schools were then assured admission to the universities.[49]

The rapid growth of high schools fueled an effort to accommodate an enormous range of student interests and needs. But, as historian Patricia Albjerg Graham has noted, policies and practices "intended for 250,000 students might not be appropriate for a student body nearly ten times that size and growing rapidly."[50] Gerald Gutek has noted that the high school has always been driven by the tensions evident between views of the Committee of Ten and the Cardinal Principles, between those who saw it as a "college-preparatory institution" and those who sought "a 'people's college' offering manual, industrial, commercial and vocational programs."[51] By the middle of the twentieth century, Cardinal Principles–inspired schools designed to serve everyone had given rise to an incoherent and less than rigorous high school curriculum.[52]

Efforts to shape the high school have been a project of competing pet agendas at least since the World War I era, when some reformers sought to strike German as a foreign language, while others pushed to expand physical education programs to equip potential inductees for the armed services.[53] The pushing and pulling eventually yielded the "shopping mall" high school, where students are offered an assortment of programs, electives, instructional approaches, and related services under one roof. The result is a school where it is difficult to establish clear priorities, a coherent course of studies, or disciplined instruction.[54]

More recent efforts to reform high schools have been driven by proponents of the "small schools" movement, which has sought to break up into smaller, less anonymous institutions the massive high schools that were built in the 1970s and 1980s. Such schools would shrink down to a few hundred students each, and then subdivide into smaller groups of four to five teachers with 80 to 120 students in order to individualize curriculum and provide more attention to students.[55]

Ironically, the giant high schools that today's reformers decry were themselves a product of the reform orthodoxy of an earlier era: the research-based reform agenda advocated by former Harvard University president James Conant in the 1960s. Conant concluded that the primary problem with American high schools was their size—but he thought the schools of the day were simply too *small*. Conant spearheaded a successful effort to *increase* the size of high schools and consolidate thousands of tiny schools. Each grade level, Conant recommended, should have, at a minimum, one hundred students. He recommended that the number of high schools be cut from 21,000 to 9,000, so that states might centralize resources in order to boost educational quality.[56] Conant was careful to indicate that he only wanted schools large enough to ensure the provision of a full academic core, and his recommended minimum school size of four hundred would strike later "small school" advocates as just fine. Nonetheless, a wave of enormous mega high schools were erected in the decades to follow, suggesting how readily potentially sensible reforms can become distorted and adopted as new conventions.

The small-school crusade of the early 2000s fell victim to the same kinds of problems that plagued Conant's efforts. The critique of the mega high school made sense, as did the case for strengthening rigor, relevance, and relationships. Some small high schools, especially those led by committed leaders and pursued with autonomy and focus, showed some impressive results.[57] Yet, as the idea gained sway, claiming foundation support and winning enthusiastic adherents in several large districts, there was a rush to hurriedly refashion hundreds of existing high schools into thousands of new small schools. Eventually, the wave floundered, as it proved difficult to get the personnel, resources, and flexibility to make the model work within the confines of existing policy and practice. Small schools lost their luster and were soon regarded by most as one more passing fad.

Competing notions of what high school students should know, what skills they need, and how best to teach them have been up for debate since the first high school opened its doors. But we have tended to focus on wholesale new solutions, such as determining an optimal curricula or size. It may make more sense to inquire how to empower a variety of schools and providers to serve students' discrete needs. If the question that should guide high school reform is "What are we trying to accomplish?" the answer is probably, "It depends." Namely, it will depend on the students in question, on their needs and goals.

If the essential elements of high school are that all children should be served, master core academic content and skills, and be prepared for college or work, then the range of experiences that might fit the bill is pretty big. To take just one example of an alternative high school model that reimagines structure as well as pedagogy, consider the "Starbucks School" dreamed up by Michael Goldstein, founder of the Boston-based MATCH charter school. If the goal is to provide personalized instruction and support to at-risk youth, the regimented school day with its rotating cast of teachers is probably a poor fit. The Starbucks model would give up on dragging these students into the local school and instead focus on matching the smallest possible group of students with a skilled, dynamic teacher in a comfortable environment. What is most interesting here is not the particular model, which bears more than a passing resemblance to previous alternative school models, but the larger shifts in governance, organization, funding, and staffing that make it a coherent option capable of growth at scale—rather than one more boutique program tucked into existing offerings.

Goldstein has posited that, for the same $20,000 or more that a city like Boston spends annually on a typical at-risk high school student, it could create a class of eight students, buy each a laptop and a bus pass (and maybe a Starbucks card), secure them a block of online tutoring time from a provider like Smarthinking.com or Tutor.com, and pay a top-shelf teacher $110,000 plus benefits to meet them each day at Starbucks or a YMCA. Perhaps $16,000, 10 percent of the total per student outlay, would flow back to the central district for fixed costs, oversight, assessments, and such. Hours could be designed flexibly, at the teacher's discretion, and instruction would be organized around student need. Students need not progress at the conventional, stately, age-graded pace. They could move more slowly or more rapidly, depending upon the subject and their performance.

The goal would be to help the students finish their high school courses and master the essential content. Consistent with that, the teacher's salary might be structured as an initial base salary of $50,000 or $60,000, along with a bonus for each state-mandated graduation exam that a student successfully completes and for each student who is enrolled in college or ensconced in a job the following September. The result would be a well-compensated, enthusiastic teacher who was deeply invested in the success of each student, backed up by subject expertise when necessary. Dumping the rest of the district operation means that intimate class size, personal support, high-quality laptops, and the rest could be paid for with no additional dollars.

What about students who wanted to play football, or the flute? First off, let's not allow our visions of the ideal stifle better solutions. The reality is that few at-risk students are engaged in these kinds of activities. But that's not a very satisfying answer, and it needn't be. After all, it's not clear why students need to sit in thirty-person science classes in order to show up for football practice. There's no reason, other than bureaucratic inertia, why it should be a problem for a sixteen-year-old to be taught at the library or the coffee shop and then arrange to be at school for band practice. If creating room for this kind of scheduling requires that some schools alter familiar schedules or shift electives from the academic day to the hours after school, then that's worth exploring.

While we typically think of such models as boutiques, there is nothing about the Starbucks model that could not be scaled, given adequate accountability systems, a reimagined teaching profession, and retooled systems of governance and student funding. Because the model does not require official school facilities but can make use of any available space, it can be configured for various communities. Asking local school districts to recruit and train teachers with the requisite skills might be prohibitive, but one could readily imagine a national provider that would recruit, train, and deploy such teachers to communities. If it is too onerous for local school districts to keep track of the progress of these students in their unconventional role, that same provider could provide all necessary assessments and monitoring. In fact, the Starbucks school provider could essentially operate as a non-geographic school district, hiring and preparing faculty, supplying services, managing funds, and providing assessment and support.

The point is not that there is anything magical about this particular solution; it is merely one illustration of the kind of (potentially) effective solutions that become possible if we relax our assumptions about how teens ought to be educated. If the concern is that such diversification yields stratification or fragmentation, then let us take care to judge all forms of provision by that same standard. Let us not presume that deconstructing comprehensive schools will aggravate concerns but judge all forms of provision with the same measuring stick. High school has been the victim of wave upon wave of faddism, but most of it has focused on tinkering with the size, shape, and organization of a confused enterprise, rather than asking how to reshape that institution for the work it is being asked to do.

TURNING THE PAGE ON THE SCHOOL CALENDAR

In the past two decades, a drumbeat of reports has shown that U.S. students fall short on international assessments. While there are a number of potential explanations for relative performance, from cultural norms to pedagogical approaches, one obvious factor is that U.S. students spend substantially less time learning than do most of their peers around the globe. If our schools are consistently failing to ensure that many students master the requisite content and skills, it is worth asking whether our arrangements are ensuring that those students are getting all the instruction they require.

Today, the U.S. school year is remarkably immutable and consistent—180 days from fall through spring, regardless of student need or community context. The school year averaged 130 to 135 days between 1870 and 1890, stretched to 160 days by 1920 and 178 days by 1950, and has hovered there ever since. The average number of days attended per pupil grew from 78 in 1870 to 121 in 1920, to 158 in 1950, and then settled down at about 161.[58]

Recent reform proposals have called for extending the average school day and school year, particularly for underachieving students who often need extra assistance and don't have supervision at home during the summer months. Some promising efforts along these lines include the extended school year (and school day) employed by the KIPP Academies and the 30 percent boost in learning time provided at some schools via the nationally noted Mass 2020 "Extended Learning Time" pilot in Massachusetts.[59]

The current wave of efforts to rethink the school calendar was energized by the final report of the National Education Commission on Time and Learning in April 1994, which observed, "Learning in America is a prisoner of time. For the past 150 years, American public schools have held time constant and let learning vary. The rule, only rarely voiced, is simple: learn what you can in the time we make available. . . . Our time-bound mentality has fooled us all into believing that schools can educate all of the people all of the time in a school year of 180 six-hour days. . . . We have put the cart before the horse: our schools and the people involved with them—students, parents, teachers, administrators, and staff—are captives of clock and calendar."[60] Not a bad summation of emancipatory thinking, at that.

Today, "modified-calendar" schools enroll barely 2 million kids—about 5 percent of all K–12 students.[61] About 50 million children have summer vacation every year across the United States. But there is nothing sacred about the calendar we have today. Indeed, it has been questioned, altered, and used as a tool for education reform throughout American history. Kenneth Gold of the City University of New York has pointed out that, through the first decades of the 1800s, the summer term was a "vital part of both urban and rural school years," and was attended by roughly the same students, in the same numbers as in other sessions.[62]

Charles Ballinger and Carolyn Kneese, authors of *School Calendar Reform: Learning in All Seasons,* have reported, "From the 1840s onward, schools in America's largest cities were open 11 or 12 months of the year. New York City offered classes for 245 days annually; Chicago, for 240; Detroit, 259; and Philadelphia, 252."[63] At the same time, school years were much shorter in rural areas, where populations were less dense, schooling was less organized, and schools were frequently open three to six months a year.[64]

The traditional school year—fall through spring, with long summers off—was a triumph of Common School engineering, reflecting a desire to systematize schooling, preserve children's health, and apply scientific thinking regarding the needs of child and teacher. Contrary to common perception, this schedule was not a remnant of an agrarian calendar. After all, summers were not the busiest time of year for farmers. Spring, when crops were planted, and fall, when crops were harvested, were the times when farmers had a pressing need for their children's assistance—and rural education accommodated with frequent and appropriately lengthy breaks. Summer vacation as we know it is more accurately understood as the product of a confluence of factors specific to nineteenth-century urban life.

In particular, fears of mental fatigue and overtaxing work, along with the emergence of a middle class and the rise of new forms of travel, spurred the emergence of vacation for adults and children. The Common Schoolers and the first generation of professional educators believed that too much schooling would impair the health of teachers and children.[65] In 1870, the *New York Times* reported, "The theory among physicians and prudent parents is that the quality of the work of the children's brain, during the remaining nine months, is such as to make up for the diminished quantity . . . and probably among women of culture, there is no branch of employment so trying to the nervous system."[66]

Popular conceptions regarding the dangers of overtaxing one's mental capacities reflected a society, in the phrase of the University of Toronto's Joel Weiss, "coming to terms with the psychological necessity of relaxation for a large middle class."[67] Moreover, in the era before air-conditioning, school buildings were not pleasant or particularly healthy places to be in hot weather. Weiss emphasizes the considerations about disease, quoting records from the Victoria Public School, Brockville, 1860: "The midsummer being the period of epidemics, and most fruitful of diseases generally, many children are either kept at home, or are sent out into the country, or visit the various watering places with their parents."[68]

Once the now traditional calendar was set, the desire to professionalize teaching and promote administrative convenience helped to cement it in place. Summer sessions were "used for professional education courses and for teachers upgrading to baccalaureate degrees."[69] But changing academic expectations, second thoughts regarding the fragility of women teachers and students, the invention of air-conditioning, improved hygiene, and the urbanization and the suburbanization of the nation mean that the forces that once dictated the traditional school calendar no longer make much sense.

There are good reasons to rethink the school calendar. Today, two-thirds of children are growing up in households with a single working parent or where both parents work. These children are often left to their own devices after school or in the summer. Low-income children, who lack access to camps, travel, or other world-expanding activities, suffer particularly high rates of "summer learning loss."[70] They may be loitering in parking lots and shopping malls, cruising iffy websites, and slouching toward academic disaster. Meanwhile,

C. S. Mott Foundation program officer An-Me Chung has noted that children in more affluent families "basically have their own extended day that their parents have put together for them."[71] These children spend their summers discovering new interests at summer camp, playing ball at the YMCA, or traveling with Mom and Dad.

Especially for those children lacking a slate of compelling summer activities, it's time to take a fresh look at the traditional summer break. An oft-cited 2007 Johns Hopkins study calculated that 65 percent of the differences in ninth-grade academic achievement between low-income and high-income youth were attributed to summer learning differences in elementary school. "Since it is low SES [socioeconomic status] youth specifically whose out-of-school learning lags behind," the report concluded, "this summer shortfall relative to better-off children contributes to the perpetuation of family advantage and disadvantage across generations."[72]

Summer vacation can also create difficulties for today's working families. As recently as the 1960s, the traditional summer vacation was still a good fit for most families, as 57 percent of children lived in non-farming households with a homemaker mother and breadwinning father.[73] Today, however, two-thirds of American children live with two working parents or with a single working parent, which means that no one is home to supervise children during the summer.[74] For these families, summer vacation can be more obstacle course than respite. Parents struggle to occupy their children's time and to monitor their socializing and Web usage from work.

The Urban Institute has estimated that just 30 percent of school-aged children in families with an employed primary caregiver are cared for by a parent during the summer. Thirty-four percent of other children are taken care of by a relative, with another 30 percent enrolled in at least one organized summer program, such as a summer school or camp.[75] The cost to families is substantial, with 41 percent of working families with school-age children paying for child care; on average, they spend 8 percent of their summer earnings on child care.[76] Meanwhile, expensive school facilities and assets, such as computers, texts, and transportation, frequently sit idle. Other advanced nations, including the United Kingdom, Germany, France, Russia, Australia, Japan, and Korea, don't provide an American-style summer vacation, with most offering no more than seven consecutive weeks of vacation.[77]

Conventional notions of universal summer vacation made more sense when academic achievement mattered less, when we didn't expect schools to serve as engines of equal opportunity or to address "achievement gaps," and when more children had a parent at home every afternoon. Today, things have changed. Summer vacations risk knowledge loss rather than provide the healthful benefits as believed in an earlier era. We know that knowledge and academic skills will be critical to the future success and happiness of today's children. Programs with extended school years, such as the KIPP Academies, have had much success in boosting the achievement for disadvantaged kids.

Yet inertia has ruled, especially in the face of resistance to even sensible change. We have been slow to rethink the calendar, in part due to resistance among parents, educators, and public officials who are reluctant to upend familiar routines. The "summer recreation industry," including golf courses, amusement parks, movie theaters, summer camps, and beachside resorts, resist change, as they depend heavily on a clientele of families with children or on employing a cheap teen workforce. Teacher unions, too, are reluctant to see the school year extended, with efforts to add even two or three days to the academic year typically provoking angry opposition from union officials.

The challenges posed by the school calendar are not uniform; they vary by community, student population, and instructional model. The solutions need not, and should not, be national or uniform. Summer vacations are still a boon and a welcome window for many families and communities. The need is not for systemic moves to "fix" the school calendar but to acknowledge that this nineteenth-century school practice may be a poor fit for many of today's families. Further, additional schooling should not be an invitation to drudgery or an attack on childhood. It is not the changing of the calendar that matters but what educators do with the new opportunities. An extended year should give teachers more time to conduct rich and imaginative lessons and provide more time for music and the arts. Summer vacation can be a grand thing. But for many children and families in the twenty-first century, it can also be a dangerous anachronism.

CONCLUSION

Arrangements controlling time, governance, or school configuration determine the contours of K–12 schooling. This signals the importance of provisions that suit our ambitions rather than the schools we have inherited. We need a way to respect the purposes of schooling without feeling obliged to mimic the "grammar of schooling," in David Tyack's memorable phrase.[78] Even when we recognize that old routines and assumptions may no longer hold, we too often shrink from structural change or turn potentially sensible innovations into iffy new best practices. Rarely do we consider whether arrangements devised to answer particular challenges still make sense, or what that implies for how we might put dollars, time, and energy to better use. As a result, revamping culture and practice becomes an attempt to construct twenty-first-century learning organizations within the forms of industrial-era bureaucracies. The result is akin to Sisyphus's endless struggle to roll a boulder up a hill.

Altering arrangements or institutions does not miraculously or directly improve teaching and learning. It can, however, enable organizational and cultural shifts that make sustained progress a possibility. Absent such larger shifts, energy and enthusiasm will yield occasional glimpses of promise, only to soon peter out. Especially problematic is the constant struggle to maintain buy-in among teachers, public officials, and parents dubious about the pedagogy or approach in question. Structures determine how difficult it will be to make solutions stick and whether inertia will support or erode them. Arrangements that better insulate teaching and learning organizations from political tussling, and which make it easier to attract educators and families committed to a shared vision, can facilitate the kind of instructional coherence and clear expectations that reformers spend so much time and energy trying to manufacture.

Observing that geographical districts or the familiar high school can make it tough to solve important problems does not mean that these should be summarily discarded. It means that we should cease imagining that familiar arrangements are the only legitimate ones and that we should explore, weigh, and employ alternatives. Yet, the lust for the quick fix or the "more, better" mantra typically wins out. Might there not be a more promising path?

8 Finding a New Path

"Pathwalker, there is no path. You must make the path as you walk."

—Antonio Machado

Reformers like to imagine that retooling American schooling is a matter of caring enough, agitating enough, spending enough, and seeking out the right recipes. Surely, they imply, these strategies will equip our schools for the challenges we ask them to shoulder. If the schools erected over centuries past were a road map for the system of schooling that we want, the strategy of walking the same path faster and more energetically would have much to commend it. But our schools do not provide that road map. They were never intended to take us where we now desire to go. Our schools are not a solid foundation for twenty-first-century schooling but a rickety structure that wobbles under the weight of each new addition.

As American schooling took shape, reformers employed the popular tools of their time—notably industrial bureaucracy, scientific management, and cheap labor. Today, despite new tools and technology, our institutions still closely resemble those built in the industrial era. Striking out for a new destination will require a new path; finding that path requires that we first survey the terrain. To recap: counting from 1647, when Massachusetts enacted the first educational statute in the American colonies, it took a little over three centuries to build a school system that enrolled three-quarters of our youth on a regular basis. During this time, schools were expected to mold youth into God-fearing, authority-respecting citizens with little concern for academic performance or promoting economic opportunity.

Just when we figured out how to enroll most children in schooling—well into the twentieth century—the pool of talented female labor that had been sustaining those schools for almost a hundred years began to thin out. Simultaneously, values that had undergirded those schools started to dissolve amidst changing cultural norms. We radically expanded the number of teachers we hired; repurposed schools to address the legacy of slavery and racial inequality; redefined the moral purpose of schools from promoting "Americanism" to appreciating diversity and tolerance; within a generation, proceeded to declare education the "new civil right"; promised to educate every child to a high level of proficiency; and asked schools to equalize opportunity so that all students might have a chance to succeed in a knowledge-based economy.

Whew! And the glaring irony is that the elaborate system of schooling built over those three centuries—now employing 3.3 million teachers in 95,000 buildings and governed by countless rules and routines—was built to simply ensure access to the rudimentary three Rs. This was a sensible system to serve Benjamin Rush's hope to indoctrinate young republicans in an era when literacy was defined as the ability to sign one's name. But it is not at all clear that our elaborate pastiche of public monopolies is an ideal model for delivering an education that shrinks from religious dicta and patriotic fervor, while focusing on equalizing opportunity and preparing students for a knowledge-based economy.

Common Schooling sought to promote norms and beliefs that would knit together a young nation lacking much in the way of central government or common institutions, and where communications and culture were intensely local. Today, diversity and multiculturalism have been publicly embraced by mainstream leaders of the U.S. military and the U.S. Chamber of Commerce. Meanwhile, more than two centuries of tradition have yielded strong national institutions, and advances in communication and transportation have forged countless bonds between North and South, urban and rural, and black and white in a manner that would have astonished even two generations ago. In other words, much that the Common Schools were asked to do has now been accomplished, through their efforts and through broader social changes. Indeed, this triumph can be glimpsed in the simple fact that it is now the most ardent champions of public school systems who tout the importance of celebrating difference. The Progressives sought out to universalize schooling, so as to get students out of the labor force and to teach them necessary skills. They systematized school management, counted everything from enrollment to books, and managed to build an educational system that turned school attendance into one of life's unexceptional routines. Today, more than 95 percent of American children regularly attend school, concerns about child labor are more often about the impact of jobs on high school performance than about youth competing against adults for scarce work, and the challenge of the hour is one of educational quality rather than quantity. The very success of the Progressive agenda can be seen in today's casual assumption that schooling is not a privilege but a basic right, and the charge that every child is entitled not only to an education but to a high-quality education that prepares them for citizenship and for college or a career.

Would-be reformers and policy makers have made grand promises while taking care not to ask whether our heavy-footed school systems are capable of achieving the promised ends. It is an unpleasant position for the educators caught in the middle. Can the bureaucracies erected by Common Schoolers to solve the administrative challenge of compulsory enrollment be repurposed to serve contemporary reformers? Is the universalization pushed by the Progressives capable of serving heterogeneous needs, leveraging new tools, or moving past paralyzing stalemates?

Unfortunately, the answer may well be "no." Would-be reformers would do well to heed the caution that historians Robert Church and Michael Sedlak penned decades ago: "The tragedy has been that in the face of common schooling's inevitable failure to fulfill [disparate] goals schoolmen and citizens alike have failed, for generation after generation, to reassess either the viability or the desirability of the objectives set for public schooling at the start of the common school movement. . . . Instead, [they] have agreed that success is just around the corner if only the common school system could be made a little larger and a little more powerful."[1] In our enthusiasm for quick fixes, we have glossed over such warnings. The results should not surprise, as a half-century of organizational sociology has made clear that large organizations have a powerful inclination and good reason to keep doing what they were originally built to do.[2]

In confronting the stubborn challenges of our system of schooling, we generally make two kinds of mistakes. More common is that made by defenders of the status quo, who imagine that more money, expertise, and support will see us through. Among those convinced of the need for dramatic change like today's New Progressives, however, there is a parallel mistake—a hankering to replace stifling policies and practices with new orthodoxies. An emancipatory reformer believes the way out of this thicket begins not with haste but with diagnosis and deliberation.

This volume is not intended as a work of history; many finer and more fastidious histories are available. History is approached here as a tool for rethinking structures, policies, and practices as a means to help parents, practitioners, policy makers, and would-be reformers step back from the pressing concerns of the moment. My hope is that interested readers will regard this work in the manner that a weary traveler looks upon a butte—as a chance to rise above the thicket in order to glimpse the horizon, gain a sense of the landscape, and scout a more promising path for the journey ahead.

GETTING OFF THE TREADMILL

Because we forget how radical the ambitions of the Common Schoolers and the Progressives really were, we invest their handiwork with a permanence that fails to ignore the extraordinary complexity of the challenge they tackled. In *Popular Education and Its Discontents*,

Lawrence Cremin argues, "Popular schooling is as radical an ideal as Americans have embraced [and] we have made great progress in moving toward the ideal, however imperfect the institutions we have established to achieve it."[3] That ideal is now firmly rooted. The issue is how to secure it. And, on that score, there is too often a temptation to crouch behind the ideal and use it as an excuse to flaunt moral superiority, promote self-interest, and excuse incoherent policies and practices.

Our frustrations have led some to suggest that we can solve our problems simply by returning to the ways of an earlier time. Such a strategy is misguided. Diane Ravitch has explained, "Each generation supposes that its complaints are unprecedented. . . . But those who seek the 'good old days' will be disappointed, for in fact there never was a Golden Age. It is impossible to find a period in the twentieth century in which education reformers, parents, and the citizenry were satisfied with the schools."[4] While our arrangements may have functioned adequately a century ago, they are desperately inadequate by today's standards. As Richard Rothstein echoes Ravitch's rebuke to this overly rosy brand of nostalgia, noting with more than a hint of vitriol in *The Way We Were?*, "If students learn less today than their parents did in the 1950s and 1960s, and if their parents learned less than their own parents . . . one should discover an age when all students learned to read, calculate, and think . . . But such an age never was. In 1900, for example, only 6 percent of all young people graduated from high school; more than half failed to get as far as eighth grade."[5]

When the past fails to deliver the solution we seek, many look abroad for pat fixes. Enthusiasts and reputable experts look to Finland or Singapore and insist that, if we would only imitate their best practices, that will make all the difference. We have spent much time discussing the difficulty of imitating and importing best practices into our schools, and I won't rehash those points. Instead, I'll note that such remedies are curiously detached from our own American institutions, traditions, and strengths. The United States is a nation with a powerful tradition of decentralization and localism, a dynamic economy with profound attachments to individualism and entrepreneurship, and a richly diverse population. I find it peculiar when reformers champion uniform, centralized strategies that will be difficult to implement effectively in the American system and that cut across the grain of the American ethos.

If looking backward or looking abroad turns out not to offer simple solutions, we must look elsewhere for guidance. Unfortunately, efforts to envision the future wind up rehashing long-standing trends regarding demographics, marketable skills, or international competitors, and then leaping to romanticize the latest reform proposal or technology of the moment. The result is a succession of ill-designed or oversold schemes that, as with teacher career ladders in the 1980s or site-based management (SBM) in the 1990s, take good ideas and then try to supersize them into new orthodoxies that can be latched onto the status quo. Thus the sensible notion that school leaders should be granted more autonomy to select faculty and allocate resources, should do a better job engaging the community, and should be monitored on the basis of performance rather than process morphed into an SBM regimen of dysfunctional school councils with little power in systems that pretty much managed and monitored schools the way they always had. The experience neither proved nor disproved the case for decentralized management; it mostly showed that labeling half-baked notions with new jargon doesn't improve schooling. Emancipatory intuitions emerge, only to be packaged as fads, stripped of their power, and adopted crudely, yielding disappointing results and triggering a search for new fixes. We're once again seeing the early signs of these in the efforts of today's New Progressives.

Mayoral Control

Mayoral control provides a terrific illustration of how the enthusiasm for surefire new solutions can lead to troubling blind spots. As we've covered, a century ago, Progressives sacrificed flexibility to advance "nonpolitical" control and to promote "scientific" notions of efficiency and uniformity by turning school boards into apolitical, more professional bodies. Unfortunately, while mayoral control seeks to address the problems of ineffectual political leadership, its proponents too frequently skirt past the larger problems of structural rigidity that have remained in place and largely unquestioned since the Progressive era. Should school systems continue to be staffed by public employees governed by complex contractual and statutory rules? Is the hierarchical Progressive-era model governed by the dictates of 1920s-style scientific management suited to seizing today's opportunities? Are the rigid administrative systems the Progressives constructed compatible with contemporary tools and needs?

It is valuable to recognize, as champions of mayoral control have made clear, that urban school districts are political entities and that governance must address that inevitable reality. Indeed, mayoral control is likely a sensible reform in some locales, and it is an idea that I have sometimes advocated. Equally problematic, and left unaddressed by mayoral control, however, is the legacy of rigidity and uniformity that infuses management, staffing, compensation, and the broader educational enterprise. If pursued with an eye to these constraints and questions, mayoral control can be a sensible step; pursued as an alternative to addressing them, it becomes a distraction.

Merit Pay

Another telling example is playing out in the case of merit pay. Barack Obama sounded powerful chords on teacher pay while running for the presidency in 2008, signaling his belief that effective teachers, those with critical skills, and those serving in tougher environments ought to be paid accordingly. President Obama's secretary of education, Arne Duncan, made similar proclamations in 2009 when he declared that we should "reward those teachers and those principals that are making a huge difference in students' lives."[6]

However, the response to this charge is too often a crude effort to sprinkle cash rewards for higher test scores atop existing salary schedules that base teacher pay on seniority and college credits. Notably absent from such efforts was any attempt to push states to revisit the underlying compensation system or to nurture alternative, sensible approaches to rethinking pay, nor did advocates express much concern that state officials and school bureaucracies might misapply, distort, or use these measures to lay the basis for problematic new standard practices. This ardent effort to trumpet a particular and potentially problematic vision of "best-practice" reform displayed all the sophistication of the pay-per-unit model used to compensate aluminum siding and encyclopedia salesmen half a century ago.

Linking teacher pay to student outcomes is useful and appropriate if it constitutes one part of a broader effort to pay employees with regard to their different responsibilities, expertise, and abilities. But transformative pay reform cannot simply be superimposed on current work arrangements in which 3.3 million teachers labor under roughly identical job descriptions; it must be flexible and create room for value and performance to be responsibly evaluated and rewarded. It should be approached as an integral part of rethinking how to create jobs, leverage the available talent, and pay accordingly. Merit-based pay is fine if promoted as one small piece of that effort; but, too often, it has substituted for a broader rethinking.

Extending Learning Time

Reformers, including President Obama, have rallied behind the sensible push to extend the school day. As discussed in chapter 6, the old school calendar makes little sense today—and the same can be said of the school day and the expectation that we can attain more ambitious goals in the amount of time prescribed decades ago. More time certainly can be a good idea, especially when schools know how to use the hours, when talented teachers have useful ideas and energy, and when families think the student would benefit.

If executed with the same teachers, materials, and techniques, however, there is reason to doubt whether the significant supplementation of existing resources would result in something other than more of the same. National adoption of the extended-day model used by schools in the Massachusetts 2020 Expanded Learning Time Initiative, for instance, would cost the same amount as doubling the salaries of the nation's 1 million best teachers.[7] In KIPP charter schools, where a longer school day and Saturday instruction are defining characteristics, the recipe also calls for talented and impassioned faculty, firm discipline, a powerful school culture, and students who have chosen to be there. Unfortunately, the champions of added time tend to overlook the significant financial, structural, and human capital resources that would be required for the recipe to work. Before embracing expensive new policies, wedging kids into lousy schools for hundreds of extra hours, disrupting fruitful existing afterschool activities, and imposing substantial new demands on teachers, it is worth ensuring that extended time serves as an opportunity for rethinking and not as an alternative to making good use of the time schools already have.

More "Equitably" Distributing Good Teachers

Another illustration is the effort to "equitably" distribute good teachers across school systems, as encouraged by the U.S. Department of Education's 2009 Race to the Top fund.[8] On the one hand, attracting talented teachers to needy schools makes obvious sense. That said, seeking to force-march good teachers into high-poverty schools shows all the classic hallmarks of a good idea gone awry. Ill-conceived policies can encourage districts to move teachers from schools and classrooms where they are effective to situations when they are less effective, as well as driving good teachers from the profession.

The unfortunate reality is that we are still largely unable to identify "effective" teachers other than by looking at reading and math test scores. The particular problem this poses is that the skills that make a teacher effective in one school or system won't necessarily make them successful in another context. As we noted in chapter 5, instructional techniques effective with proficient, affluent students, for instance, may not translate to schools serving disadvantaged populations. The highly structured instructional strategies employed successfully with low-income students by charter school providers like KIPP or Achievement First are far less welcome in more affluent environs.

Indeed, efforts to redistribute teachers without attention to context and constraints could readily reduce the overall quality of teaching, as talented teachers shifted to low-performing schools may be more likely to depart for other work.[9] Thus, ill-conceived efforts to move seemingly effective teachers to more disadvantaged schools may prompt them to leave the profession at higher rates. As University of Pennsylvania's Richard Ingersoll has observed, teachers in high-poverty schools are almost twice as likely to leave teaching as teachers in medium-poverty schools.[10] It would be a self-defeating, shortsighted strategy to systematically shift seemingly effective teachers to the schools where they are most likely to leave the profession.

Accountability

To take one final example, the No Child Left Behind Act is a powerful and familiar cautionary tale of a good idea applied recklessly. In 2001, the Bush administration, along with respected Democrats like Congressman George Miller and the late Senator Ted Kennedy, took the sensible and broadly supported notion of holding schools accountable for outcomes. They then pursued the vision in a prescriptive and overwrought fashion, with a framework driven more by their grand ambitions than by a coherent rendering of how such systems can work effectively. As a result, nine years later, most of the country wants to see No Child Left Behind overhauled or dumped outright.

After years of discontent and disparagement, it is easy to forget that NCLB was once enormously popular. In Bush's first few years, the law was touted as a triumph of bipartisanship and a signal accomplishment. But the law faltered because it forced a jury-rigged system of targets, rules, and procedures on the states without attending to the incentives or organizational dynamics involved in making it work. NCLB's champions learned that while the federal government can force states and school districts to do things they don't want to do, it can't force them to do those things well. Every state now has standards and tests for reading and math in grades three through eight, a definition of "Adequate Yearly Progress," and a system of free tutoring for poor students in schools that don't make the grade. But most of those standards and tests are set at laughably low levels, the definitions of AYP are riddled with holes and twisted by game-playing, and the free tutoring reaches only a minority of the intended beneficiaries. States followed the letter, but not the spirit, of the law.

NCLB enthusiasts bemoaned the intransigence of states and districts, but *what did they expect?* The whole point of performance-based accountability is to hold providers responsible for outcomes while relaxing direction as to how they go about producing those results. Instead, NCLB superimposed a system of test-based accountability on top of all the existing rules and strictures—and then added some new rules and mandates, to boot.

When we look at the difficulties implicit in efforts to promote measures like mayoral control, merit pay, extended learning time, and accountability, we see that sensible ideas are often implemented haphazardly and ineffectually. The lesson is not that these notions are bad ideas. It is that discretion and judgment are the watchwords of smart reinvention. After all, existing arrangements that are problematic on the whole may work perfectly well in certain locales or for certain purposes. Solutions for problems as nuanced and varied as those plaguing schooling are unlikely to work equally well in all settings; the aim is not new universal practices, but problem solving attuned to the challenge at hand. In seeking to claim the necessary support from officials or the public, would-be reformers have turned to scientific research in the hope it will prove that their proposals are sound.

CAN'T SCIENCE SAVE US FROM ALL THIS BOTHER?

Can science help us identify what works, how schooling should be arranged, or who should teach and how teachers should be paid? Well-designed and carefully interpreted research is a valuable tool. It is too much to hope, however, that even terrific research will settle the crucial philosophical debates over priorities, practices, and pedagogies that have been brewing since the dawn of Western civilization. Education is a value-laden enterprise that requires us to make decisions about what we deem most important and what we value. Measurement is a powerful tool—so long as we are measuring what we value. Too often, however, we have fallen into the trap of valuing what we can readily measure.

Contemporary reformers are not the first to put faith in the power of evidence to prescribe solutions. As we saw in chapter 5, the Progressives were confident that science would allow them to unlock the secrets of properly and efficiently delivering education. Indeed, in all their bureaucratic, micromanaging glory, they were fascinated with data and research.[11]

The promise of influential, pedigreed science often looks better in the moment than in the rearview mirror. In the latter half of the nineteenth century, the question of what women should learn and could master was a question of pressing scholarly interest. One attempt to answer such questions was an influential 1873 study by Edward C. Clarke, a professor at Harvard Medical College. As Margaret Nash noted in *Women's Education in the United States, 1780–1840*, the study reported that females who studied too much "misdirected blood from their 'female apparatus' to their brains, resulting in 'neuralgia, uterine disease, hysteria, and other derangements of the nervous system,' along with eventual sterility."[12] Clarke's report was so popular that it went through twelve printings in its first year.[13]

Okay, we can readily agree that Clarke's stuff was self-evidently silly. But with New Progressives exulting in the promise of testing and measurement, we would do well to regard Clarke as a cautionary tale. Today, reformers forget that their predecessors had imagined these battles fought and won several generations ago. Testing and measurement aren't quite as brand new as some may think. A century ago, in 1913, Leonard Ayers of the Department of Child Hygiene at the Russell Sage Foundation opined that where "methods for measuring the work of school children . . . exist let us use them, and where they do not yet exist let us strive to develop them. . . . Bear steadfastly in mind that economy of time in education is to be reached thru measuring the results that we are getting, rather than thru arguing about the methods that we might be using."[14] It's best to recall the boasts of that earlier era, if only to ask why those victories proved less satisfying than anticipated.

New Progressives seem bent on applying the methods of medical research in their desire to determine what "works" in schooling. The medical model, with its reliance on trials in which therapies are administered to individual patients under explicit protocols, is enormously powerful and prescriptive when recommending interventions for discrete conditions. Such a model can be equally useful for assessing specific interventions that seek to increase measurable knowledge and skills by applying discrete treatments to individual students under controlled conditions. However, just as few observers imagine that medical trials can authoritatively gauge the merits of universal health coverage, how to pay doctors, or how best to hold hospitals accountable, so, too, is such research limited when it comes to educational reforms that concern structural matters such as governance, accountability, staffing, and compensation.

Scientific research is a powerful tool, but we should have no illusions that researchers will settle value-laden debates or identify the "correct" way to arrange, govern, staff, or provide schooling. An emancipatory course requires that we not try to delegate responsibility for decisions to researchers but that we take ownership of our path and the implications that follow.

AN EMANCIPATED SYSTEM OF SCHOOLING

If science alone cannot deliver us clear direction, what can point us toward the trailhead? How do we know what arrangements to change? How do we know where to start? An emancipatory reformer begins with the humble task of removing barriers and clearing the detritus that stifles new solutions. The premise is that such prosaic problem solving, not excited rhetoric, holds the key to excellence. While we have spent the first decade of the twenty-first century enmeshed in a fierce debate regarding the merits of widespread testing, for instance, the point often lost amid the furor is that these assessments are a tool. They are not innately good or bad—they are both, with their value depending on the students and aims in question.

This is exactly what one would expect of any tool; the utility of a saw depends on its sharpness and suitability for the job at hand. These tests have been enormously successful in focusing time, energy, and instruction on previously overlooked students, but the change in focus can ill-serve those children who start school with larger vocabularies, greater bodies of knowledge, and more academic skills. Whereas the search for a new orthodoxy inevitably provokes heated debate as to whether testing is "good" or "bad," it is worth inquiring if we might not design a system of schooling so that the two can productively coexist. Learners clearly must master a certain threshold of basic skills. This postulate is hardly contentious; it has been endorsed over the centuries by libertarian icons John Stuart Mill and Milton Friedman, and even by Revolutionary pamphleteer Thomas Paine. The hard part, of course, is determining what the threshold should be and then gauging whether students have indeed surpassed it. However, if we can arrive at a rough, workable consensus as to what the minimal threshold is and how to measure it—a task with which we are enjoying substantial success in reading, math, and science—there is little cause to worry about where or how students learn. Moreover, to an emancipatory reformer, the precise composition of the core is less important than its ability to provide some agreed-upon basis for transparency and accountability across varied forms of provision.

Crucial to that exercise is distinguishing between what all students need to learn, and what some—but not all—need to learn. The millennia-spanning impulse is to pursue uniformity in the hope of teaching every child everything. This turns education into a cultural battlefield. There are some things that all students need to master, but there are many laudable academic accomplishments (like the ability to speak Chinese, calculate differential equations, or pen sonnets) that not every student needs to be able to do.

Such a postulate ensures, of course, that some children are going to be left behind. An unfortunate but essential reality is that children will continue to be left behind in the twenty-second century and in the twenty-third century. Rather than hide from this harsh reality, the question is whether new arrangements might enable us to do as well as possible by as many students as possible in as many different ways as possible. Any meaningful standard of excellence necessarily presumes that some children are going to fall short.

This seemingly radical bit of straight talk really should be far less controversial than it might seem. A quick look at international student achievement should suffice to make this point. When researchers gauge the achievement of the nations that fare best on international assessments against existing U.S. standards, not even in the most successful do more than 73 percent of students (in Singapore) perform at the level the National Assessment of Educational Progress deems "proficient" in mathematics. Indeed, only six countries, including Singapore, had more than 50 percent of their students performing at the level the United States deems proficient.[15] The bottom line is that large numbers of children will continue to fall short of our stated goals.

Since our measures gauge performance in reading and math, we've seen a predictable inclination to focus energy and attention on those. Nowhere has this been more evident than in efforts to gauge teacher quality using "value-added" metrics that measure only reading and math achievement, leading to a default definition in which quality teaching is increasingly defined almost entirely in terms of reading and math test scores. The push toward standardization has shortchanged advanced students and gifted students, fostered pushback, and bred fierce conflicts over testing. A more circumscribed set of universal aims, greater comfort with the diversity of student abilities and needs, and heightened respect for the array of potentially effective instructional strategies could allow more forms of excellent teaching and learning to emerge and to coexist.

DIVERSE SCHOOLING AS AN ASSET

Anything other than the effort to continually expand the reach of common expectations is typically regarded as defeatist. Yet more than twenty years of efforts to promote greater "coherence" and "alignment" across schools, districts, states, and nation have left overall performance largely unchanged. Perhaps the grand pursuit of "system-wide coherence" is a chimera so removed from what educators do and how schools are managed, and so removed from the realities of American government and institutions, that it amounts to little more than a distraction.

It is not only pragmatic but also prudent to embrace a system of schooling that nurtures a diverse set of skills, knowledge, and habits of mind. It can be prudent because it allows us to foster intellectual diversity and can free up energy that is otherwise siphoned into bitter wars for control of the curriculum. It allows for individual schools, educators, and providers to excel at something, rather than asking every school to excel at everything. It can be pragmatic because we cannot know the future and will fare better if we cultivate multiple kinds of excellence.[16]

We are well advised to exercise sensible restraint when seeking to determine what skills, subjects, or knowledge will be vital in the years ahead. After all, as we like to remind ourselves, education is an investment—and the bedrock principle of sound investing is diversification, because the vagaries of life are such that it is never clear which investments will pay off.

The problem is that the world is unpredictable. We have been known to change our minds over time as to what skills or knowledge are essential, and we have a dubious track record on anticipating what will prove important or useful two decades hence, so it's important to diversify offerings in order to increase the chances that one of the gambles we take will pay off.

There is no need to take my word for it. Consider a few of the more amusing anecdotes regarding efforts to predict what the future holds or the implications of new technology. Ken Olson, founder and president of computer-maker Digital Equipment Corp. (DEC), insisted at a World Future Society meeting in Boston in 1977, "There is no reason for any individual to have a computer in his home."[17] *Business Week* reported in 1968 that "with over fifteen types of foreign cars already on sale here, the Japanese auto industry isn't likely to carve out a big share of the market for itself."[18] In 1927, H. M. Warner, co-founder of Warner Brothers, argued that it would be pointless to start producing movies with sound, asking, "Who the hell wants to hear actors talk?"[19] And in a memorable show of expertise run amok, Surgeon General William H. Stewart told the U.S. Congress in 1969, "We can close the books on infectious diseases."[20]

Our grand innovations have a way of lingering on, even once they have proven unhelpful. For example, of American high school students studying a foreign language today, three-quarters are studying Spanish or French—and less than 1 percent are studying Farsi, Japanese, Korean, Russian, or Urdu.[21] These enrollments are in part a legacy of the National Defense Education Act of 1958, which invested tens of millions to expand modern language teaching—when the most popular languages of the time were Spanish, French,

German, Russian, and Italian.[22] Of those languages, only Russian is found on the federal government's current list of most critical languages (which includes Arabic, Chinese, Dari, Hindi, Farsi, Pashto, Persian, Punjabi, Russian, and Turkish).[23] Just as needs have shifted again and again since 1958, so will they shift in the years ahead. Given the difficulty of guessing the future or honing curricula in anticipation of future trends, we are perhaps better served by focusing on cultivating excellent teaching and learning in all its varieties rather than trying to fine-tune instruction to match anticipated trends.

Amidst all the encomiums to tolerance and cultural diversity proffered by defenders of the status quo, few recognize the potential virtues of tolerating a diversity of educational institutions and arrangements. Allowing varied forms of teaching and learning to prosper side by side not only reduces the fierce trench warfare that consumes our schools, but also can foster the heterogeneity of thought that enriches civil society. University of Michigan social scientist Scott Page argues compellingly in his book *The Difference* that our collective wisdom exceeds the sum of its parts, and he uses simple formulas and a raft of examples to show why teams composed of individuals with varied perspectives, abilities, and habits of mind are likely to devise better solutions than brilliant individuals working in isolation or even groups of like-minded experts. The key is not racial diversity but the ability of contrarian voices to surface new ideas and counter the tendency toward groupthink.[24]

Allowing various definitions of quality to flourish can stifle the kinds of knockdown brawls that have so often fueled the math and reading wars and that have characterized schooling since the time of the Greeks. The funny thing is that, as noted in chapter 5, even the most conscientious efforts by national panels convened to sort through the competing claims regarding math and reading instruction have concluded that there is merit in multiple approaches. The experts keep coming to the unsurprising conclusion that various approaches may be more or less effective depending on the child in question, the grade level, the classroom context, and the teacher's skill.

Welcoming pluralism provides an institutional mechanism for permitting competing notions of the good to flourish. This is not so much a Darwinian argument that the "fittest" will win out as it is a conviction that there is value in nurturing diverse intellectual traditions, models of thought, bodies of knowledge, and modes of learning. It is necessary and appropriate that the public impose baseline requirements of what all students should learn, but welcoming a diversity of arrangements and institutions may be both prudent and pragmatic.

CONCLUSION

Repurposing old institutions is much harder than we might wish; in the vast majority of the large, established, aged, and politically governed enterprises that are our state systems and school districts, it is likely to be impossible. I wrote this book hoping to encourage those willing to search for an alternate trail to do so, and to suggest some promising paths they might explore. I do not claim to know precisely the shape that the trails ahead should or will take. That said, emancipatory reform starts from the premise that we ought not merely strive to replicate what is thought to work in differently configured systems in nations with centralized governments, less diverse cultures, and less individualistic traditions. It presumes not that these traits are frailties to be overcome but that they are strengths to be leveraged.

There are, of course, many in the world of policy who claim to know what schooling should and will look like in a generation's time. They are confident in their vision, impatient with delay, only too eager to issue marching orders. I am skeptical of their grand designs. History humbles those claiming to be prescient over and over again. In sector after sector and era after era, those who claim to know the shape of things to come have been mistaken time and again, while one revolutionary change after another has arisen unlooked for. Rather than education reform again being, as in the 1980s, a matter of prescriptive state policies on teacher ladders and additional course requirements, or, as in the 2000s, a matter of accountability systems and mandated interventions in low-performing schools, perhaps it is time for an agenda that creates room for problem solvers rather than prescribing solutions.

Even those who can carry a tune may stumble on the words. Even those who decry the status quo as anachronistic can fail to grasp how limited their preferred solutions are and how heavily they rely on policies and practices designed for another era. The disconnect is especially disconcerting given the scope of our new ambitions. As Patricia Albjerg Graham has reminded us, "The movement for academic achievement for everybody is by far the most radical and difficult of all the educational efforts of the twentieth century."[25] Let us not kid ourselves about the size of the task we have undertaken.

Yet we continually shrink from the task we have set out for ourselves. We stubbornly imagine that comfortable old machinery can serve dramatic new ends. We try to avoid confronting the fact that education is a value-laden enterprise. A heavy cost is that would-be reformers hesitate to say that math teachers should be paid more than gym teachers because they are more important. Instead, they seek to delegate the moral responsibility for their choices to science— demurring that they only want to do what is "evidence-based."

The frustrating truth is that there are no permanent solutions in schooling, only solutions that make sense in a given place and time. There are fundamental principles, but how these should be interpreted or pursued in a given era is anything but certain. This state of affairs is, to say the least, challenging. It is doubly so when schooling is the charge of public officials who have reasons to prefer grand "more and better" solutions provided by public employees who have good cause to avoid risks, abide by rules, and hew to routine. The resulting tension can readily yield a parody of swell-sounding reforms that amount to little.

A century ago, Progressives deemed rigid, bean-counting bureaucracies the modern and scientific way to promote more uniform, universal schooling. They rejected flexibility in the name of efficiency and uniformity. Their push to systematize and depoliticize publicly governed systems has today yielded ineffectual petty politics dominated by vested interests and aggrieved parties. Their legacy of rigidity and uniformity suffuses management, staffing, compensation, and the educational enterprise down to this day. Rather than seeking ways to nudge this limping jalopy a few feet forward, it may be the better part of wisdom to step back from yesterday's schools and pursue solutions that might live up to our grand new ambitions.

A century. That's a long time to do things a certain way. As we noted, way back in chapter 1, most Fortune 500 companies only make it half that long. And much of our school model has a history far longer than that. There is a great deal to rethink and a long way to journey, not because some flavor-of-the-month pop intellectual has announced that our civilization is at stake, but because perhaps our greatest democratic legacy is a confused, anachronistic, and barnacled mess. We've bustled to "fight for our children" and "eliminate achievement gaps" because "our kids deserve it," because "our economy demands it," and for a dozen other impassioned reasons. Unfortunately, all this frenetic bounding hasn't added up to much. The faster we've sought to run, the harder it's been to recognize the treadmill on which we're running. Perhaps it's time to simmer down, think more, proselytize less, and gird ourselves for a long journey. The Chinese have an adage that a journey of a thousand miles begins with but a single step. It is past time that we take that step.

Epilogue: A Few Thoughts on Making This Work

"Perhaps the greatest idea that America has given the world is the idea of education for all. The world is entitled to know whether this idea means that everybody can be educated, or only that everybody must go to school."

—Robert Hutchins, former president of the University of Chicago, 1951

"Insanity: doing the same thing over and over again and expecting different results."

—Albert Einstein

The notion that in 2040, busloads of twelve-year-olds will be boarding a bus at 7:30 A.M. for a ride to a comprehensive school building where they would bend over texts and notebooks from 8 until 3 now makes about as much sense as expecting that those same students will be delivering rubber-banded newspapers to their neighbors by bike or heading to the public library so that they can track down resources through the card catalogue. The seismic shifts in society and culture are well under way, shaping the interests, behavior, and even the dating habits of today's students. The question is whether we will harness new opportunities and tame them to serve our educational needs. If we do not, we will not stop the gradual changes under way. But we will ensure that, like previous waves of reform, new efforts are the work of opportunists and tinkerers working at the margins.

Rethinking today's arrangements starts not by embracing this or that new measure, but by revisiting our notions of what schooling is and should look like. Schools look the way they do because of long-ago agendas, inertia, and efforts to meet the challenges of earlier eras. Tackling today's challenges starts by asking what it is we hope to accomplish, and then reimagining schooling to suit those purposes. In pursuing this "unbundling" of the schoolhouse, it is useful to think along two dimensions. One is rethinking the structure of schooling: how schools are governed, what teaching entails, how to configure the school day, and so forth. The second dimension involves rethinking the content of schooling: what students learn, when they learn it, how curricula are sequenced, and so forth. An easy way to understand the distinction is to recognize that a virtual school in which students are taught entirely by online instructors has obviously overhauled the structure of schooling, but is probably still using a scope and sequence of learning that reflects the norms in local brick-and-mortar schools. Unbundling that second, content dimension requires not just rethinking the governance or delivery of schooling, but envisioning ways to use new tools to customize instruction to the needs, strengths, and interests of individual students.

Unbundling means regarding schools not as self-contained boxes that have to meet every need for every child, but as one option among many—with many schools also serving as brokers of instructional services, coordinating stand-alone providers to deliver instruction and support under their roofs. Music teachers in the community might provide instruction in lieu of the school's music program, or a district might turn its foreign language instruction over to a contractor that handles faculty and online support.

One eye-opening example of how this might all work is provided by the fascinating School of One experiment in New York City. The School of One, created by the New York City Department of Education in partnership with for-profit provider Wireless Generation, starts from the presumption that new technologies mean we no longer have to teach classes of twenty-five students the same thing at the same time. Rather, it should be possible to customize what a student learns each day based on what she has already mastered and needs to learn, to do so with an eye toward the ways in which that student learns best, and to do so in a way that maximizes the efficient use of school resources. The School of One manages this feat (currently, just for middle school math) by collecting data on which learning objectives students have mastered and how they like to learn, and then assigning them each day to appropriate lessons. On a given day, depending on the content in question, a student might learn in a large group, from a tutor, in a small group, using a computer simulation, or any number of other ways. A student's mastery of each learning objective is gauged using an assessment, and students aren't sent on to the next objective until they've learned the present one. Rather than one teacher having to shepherd twenty-five students through the curriculum from start to finish, teachers can now swap lessons and focus on those they teach best—while advanced students can move more rapidly and lagging students can get extra instruction. The result allows students to move at their own pace, teachers to concentrate on teaching to their strengths, teacher aides to provide targeted support, students to spend more time learning in the manner they like best, and makes it harder for kids to get lost in the shuffle. Am I suggesting that the School of One is "the answer" or the wave of the future? Of course not. But it does provide a powerful example of how unbundling can give us leave to start using tools and talent in smarter ways.

Even if we wished it were otherwise, financial pressures, a changing labor market, new technologies, and the inadequacy of our old model means that schooling will inexorably change. Our choice is not whether change will come, but the pace and manner in which it comes. Making change work for our ends requires not an eager new orthodoxy but a commitment to unshackle ourselves from entrenched debates, outdated arrangements, and misplaced fears. It requires getting past the desire for mushy, a-bit-of-this-and-a-bit-of-that consensus and by addressing legitimate concerns about whether a less constricting world of schooling might aggravate social stratification or yield to profiteering. And it requires approaching questions of talent, financing, technology, and coordination in a manner that can provide essential support and quality control.

GETTING PAST THE SEARCH FOR "MIDDLE GROUND"

In a 2009 *New York Times* book review essay entitled "Dreams of Better Schools," Andrew Delbanco discussed two recent books, one by left-leaning education professor, veteran educator, and standards critic Mike Rose and another by E. D. Hirsch, the Core Knowledge champion and prominent critic of education schools whom we encountered in chapter 5.[1] On the surface, the two books appear to be resolutely anchored in the stale debates of recent decades. In *Why School?*, Rose frets that excessive testing and standardization stifles learning; in *The Making of Americans,* Hirsch worries that romantics like Rose are dismissive of curriculum and content.

But looking further, Delbanco suggested that both volumes "get a lot of things right," especially in flagging "universal education for citizenship as indispensable for democracy," in Rose's concession that some testing can be useful, and in Hirsch's willingness "to end the standoff between left and right." Delbanco concluded, "If there is to be progress in the schools, we need more of this kind of moderation. Otherwise we will remain caught between the usual warring parties: pro-teacher-union versus anti-union groups; those who favor mayoral control against those who prefer community control. . . . The disputes have gotten tired, and Hirsch and Rose know it. Almost in spite of themselves, they give hints of a middle ground."

The problem with Delbanco's reflexive plea for "middle ground" solutions is that this comfortable, appealing mantra too often summons new orthodoxies rather than questioning the old. The problem with seeking middle ground between champions and critics of the teacher unions, mayoral control, or standardized testing is that the easiest way to compromise is by leaving the old regularities intact and sprinkling in a handful of new resources, programs, and initiatives. Lord knows there's nothing wrong with centrism and moderation. But, over time, we have seen middle-ground, centrist solutions such as teacher "career ladders" and magnet schools plopped atop existing systems that remain unchanged, only to amount to one more fad.

Emancipatory reform is not about finding a middle way but about stripping away old routines, rules, and habits of mind to create new room for educators and problem solvers to do profoundly better.

GETTING PAST "WHOLE SCHOOL" IMPROVEMENT

Today, we ask school systems to tackle a vast array of responsibilities, making it difficult for them to do anything particularly well. Schools are expected to hire faculty who can provide instruction for the diverse needs of English language learners, special needs students, and gifted students; to provide students with physical education, extracurricular supervision, counseling, and other services; and to excel at all of this. Once upon a time, when most industrial enterprises adopted the same organizational logic and for the same reasons, this arrangement seemed sensible enough. Now, however, it is an anachronistic burden on educators in a century where providers can offer specialized services across geographic boundaries and where even such trivial products as cell-phone plans can be intensively customized.

The "whole school" expectation makes it harder to specialize or focus on particular needs. Even if their expertise is in designing curricula for middle school math or helping ELL students master English or recruiting and training alternative educators, new providers find themselves struggling to launch new schools and tackling everything from facilities to information systems. No one suggested that Amazon creator Jeff Bezos travel around the country shilling his new plan to sell books and music online to already established stores until he found a taker. Nor was he told that the only way for his plan to be taken seriously was if he would agree to also launch a chain of brick-and-mortar stores that could do everything Barnes & Noble and Borders already did, but better. This would be a recipe for stagnation; yet, in schooling, it stands as the norm.

Finding a new path requires shifting from a world where public officials provide access to "a school" to one where their aim is ensuring that all students benefit from schooling that serves their needs. This entails abandoning the industrial model where each school aspires to be a self-contained provider of manifold services. Today, because we regard each school in this manner, we speak of educational choice as the ability of families to choose school A rather than school B. Such options are relevant only to a limited slice of the population; many families may be less interested in shuffling their child among schools than in merely helping her obtain better math instruction, more convenient and intensive tutoring, or richer instruction in the arts. Indeed, providers like Tutor.com or Smarthinking can provide families with tutoring in a variety of subjects, twenty-four hours a day. For many middle-class families, the more relevant choice may be not the option to switch schools but the ability to tap school spending to purchase one-on-one instruction in biology or chemistry in lieu of enrolling their child in this or that school-offered elective.

Allowing broader choices among approved providers means that students will increasingly benefit from various providers—either within the schoolhouse or without. Is it possible that today's schools, states, and districts can do this? In theory, of course it is. But the reality is that established organizations have enormous difficulty taking advantage of new tools or technologies that would require the dismantling of entrenched routines, pecking orders, expectations, and rules.

GETTING PAST GEOGRAPHY

From the tribe to the village to the nation-state, political communities have always been defined by geographic space. For most of human history, such an arrangement was sensible and, really, inevitable. Organizing schools and school districts thusly was a no-brainer for Common School and Progressive reformers, who made geography an organizing principle in everything from attendance zones to district governance. At the same time, while we've historically organized communities spatially, alternatives have always existed. Private groups like the Masons or the Catholic Church have formed communities, chosen officials, and governed themselves across great distances and formal lines of governance.

Today, advances in communications have given rise to new, virtual communities. However, even communities as seemingly decentralized and nonhierarchical as Wikipedia have tempered their initial laissez-faire instincts and, over time, developed governance structures to protect against abuse and to police quality. The growth of national and international networks in education and schooling means the question is not whether they will exist but whether it is possible to devise meaningful governance beyond what is hard-wired into existing geographical units.

The nature of contemporary technology and transportation, however, is that they lessen the significance of geography and physical space. Virtual communities among those with similar interests are now commonplace; two decades ago they belonged to the realm of science fiction. Rather than seeking dates at the local bar, singles searching for romance and a life partner turn to online dating services. One can now routinely travel from New York to Beijing in less time than it took a nineteenth-century educator to travel from New York to Chicago. Clearly, a growing share of complex transactions that once depended on face-to-face relationships with local professionals can be completed online, even as the reality of modern air travel can allow a data maven to sit down with educators in Baltimore, Boston, and Buffalo in the space of a single day. Yet, even as these revolutionary developments have triggered seismic shifts outside of schooling in finance, trade, industry, and culture, educational debates regarding school choice, governance, and instruction remain rooted in arrangements that are shaped primarily by geography.

Much of schooling obviously can and should always be organized spatially. For those disturbed by all this talk of technology and virtual communities, it's useful to note that personal interaction will always be a vital part of schooling, especially for younger children or those lacking strong adult figures in their lives. But, keep in mind how much socializing (e.g., Facebook), matchmaking (e.g., eHarmony), and professional networking (e.g., LinkedIn) have migrated online in the past decade. In the same way, many tasks central to teaching and learning, such as lecturing, tutoring, and assessment, might be pursued more powerfully (and certainly more cost-effectively, more conveniently, and in a more customized fashion) through Web-based technologies.

ADDRESSING CONCERNS ABOUT SEGREGATION AND STRATIFICATION

Even if we free ourselves from some of these mental traps, legitimate questions emerge as soon as we start rethinking the organizations of schooling and teaching. Skeptics fear that alternative schooling arrangements that allow this kind of heterogeneity will lead to self-selection or other forms of stratification. This is a concern that resonates in an age marked by concerns about home-grown terrorists and stark political divides between "red" and "blue" America. I'd argue that the problem is far less worrisome that many might imagine—and that legitimate concerns can be addressed through smart policies that still allow for institutional redesign.

Social divides are a subject of real concern, but there is dreadfully little reason to believe that traditional school districts with their catch-all facilities and millions of conventionally employed teachers are particularly good at combating these tensions. In 2008, the U.S. Department of Education reported that 70 percent of white students attend schools that are at least 75 percent white; while other research shows that, in industrial states, over half of all black children attend school that are over 90 percent minority.[2]

The vast majority of families already exercise school choice, with more than 50 percent doing so by choosing their residence partly in order to choose a school.[3] Those are families that can afford to do so by buying homes in communities known to have good schools. In other words, as Milton Friedman surmised a half century ago, when school assignment and quality is bundled in with one's housing purchase, we create strong incentives for the affluent to self-segregate while fostering stratification and isolating the disadvantaged.[4] The familiar machinery of school districts, attendance zones, and "whole-school" provision reinforces these patterns and strengthens this dynamic.

There is a simple reason that suburban families and the affluent don't clamor for school choice: they already have chosen their school and are reasonably satisfied with it. Generally satisfied with but not necessarily delighted by the schooling they receive, the affluent have routinely supplemented their children's schooling with tutors, college consultants, and musical instruction. This allows them to privately address any concerns.

Ultimately, vague concerns about stratification or segregation should not be a reason to cling to the status quo, or to reject it. Public funding, monitoring, and accountability can be designed to address such concerns. If the fear is that providers will shortchange low-income children or those with special needs, weighted funding formulas can direct more dollars to those who serve them. Such systems are up and running in districts like Houston and Seattle. Eligibility for some programs can be reserved for the less affluent, as with the Milwaukee Parental Choice Program, or for children in persistently low-performing schools, as with Florida's voucher program. Such solutions are a matter of program design, about which reasonable people can disagree. But it is ultimately more fruitful to debate such policies in terms of potential costs and benefits than by suggesting that some of the options are somehow illegitimate or intrinsically dubious.

ADDRESSING CONCERNS ABOUT QUALITY CONTROL

Opening up state-run, bureaucratically managed systems to a variety of new providers also creates obvious concerns that new providers will manipulate circumstances for their own advantage. I obviously have little sympathy for claims that "nontraditional" providers (for-profit or nonprofit) are darkening the previously pristine world of schooling with the stain of self-interest. American education has long been dominated by unions, neighborhood groups, and administrators as self-interested and greedy as anybody in the private sector. That said, any call to shift from state-operated schools ruled by familiar patterns must wrestle with the potentially adverse consequences of self-interested sellers and quick-buck artists.

Just as is true today, some for-profit and nonprofit operators will be self-promoters out to make a buck, and others will be little more than snake oil salesmen. Even if these constituted only a tiny handful of providers—and they represent much more than that—it would be necessary to safeguard children and taxpayers against unacceptable behaviors. The ink was scarcely dry on the No Child Left Behind Act before its provision allowing federal funds to pay for private-tutoring providers yielded large numbers of dubious operations. A world that welcomes more such activity must do a far better job ensuring that money is spent wisely and well, and that providers are accountable for delivering good value at a good price.

In the long run, whether children and taxpayers benefit depends on the wiles of buyers at least as much as on the scruples of would-be sellers. The biggest problem we face today, in policing the quality of charter schooling or NCLB tutoring, is that so many of today's buyers are inept. For instance, the vast majority of charter school authorizers are traditional school districts for whom this is a peripheral responsibility of modest import. Most of today's buyers are themselves creatures of the status quo. They are mostly state and district officials, and sometimes school leaders, with scant experience at gauging value-for-money. They're only sporadically accountable for the wisdom or efficacy of their purchasing decisions. They're not rewarded for cost savings or dinged for failing to deliver. Addressing the quality-control challenge begins by ensuring that those charged with approving and overseeing providers take that work seriously and have the expertise and resources to do it well. Some of today's best charter school authorizers, and especially the criteria sketched out by the National Association of Charter School Authorizers, offer some terrific guidance on this score.

When it comes to promoting quality and accountability in a more dynamic system, there are three particular cautions worth keeping in mind. The first is that public education involves public funds and therefore necessarily invites appropriate public oversight. The second is that markets work as intended only when consumers have access to good and useful information. The third is that where there is so much fragmentation or ambiguity that costs and benefits are hard to judge, and where the opportunities for chicanery are real, requiring providers to be approved in some fashion can make sense.

In practice, policing against the waste of public funds will require empowering district and school leaders to be more vigilant procurers of services and then holding them accountable for their results. At the same time, allowing providers to deliver instruction or other services to families will call for some kind of "approved provider" list. The intuition is simple; the mechanics of how this might be approved less so. When public funds support schools or service providers that aren't state-operated—as they do today in the case of charter schools, publicly funded vouchers in Milwaukee or Florida, or tutors operating under the No Child Left Behind Act's "supplemental service" provision—there is a need to determine who should be eligible. This requires establishing criteria governing finances, operations, and performance. It also means deciding how much freedom operators will have and how closely they will be monitored. Finally, it entails deciding what conditions or performance outcomes will be expected if providers are to retain their eligibility.

None of this is novel or needs to be created whole-cloth. These same determinations are made routinely in fields like health care, when insurers decide on lists of eligible providers. The Department of Defense and the Environmental Protection Agency, just like any state and local government, have processes for tackling these challenges. The need is to thoughtfully translate these models to schooling in ways that respect the challenges at hand.

If the aim of emancipating our schools is, in part, to move past the false faith in uniform provision, it is important to craft metrics that reflect the instruction or service they are providing. An insistence on uniform metrics implies a uniformity of provision. This means the performance measures that might be contemplated for providers of music instruction can and should be quite different from those that provide reading. The need is not for new one-size-fits-all federal or state rules, but for states, communities, and third parties to design systems that promote transparency and accountability without imposing new orthodoxies.

As families gain more leeway to steer public dollars to providers other than district schools, the public has a right to insist that providers meet reasonable conditions. Exactly what those conditions should look like is the kind of crucial conversation that we have not yet embarked upon. The degree to which those regulatory conditions ought to be primarily fiduciary, as with government contracting; to be based on professional qualifications, as in medicine; or to be based upon measured performance will depend on context and will have to ultimately be resolved through experimentation and trial and error. None of this is self-executing. Public officials still need to play a crucial role, but it will be increasingly as monitors and decreasingly as monopolistic operators.

THE TALENT CHALLENGE

It's often said that teachers deserve to be paid like rock stars. Of course, if Bruce Springsteen or Beyonce weren't allowed to sell albums and could only perform for audiences of twenty or twenty-five fans at a time, they'd be paid like teachers. The riches enjoyed by rock stars are a consequence of their ability to entertain audiences of 20,000 or more while selling their music to millions. It is the tools and technologies that extend their reach that make this possible.

Supported by teams of assistants, equipment specialists, agents, bookers, and handlers, the musicians themselves are actually the face of complex organizations that have learned to leverage modern tools. Drawing from this example, the most obvious opportunities ahead for making similar gains in schooling are those that take advantage of rethinking careerism, specialization, and how new providers might augment schoolhouse instruction.

Rather than try to convince today's twenty-two-year-olds to enter—and remain in—teaching, we might do better if we rethink the profession with an eye to the contemporary talent pool. There is enormous interest in teaching among talented college graduates, but not necessarily as a lifelong vocation. This is not surprising, as the Bureau of Labor Statistics has reported that the typical college graduate today holds six jobs by the age of thirty-two.[5] Mid-career professionals also express a great deal of interest in teaching—but don't necessarily want to abandon their current careers, have little stomach for teacher training programs (even those of the "alternative" variety), and may be more interested in teaching a few hours a day, or a week, than in becoming "teachers."

The realities of the modern labor market argue for freeing ourselves from the expectation that teaching should necessarily be a full-time, careerist endeavor. One approach is being pioneered by Boston-based Citizen Schools, which recruits adults from a wide variety of occupations to design apprenticeship after-school experiences for middle school kids. Internships, work-based learning, and service-learning opportunities would seem an integral component of many redesigned high schools, all of which happily can expose students to other adults who care about what they are doing and can provide low-stakes mentoring and career advice. Such avenues suggest exploring the potential of relying upon a smaller, more selective, specialized and professionalized core of tenured careerists, supplemented by more support staff in the schools and a much wider array of adults who help to support student learning outside the schoolhouse walls.

Today, our aim is to find 3.3 million teachers who have completed roughly similar training in order to fill 3.3 million broadly similar roles. Instead, just as registered nurses and thoracic surgeons work side by side in an operating room, we might envision schools where the exquisitely trained work alongside those with more rote preparation. And, just as in a hospital, we might have no difficulty recognizing that one has a skill set that is scarcer and required more training than another, and alter duties and compensation accordingly. Rather than hire them in the same fashion or envision their roles as different rungs on a career ladder, we might comfortably recognize that they are on distinctive tracks. Such a step would not require that we find 3.3 million equally skilled teachers, but instead allow us to focus on seeking a much smaller body of highly skilled teachers and *then* an army of other educators who could complement them in a variety of roles.

Specialization inside schools mirrors the opportunities to do the same outside the schoolhouse. The familiar staffing model requires schools with many classrooms, each featuring a teacher working face-to-face with a particular group of students. This "people-everywhere" strategy was a natural for the Romans or America's founders, but we have devised some new tools in the past few decades. People-everywhere is expensive, does little to leverage the strengths or expertise of individual instructors, and limits the available talent pool in a given locale to the educators who will live there. Why not take a page from Washington, D.C.–based Smarthinking, which uses tutors with advanced degrees in the United States and a number of other nations to provide intensive instruction to students, twenty-four hours a day, seven days a week, and in about two dozen subjects?

THE TECHNOLOGY CHALLENGE

Quantum leaps in productivity are always about using new advances in technology and management to render skilled employees more productive. Unfortunately, our approach to schooling has long reflected the admonition written into the Elementary and Secondary Education Act of 1965: "supplement, not supplant."[6] Technology has not been used to allow educators to slough off rote duties and focus on what they do best or to allow schools and systems to shuck unnecessary personnel.

Schooling has proceeded under the assumption that each year requires as many people—or more—as it did the year before, and technology is regarded as a perpetually "second-best" option. Consequently, new technological delivery is generally treated as an unattractive alternative rather than a lever that can help transform. Technology has persistently disappointed as film projectors, televisions, computers, and the Internet have largely served as a series of expensive baubles shoveled into otherwise unchanged schools and classrooms,[7] but this should come as no surprise. Harvard Business School professor Clay Christensen has argued that the instinctive response of any established organization when innovations emerge is to cram them into the existing model in order to do the familiar a little bit better. He has consequently advised, "The way to implement an innovation so that it will transform an organization is to implement it disruptively."[8] Harnessing the power of Web-based instruction and other new tools is only possible if they begin to displace, and not merely augment, traditional routines.

Substituting technology for laborious tasks can remake schooling by shifting away from the traditional shape of the schoolhouse and school district in a number of scenarios. For example, allowing graduate students in Boston or New York to tutor students in rural communities requires Web-based communication to match students in need with instructional expertise—wherever that expertise can be found. Finding ways for highly skilled teachers to instruct hundreds (or even thousands) of children at once requires staffing and instructional strategies that rethink how teaching talent is used. Enabling school "systems" to operate networks of similar schools that are dotted across multiple communities requires a new concept of what constitutes a school district. Of course, none of these benefits come easily.

THE FINANCING CHALLENGE

The existing school funding model grew haphazardly from its local-ist origins. The earliest schools in colonial America were funded by local sources. Over time, the state took on an increasing role in sup-plementing these funds. In the early twentieth century, local dollars still accounted for the vast majority of spending, but by century's end, the state and local share was a rough split—with most state aid intended to help equalize disparities in funding due to intrastate vari-ations in local wealth. Meanwhile, the federal government first got substantially involved in school spending in the 1960s, with most of its dollars going to support low-income students and a slew of cate-gorical programs. Today, Uncle Sam accounts for about one-tenth of the nation's $600 billion in K–12 spending. Most of this money is tied up in district salaries and in formulas that allocate staff to schools based on class size and staffing formulas.

All of this is intended to provide schools to all children and to provide a more equitable distribution of dollars. This system, with its emphasis on enrollment, funding categories, and intricate formulas and rules, is hostile to efforts to rethink staffing or schooling. As I write, the cutting edge of finance reform is thought to be efforts to make sure that poor schools get their fair share and to adjust fund-ing so that dollars more accurately follow the students. This approach to weighted student funding is certainly an improvement over tradi-tional funding models, but it still envisions nothing more than the government's funneling of a block of money to a school for each child who attends.

Other models, more similar to a flex-spending account, promise to create more opportunities to help families secure the instruction and services they need—whether that involves academic tutoring or musical training, whether virtual or live. One place to look for an example of empowered consumer spending that could be applied to education is health savings accounts. Health savings accounts (HSAs) are one option in the world of health insurance designed to give individuals greater control over their money. Created in 2003, HSAs allow individuals to pay for qualified medical expenses.[9] Individuals wind up with greater control over medical care purchases and greater incentives to shop around for better care and to save for future health costs.

Applied to education, such an approach would allow families to be free to procure services from an array of approved providers with some or all of their child's school funding. A given family could procure music instruction from tutor X, athletic involvement from program Y, and academic services from school Z. A family would have an allotment of money to be spent on a child's schooling, and those dollars could be steered to approved providers in a variety of ways, depending on the child's needs.

Allowing families to redirect the money they save from one educational need to another can create incentives to think about costs and benefits more carefully. Currently, families have no reason to know or to care if a district reading program costs $1,000 per student or $4,000 per student. Consequently, there's a natural bias toward time- and labor-intensive programs, as these seem "better" to parents than alternatives. Such parental preferences make it harder for school and district leaders to employ more cost-effective alternatives, and give them less incentive to seek out such options. Empowering parents to contemplate costs as well as benefits means that some will likely do so, and it can offer educators new opportunities to make smart decisions.

A crucial hindrance to our ability to rethink schooling is inattention to cost-effectiveness. In most of the world, we think about improvement as a matter of delivering more bang for the buck. In schooling, however, accountability and performance is judged almost entirely in terms of test scores and graduation rates—with remarkably little attention to how much it costs a school, district, or program to deliver those. Indeed, there's subtle (and sometimes not so subtle) pressure—from advocacy groups and federal policies—for states and districts to spend more money each year. Finding new efficiencies is more likely to raise eyebrows or pass unnoticed than to gain plaudits. All of this tends to stifle efforts to rethink the delivery of schooling and to discourage educators from finding more efficient ways to tap talent and technology. In a world of tighter budgets, an easy first step is for states and districts to start reporting cost per pupil as part of their accountability systems—and to recognize schools and districts which are both effective and cost-effective.

THE COORDINATION CHALLENGE

A century ago, the dominant challenge for providers of goods or services was often just getting their offerings to people. The ability to coordinate and deliver merchandise was the defining characteristic of Sears & Roebuck. Today, new transportation, communication, and management tools mean that coordination and delivery can be pretty readily outsourced—enabling providers to focus on quality. In schooling, however, the pressure on each school and district to deliver a raft of services to an array of students with various needs means there's a need to invest enormous time and energy in coordinating delivery before turning to quality. Obviously, importing a math provider to hire and train the math teachers charged with providing middle school algebra pose new challenges, as does giving families more leeway to purchase tutoring from approved providers with public funds, but it's very possible that these challenges will prove more tractable than will the question of how a-little-bit-of-everything institutions can excel.

If a family prefers having their son taught by a team of face-to-face or online tutors in lieu of a traditional school—either because local school choices are mediocre or because of the child's particular needs or gifts—there are obvious challenges relating to scheduling and quality control. Let's presume that the cost of the two options is the same. (If the unconventional option were less, it would raise interesting questions about how to reward the family's decision and what to do with the balance; if more, the state would presumably impose restrictions).

In such a case, there is a natural niche for aggregators who can schedule and certify the quality of various instructors. The reality is that very, very few families will have the time, energy, or resources to assemble a crew of four or six tutors—electronic or otherwise. So, aggregators who can recommend tutors and approaches, based upon student need and family preferences, will prove essential and will need to be accountable for their handiwork. This is a role, of course, that some existing schools or school districts might find themselves well suited to provide.

Indeed, some communities will find it advisable to retain much of the structure of systems and schools as we know them today, at least for a long stretch to come. In those locales where much of the old infrastructure is retained, the coordination of many services would be a matter of system and school leaders bringing in new providers to supplement or replace offerings, or to provide new choices. Families would lean on the familiar school and system to judge offerings, with their decisions focused on choosing between program offerings or the decision of whether to access some services (such as arts instruction, tutoring or support, or enrichment opportunities) outside the traditional schoolhouse. One consequence of releasing schooling from the old strictures is that it gives these established actors new opportunities to seize upon their strengths in new ways.

WHAT LIES AHEAD

Freeing up and unbundling schooling is less about forcing change than enabling it. If affluent communities are reluctant to exploit new opportunities, so be it; reinvention is hard enough when pursued by the committed. Systems that work passably well in those communities that attract great teachers and serve advantaged families ought not be forcibly dismantled. But for communities worst-served by the status quo, emancipatory reform could offer a much-needed alternative.

At times, I may seem to belittle those who have built the system of schooling that we have inherited. That's not my intention. Despite some quirks and questionable calls, they bequeathed us a rich heritage—a national system of staffed, funded facilities and an infrastructure of training programs, assessments, and state and local governance agencies. Ideally, this legacy should leave America enviably positioned for the twenty-first century, a time when prosperity and power will rest heavily upon learning and education. We spent more than three centuries building out a system of universal K–12 education that now encompasses rich and poor, white and black. We have a mighty infrastructure of facilities, transportation, technology, and institutions for training educators. We have millions of credentialed teachers and a vast network of school districts and funding mechanisms.

It would be a shame indeed if our seeming advantages ultimately hindered us. Yet that appears only too possible. For our vast edifice of schooling also has an enormous appetite for resources: dollars, people, and energy that are poured into programs, curricula, and professional development carried out within the confines of the status quo. We are allowing systems and schools to claim their $600 billion a year, and then fuel reinvention—whether it involves pay systems, training, school design, or technology—with dollars sprinkled around the edges. Redesign requires freeing up the dollars and talent and energy that state, local, and federal government pump into K–12 schooling day in and day out.

Because ascendant international competitors like India and China did not mirror our enormous investment in erecting school systems in the nineteenth and twentieth centuries, they find themselves today with a far less developed educational infrastructure. By clinging so fiercely to what we've built, however, we risk allowing nations less wedded to aged designs to slingshot past us. Having never made the investments in schools and teachers that we did in the pre-industrial and industrial eras, they find themselves free to erect policies and institutions particularly geared to the tools and challenges of this century. It would be a bitter irony indeed if our inability to leave behind anachronistic routines and stale habits of mind meant that the achievements of the Common Schoolers and Progressives that fueled American success in the twentieth century were to hold us back in the twenty-first. We have the power to take another road, if we find the strength to free ourselves from the heavy hand of the past. The choice that lies before us is whether or not to do so.

Preface

1. Alfie Kohn and Patrick Shannon, eds., *Education, Inc.: Turning Learning into a Business* (Portsmouth, NH: Heinemann, 2002), 101.
2. Thomas J. Sergiovanni, *Moral Leadership: Getting to the Heart of School Improvement* (San Francisco: Jossey-Bass, 1996), xiv.
3. Frederick M. Hess and Andrew P. Kelly, "Learning to Lead: What Gets Taught in Principal-Preparation Programs," *Teachers College Record* 109, no. 1 (2007): 244–274.
4. Ellwood Cubberley, *Public Education in the United States: A Study and Interpretation of American Educational History* (Cambridge, MA: Riverside Press, 1947), 527–528.
5. Diane Ravitch, *The Death and Life of the Great American School System* (New York: Basic Books, 2010), 237–238.
6. Evans Clinchy, "Reimagining Public Education," *Phi Delta Kappan* 85, no. 6 (2004): 449–450.

1. Ideas Equal to Our Ambitions

1. "Revolution on the Campus: A High-School Education Is a U.S. Civic Birthright. Why Not College, Too?" Editorial, *Life*, February 2, 1948, 24.
2. Charles M. Payne, *So Much Reform, So Little Change: The Persistence of Failure in Urban Schools* (Cambridge, MA: Harvard Education Press, 2008).
3. David Tyack and Larry Cuban, *Tinkering toward Utopia: A Century of Public School Reform* (Cambridge, MA: Harvard University Press, 1995).
4. Frederick M. Hess, *Spinning Wheels: The Politics of Urban School Reform* (Washington, DC: Brookings Institution Press, 1998).

5. Diane Ravitch, *Left Back: A Century of Battles over School Reform* (New York: Touchstone Press, 2000).
6. Chester E. Finn Jr., "The End of the Education Debate," *National Affairs*, no 2 (Winter 2010), http://nationalaffairs.com/publications/detail/the-end-of-the-education-debate, accessed May 5, 2010.
7. "A Century of Change: America, 1900–1999," U.S. Census Bureau, December 20, 1999, www.census.gov/Press-Release/www/1999/cb99-ff17.html, accessed May 5, 2010.
8. Ibid.
9. Christopher J. Lucas, *Our Western Educational Heritage* (New York: Macmillan, 1972), 468–469.
10. U.S. Department of Education, National Center for Education Statistics, *Schools and Staffing Survey, Public School Teacher Data File, 2003–2004*, Table 26, http://nces.ed.gov/surveys/sass/tables/state_2004_26.asp, accessed May 5, 2010.
11. Maris A. Vinovskis, *History and Educational Policymaking* (New Haven, CT: Yale University Press, 1999).
12. Larry Cuban, "Educational Entrepreneurs Redux," in *Educational Entrepreneurship Realities, Challenges, Possibilities*, ed. Frederick M. Hess (Cambridge, MA: Harvard Education Press, 2006), 223–242.
13. U.S. Department of Education, *A Nation at Risk* (Washington, DC: National Commission on Excellence in Education, 1983), www.ed.gov/pubs/NatAtRisk/risk.html, accessed May 5, 2010.
14. Bill Gates, Prepared Remarks to National Governors Association, (Washington, DC, February 26, 2005), www.nga.org/cda/files/eso5gates.pdf, accessed May 5, 2010.
15. Barack Obama, Speech to Hispanic Chamber of Commerce (Washington DC, March 10, 2009), www.nytimes.com/2009/03/10/us/politics/10text-obama.html, accessed May 5, 2010.
16. George W. Bush, Remarks on Submitting the Education Reform Plan to the Congress (Washington, DC, January 23, 2001), www.presidency.ucsb.edu/ws/index.php?pid=29768, accessed May 5, 2010.
17. U.S. Chamber of Commerce, *Leaders and Laggards: A State-by-State Report Card on Educational Effectiveness* (Washington, DC: U.S. Chamber of Commerce, February 2007), http://www.uschamber.com/reportcard/2007/default, accessed May 5, 2010.

18. Gates, Remarks to National Governors Association.

19. Obama, Speech to Hispanic Chamber of Commerce.

20. Bush, Remarks on Submitting the Education Reform Plan.

21. U.S. Department of Education, *A Nation at Risk: Recommendations*, www
.ed.gov/pubs/NatAtRisk/recomm.html, accessed May 5, 2010.

22. Finn, "End of the Education Debate."

23. Gerald Bracey, *What You Should Know about the War against America's Public Schools* (Boston: Allyn & Bacon, 2002), 3.

24. Paul Houston, "Pinata Beaters and the Rush toward a Narrow Self-Interest," *School Administrator* 55, no. 1 (January 1998): 38.

25. Garrison Keillor, *Homegrown Democrat: A Few Plain Thoughts from the Heart of America* (New York: Penguin Group, 2004), 208–209.

26. Thomas Jefferson, *Notes on the State of Virginia* (Richmond, VA: Chas H. Wynne, 1853), 157.

27. National Education Association of the United States, Committee on Secondary School Studies, *Report of the Committee of Ten on Secondary School Studies* (New York: American Book Company, 1894), 51–52, www.archive.org/details/reportofcomtensoonatirich, accessed May 5, 2010.

28. James Bryant Conant, *The Revolutionary Transformation of the American High School* (Cambridge, MA: Harvard University Press, 1959), 23.

29. Keith W. Olson, *The G.I. Bill, the Veterans, and the Colleges* (Lexington: University Press of Kentucky, 1974), 33.

30. Roger Chartier, *The Practical Impact of Writing*, from *A History of Private Life*, vol 3 (Cambridge, MA: Harvard University Press, 1989), 120.

31. John Folger and Charles Nam, *Education of the American Population* (Manchester, NH: Ayer Company Publishers, 1976), 113–114.

32. U.S. Department of Education, Institute of Education Sciences, National Center for Education Statistics, *National Adult Literacy Survey and 2003 National Assessment of Adult Literacy,* http://nces.ed.gov/naal/kf_demographics.asp, accessed May 5, 2010.

33. William Jefferson Clinton, "Remarks to the Education International World Congress, July 29, 1998," *The American Presidency Project*, www
.presidency.ucsb.edu/ws/index.php?pid=56389, accessed May 5, 2010.

34. Sonia Nieto, *What Keeps Teachers Going?* (New York: Teachers College Press, 2003), 5.

35. National Education Association of the United States, *Cardinal Principles of Secondary Education: A Report of the Commission on the Reorganization of Secondary Education, 1918*, Bulletin for United States Bureau of Education 35 (Washington, DC: Government Printing Office, 1928), 5.

36. Partnership for 21st Century Skills, "Framework for 21st Century Learning," 2, www.21stcenturyskills.org/documents/P21_Framework.pdf, accessed May 5, 2010.

37. American Diploma Project, "English and Communication Benchmarks, Grades 11–12" (Washington, DC: Achieve, 2008), 14, http://www.achieve.org/files/grades11-12.pdf, accessed May 5, 2010.

38. American Diploma Project, "Ready or Not: Creating a High School Diploma That Counts" (Washington, DC: Achieve, 2004), 67, www.achieve.org/files/ADPreport_7.pdf, accessed May 5, 2010.

39. Richard J. Murnane and Frank Levy, *Teaching the New Basic Skills: Principles for Educating Children to Thrive in a Changing Economy* (New York: Free Press, 1996), 3.

40. Ibid. 3–4.

41. Ibid., 32.

42. Plato, *Laws* (Montana: Kessinger, 2004), 90.

43. Benjamin Rush, "Thoughts upon the Mode of Education Proper in a Republic," in *Essays on Education in the Early Republic*, ed. Frederick Rudolph (Cambridge, MA: Harvard University Press, 1965), 14.

44. Horace Mann, *The Republic and the School: Horace Mann on the Education of Free Man*, ed. Lawrence A. Cremin (New York: Teachers College Press, 1957), 93.

45. David Labaree, "Citizens and Consumers: Changing Visions of Virtue and Opportunity in U.S. Education, 1841–2002" (Stanford, August 2007), 12, www.stanford.edu/~dlabaree/publications/Citizens_and Consumers.pdf, accessed May 5, 2010.

46. Alfie Kohn, "How Not to Teach Values: A Critical Look at Character Education," *Phi Delta Kappan* 78, no. 6 (February, 1997).

47. Alfie Kohn, *What to Look for in a Classroom: And Other Essays* (San Francisco: Jossey-Bass, 1998), 24.

48. Diana Selig, *Americans All: The Cultural Gifts Movement* (Cambridge, MA: Harvard University Press, 2008).

49. "Victory for Freedom of Conscience as University of Minnesota Backs Away from Ideological Screening for Ed Students," Foundation for In-

dividual Rights in Education (FIRE) press release, December 23, 2009. http://www.thefire.org/article/11420.html, accessed May 5, 2010.

50. Donald M. Fisk, "American Labor in the 20th Century," *Compensation and Working Conditions* 6, no. 3 (Fall 2001): 3–8, http://www.bls.gov/ opub/cwc/archive/fall2001art1.pdf, accessed May 5, 2010.

51. Ibid., 3.

52. Ibid.

53. Ibid.

54. Claudia Goldin and Lawrence Katz, *The Race between Education and Technology* (Cambridge, MA: Harvard University Press, 2008), 32, 34.

55. Ibid., 106.

56. Ibid., 85.

57. Ibid., 99.

58. Philip Brown, "Skill Formation in the Twenty-First Century," in *High Skills: Globalization, Competitiveness, and Skill Formation,* ed. Philip Brown, Andy Green, and Hugh Lauder (New York: Oxford University Press, 2001), 6.

59. Fisk, "American Labor."

60. Ibid., 3–4.

61. Sean P. Corcoran, William N. Evans, and Robert S. Schwab, "Changing Labor Market Opportunities for Women and the Quality of Teachers, 1957–1992," NBER Working Paper 9180 (Cambridge, MA: National Bureau of Economic Research, September 2002), 1.

62. Bureau of Labor Statistics, "Number of Jobs Held, Labor Market Activity, and Earnings Growth among the Youngest Baby Boomers: Results from a Longitudinal Survey" (Bureau of Labor Statistics, June 27, 2008), www.bls.gov/news.release/pdf/nlsoy.pdf, accessed May 5, 2010.

63. Fisk, "American Labor," 5.

64. U.S. Census Bureau, *Computer and Internet Use in the United States, 2003,* http://www.census.gov/prod/2005pubs/p23-208.pdf, accessed May 5, 2010.

65. Calculated based on phone models available from Apple Computers. Brad Stone, "Live-Blogging Apple's Music Event," Bits Blog, September 9, 2009, http://bits.blogs.nytimes.com/2009/09/09/live-blogging-apples -music-event, accessed May 5, 2010.

66. Terry Moe and John Chubb, *Liberating Learning* (San Francisco: Jossey-Bass, 2009).

67. Clayton M. Christensen, Michael B. Horn, and Curtis W. Johnson, *Disrupting Class: How Disruptive Innovation Will Change the Way the World Learns* (New York: McGraw Hill, 2008), 10.

68. Charles Bidwell and John Kasarda, "Conceptualizing and Measuring the Effects of School and Schooling," *American Journal of Education* 88, no. 4 (1980): 401–430.

69. Peter Brimelow, *Worm in the Apple: How the Teachers Unions Are Destroying American Education* (New York: HarperCollins, 2003), xvii, 1.

70. Greg Toppo, "Education Chief Calls Teachers Union 'Terrorist Organization,'" *USA Today,* February 23, 2004, http://www.usatoday.com/news/washington/2004-02-23-paige-remarks_x.htm, accessed May 5, 2010.

71. John Chubb and Terry Moe, *Politics, Markets, and America's Schools* (Washington, DC: Brookings Institution Press, 1990), 217.

72. Michael Shear and Nick Anderson, "President Obama Discusses New 'Race to the Top' Program," *Washington Post,* July 23, 2009, www.washingtonpost.com/wp-dyn/content/article/2009/07/23/AR2009072302938.html?sid=ST2009072303922, accessed May 5, 2010.

73. Clair Brown, John Haltiwanger, and Julia Lane, *Economic Turbulence: Is a Volatile Economy Good for America?* (Chicago: University of Chicago Press, 2006), 16.

74. Paul David, "Clio and the Economics of QWERTY," *The American Economic Review* 75, no. 2 (1985): 332–337.

75. "Personal Computer Announced by IBM," IBM Information Systems Division press release, August 12, 1981, www-03.ibm.com/ibm/history/exhibits/pc25/pc25_press.html, accessed May 5, 2010.

76. John Horrigan, "Wireless Internet Use," *Pew Internet & American Life Project Report,* July 2009, www.pewinternet.org/Reports/2009/12-Wireless-Internet-Use.aspx, accessed May 5, 2010.

77. Calculated based on phone models available from Verizon Wireless, AT&T, and Nextel providers accessed August 2009. "3G Smartphones," Verizon Wireless, www.verizonwireless.com/b2c/store/controller?item=phoneFirst&action=viewPhoneOverviewByDevice; AT&T, www.wireless.att.com/cell-phone-service/cell-phones; Nextel, http://nextelonline.nextel.com/NASApp/onlinestore/en/Action/DisplayPhones.

78. Arthur Krystal, *The Half-Life of an American Essayist* (Boston: David R. Godine, 2007), 18.

79. Paul Starr, *The Social Transformation of American Medicine* (New York: Basic Books, 1982), 311.

80. Joseph Califano Jr., *America's Health Care Revolution: Who Lives? Who Dies? Who Pays?* (New York: Random House, 1986), 44.

81. Ron Wyden, "The Health Care Agenda: An Invitation to Reform" (Speech to America's Health Insurance Plans 2008 National Policy Forum, Washington DC, March 5, 2008), http://wyden.senate.gov/newsroom/record .cfm?id=295998&, accessed May 5, 2010.

82. Charles Krauthammer, "Health-Care Reform: A Better Plan," *Washington Post,* August 7, 2009, www.washingtonpost.com/wp-dyn/content/ article/2009/08/06/AR2009080602933.html, accessed May 5, 2010.

83. Walter Hamilton, "In a Battered Market, Many Opt to Gamble," *Los Angeles Times,* August 25, 2009.

2. The American Education Tradition

1. David Stratman, "School Reform and the Attack on Public Education," keynote address, Massachusetts Association of School Superintendents Summer Institute, Falmouth, MA, July 16, 1997, www.newdemocracy world.org/edspeech.htm, accessed May 5, 2010.

2. Gerald Gutek, *Education and Schooling in America* (Englewood Cliffs, NJ: Prentice-Hall, 1983), 8.

3. Ellwood Cubberley, *Public Education in the United States* (Cambridge: Houghton Mifflin, 1919), 18.

4. Ibid., 26.

5. David Tyack, *Turning Points in American Educational History* (New York: Blaisdell, 1967), 120.

6. Noah Webster, "On the Education of Youth in America," in *Essays on Education in the Early Republic,* ed. Frederick Rudolph (Cambridge, MA: Harvard University Press, 1965), 66.

7. Robert Coram, "Political Inquiries: To Which Is Added, a Plan for the General Establishment of Schools throughout the United States," in *Essays on Education in the Early Republic,* ed. Frederick Rudolph (Cambridge, MA: Harvard University Press, 1965), 141.

8. Ibid., 111.

9. Ibid., 136.

10. *A Memorial Containing Travels through Life or Sundry Incidents in the Life of Dr. Benjamin Rush, born Dec. 24, 1745 died April 19, 1813*, ed. Louis Biddle and Henry Williams (Philadelphia: Sign of the Ivy Leaf, 1904), 240.

11. Alexander Leitch, *A Princeton Companion* (Princeton, NJ: Princeton University Press, 1978); David Robson, *Educating Republicans: The College in the Era of the American Revolution, 1750–1800* (Santa Barbara, CA: Greenwood, 1985), 35.

12. Alyn Brodsky, *Benjamin Rush: Patriot and Physician* (New York: Macmillan, 2004), 177, 276.

13. Benjamin Rush, "Thoughts upon the Mode of Education Proper in a Republic," in *Essays on Education in the Early Republic*, ed. Frederick Rudolph (Cambridge, MA: Harvard University Press, 1965), 3, 4, 9.

14. Hyman Kuritz, "Benjamin Rush: His Theory of Republican Education," *History of Education Quarterly* 7, no. 4 (Winter 1967): 440–441.

15. Benjamin Rush, *Letters,* vol. 30, part 2, ed. Lyman Butterfield (Princeton, NJ: Princeton University Press, 1951), 1053.

16. Benjamin Rush, *Essays, Literary, Moral and Philosophical* (Philadelphia: Thomas and William Bradford, 1806), 14–15.

17. Ibid., 75.

18. Ibid., 88.

19. Rush, "Thoughts upon the Mode," 13.

20. Ibid., 21.

21. Rush, *Essays,* 5.

22. Charles F. Arrowood, *Thomas Jefferson and Education in a Republic* (New York: AMS Press, 1971), 79–80.

23. Christopher J. Lucas, *Our Western Educational Heritage* (New York: Macmillan, 1972), 468.

24. Rush Welter, *Popular Education and Democratic Thought in America* (New York: Columbia University Press, 1962), 28–29.

25. Thomas Jefferson, "To Nathaniel Burwell," in *The Essential Jefferson,* ed. Jean Yarbrough (Indianapolis: Hackett Publishing, 2006), 247.

26. Thomas Jefferson, *A Bill for the More General Diffusion of Knowledge,* section 4, reprinted in Roy J. Honeywell, *The Educational Work of Thomas Jefferson* (New York: Russell & Russell, 1964), 200.

27. Ibid., section 6, 201.

28. Thomas Jefferson, *Report of the Commissioners Appointed to Fix the Site of the University of Virginia*, reprinted in Honeywell, *The Educational Work of Thomas Jefferson*, 250.

29. Roy J. Honeywell, *The Educational Work of Thomas Jefferson* (New York: Russell & Russell, 1964), 36.

30. Thomas Jefferson, "Letter to Peter Carr," in Honeywell, *The Educational Work of Thomas Jefferson*, 223.

31. Jefferson, *A Bill for the More General Diffusion*, section 12, 203.

32. Ibid., section 15, 204.

33. Ibid., section 18, 205.

34. Ibid., section 19, 205.

35. Honeywell, *The Educational Work*, 30.

36. Ibid., 8.

37. John Fiske, *The Critical Period of American History: 1783–1789* (Houghton Mifflin, 1916), 71.

38. Thomas Jefferson, "To John Adams," in *The Essential Jefferson*, ed. Jean Yarbrough (Indianapolis: Hackett Publishing, 2006), 215.

39. Honeywell, *The Educational Work*, 9.

40. Samuel Knox, "An Essay on the Best System of Liberal Education," in *Essays on Education in the Early Republic*, ed. Frederick Rudolph (Cambridge, MA: Harvard University Press, 1965), 271.

41. Ibid., 271.

42. Ibid., 311.

43. Ibid., 314.

44. Ibid., 312.

45. Ibid., 323.

46. William Warner, *At Peace with All Their Neighbors: Catholics and Catholicism in the National Capital, 1787–1860* (Washington, DC: Georgetown University Press, 1994), 146.

47. Allen Oscar Hansen, *Liberalism and American Education in the Eighteenth Century* (New York: Octagon Books, 1965), 139.

48. Warner, *At Peace*, 146.

49. Samuel Smith, "Remarks on Education," in *Essays on Education in the Early Republic*, ed. Frederick Rudolph (Cambridge, MA: Harvard University Press, 1965), 210.

50. Ibid., 190.

51. Ibid., 213.
52. Ibid., 212.
53. Ibid., 208.

3. The Long View

1. Christopher J. Lucas, *Our Western Educational Heritage* (New York: Macmillan, 1972), 82.
2. Plato, *The Republic,* trans. Allan Bloom (New York: Basic Books, 1986), 55–56.
3. Lucas, *Our Western Educational Heritage,* 91.
4. Edward J. Power, "Plato's Academy: A Halting Step toward Higher Education," *History of Education Quarterly* 4, no. 3 (1964): 163.
5. Ibid.
6. Ibid., 163–164.
7. Gerald Gutek, *A History of the Western Educational Experience,* 2d ed. (Prospect Heights, IL: Waveland Press, 1995), 28.
8. Lucas, *Our Western Educational Heritage,* 133.
9. Plato, "Laws," in *The Dialogues of Plato,* vol. 5, 3d ed., trans. B. Jowett (Oxford: Clarendon Press, 1862), 21.
10. Lucas, *Our Western Educational Heritage,* 57.
11. Ibid., 55.
12. Ibid.
13. Ibid., 57.
14. Linda Nathan, "A Response to Frederick Hess: The Larger Purpose of Public School," *Phi Delta Kappan* 85, no. 6 (2004): 440–441.
15. Dennis van Roekel, debate with Gary Ritter, *Issue Clash: Merit Pay,* Public Broadcasting System, April 30, 2009.
16. George Botsford and Ernest Sihler, *Hellenic Civilization* (New York: Columbia University Press, 1915), 599.
17. Henri Marrou, *History of Education in Antiquity* (Madison: University of Wisconsin Press, 1982), 138.
18. Edward Jay Watts, *City and School in Late Antique Athens and Alexandria* (Berkeley: University of California Press, 2006), 29.
19. Ibid., 32.
20. John William Henry Walden, *The Universities of Ancient Greece* (New York: Charles Scribner's Sons, 1909), 178.

21. Stephen Sawchuk, "NEA Representatives Air Their Differences with Obama Agenda," *Education Week,* July 7, 2009, http://www.edweek.org/ew/articles/2009/07/07/36nea.h28.html?qs=obama+agenda, accessed May 5, 2010.

22. Lynette Tanaka, Editorial, *NEA Today,* May 1996, 31.

23. People for the American Way, "Back to School with the Religious Right," http://site.pfaw.org/site/PageServer?pagename=report_back_to_ school, accessed May 5, 2010.

24. National Education Association Education Policy and Practice Department, *Vouchers: What Is at Stake?* (Washington, DC: NEA, 2008), 3, www.nea.org/assets/docs/mf_PB07_Vouchers.pdf, accessed May 5, 2010.

25. James Conant, "Remarks Before a Meeting of the American Association of School Administration," April 7, 1952, http://cumulus.hillsdale.edu/ buckley/Standard/downloads/originals/thetrojanhorseofamericanedu cationdotpdf_9499_buckleypublicationsbyyear1952articles/TheTrojan HorseofAmericanEducation.pdf, accessed May 5, 2010.

26. Francesco Cordasco, *A Brief History of Education: A Handbook of Information on Greek, Roman, Medieval, Renaissance, and Modern Educational Practice* (New York: Rowman and Littlefield, 1976), 14.

27. Robin Barrow, *Greek and Roman Education* (London: Bristol Classical Press, 1996), 64.

28. Ibid., 57.

29. Anthony Corbeil, "Education in the Roman Republic: Creating Traditions," in *Education in Greek and Roman Antiquity,* ed. Yun Lee Too (Leiden, The Netherlands: E. J. Brill, 2001), 269.

30. William Boyd and Edmund King, *The History of Western Education* (Forked River, NJ: Barnes and Noble Press, 1975), 66.

31. Ibid.

32. Barrow, *Greek and Roman Education,* 64–65.

33. Corbeil, "Education in the Roman Republic," 269.

34. Ibid.

35. Thomas E. Woods Jr., *How the Catholic Church Built Western Civilization* (Washington, DC: Regnery Publishers, 2005), 5.

36. Michael Williams, *The Catholic Church in Action* (New York: PJ Kennedy & Sons, 1958), 68.

37. Boyd and King, *The History of Western Education,* 103.

38. David Knowles, "The Cultural Influence of English Medieval Monasticism," *Cambridge Historical Journal* 7, no. 3 (1943): 147.

39. Ibid., 151.

40. Lucas, *Our Western Educational Heritage*, 208.

41. Ibid., 209.

42. William Haarlow, *Great Books, Honors Programs, and Hidden Origins: The Virginia Plan and the University of Virginia in the Liberal Arts Movement* (New York: Routledge, 2003), 47.

43. George Bugliarello, "A New Trivium and Quadrivium," *Bulletin of Science, Technology & Society* 23, no. 2 (2003): 111.

44. Stephen Jaeger, *The Envy of Angels: Cathedral Schools and Social Ideals in Medieval Europe, 950–1200* (Philadelphia: University of Pennsylvania Press, 2000), 47.

45. Lucas, *Our Western Educational Heritage*, 210.

46. T. G. Cook, *The History of Education in Europe* (London: Methuen & Co., 1974), 23.

47. Gutek, *A History of the Western Educational Experience*, 40.

48. John Rothwell Slater, "Printing and the Renaissance," in *Reader in the History of Books and Printing*, ed. Paul A. Winckler (Englewood, CO: Indian Head, 1978), 315.

49. Chicago Club of Printing House Craftsmen, *Printing: The Story of Its Invention and Its Service to Mankind* (Chicago: The Club, 1940), 4.

50. Ibid., 3–4.

51. Elizabeth Eisenstein, *The Printing Press as an Agent of Change* (New York: Cambridge University Press, 1980), 343–344.

52. Asa Briggs and Peter Burke, *Social History of the Media: From Gutenberg to the Internet* (Malden, MA: Polity Press, 2009), 15.

53. Fran Rees, *Johannes Gutenberg: Inventor of the Printing Press* (Minneapolis: Compass Point Books, 2006), 90.

54. Chicago Club, *Printing*, 14–15.

55. Harvey Graff, *The Legacies of Literacy: Continuities and Contradictions in Western Culture and Society* (Bloomington: Indiana University Press, 1987), 114.

56. Eisenstein, *The Printing Press*, 405.

57. Lawrence Stone, "Literacy and Education in England 1640–1900," *Past & Present* 42 (February 1969), 69–139.

58. Lucas, *Our Western Educational Heritage*, 359.
59. John William Adamson, ed., *The Educational Writings of John Locke* (New York: Longmans, Green, 1912), 18.
60. Ibid., 19; John Locke, *Some Thoughts Concerning Education* (London: C. J. Clay and Sons, 1895).
61. Ernest Bayles, "Sketch for a Study of the Growth of American Educational Thought and Practice," *History of Education Quarterly* 1, no. 3 (September 1961): 46.
62. Erwin V. Johanningmeier and Theresa Richardson, *Education Research, the National Agenda, and Educational Reform: A History* (Charlotte, NC: Information Age Publishing, 2008), 97.
63. Jean-Jacques Rousseau, *Emile* (Charleston, SC: BilioBazaar, 2008), 31.
64. Jean-Jacques Rousseau, "Considerations on the Government of Poland," in *The Social Contract and Other Later Political Writings,* ed. Victor Gourevitch (Cambridge: Cambridge University Press, 1997), 190.
65. Ibid., 189.
66. Jean-Jacques Rousseau, "Considerations on the Government of Poland," in *Jean Jacques Rousseau: Political Writings,* ed. Frederick Watkins (Madison: University of Wisconsin Press, 1986), 176.
67. Rousseau, *Emile*, 9.

4. The Common Schoolers and the Push for Uniformity

1. Forest Chester Ensign, *Compulsory School Attendance and Child Labor* (New York: Arno Press, 1969), 13.
2. R. Freeman Butts and Lawrence A. Cremin, *A History of Education in American Culture* (New York: Holt, Rinehart and Winston, 1953), 102.
3. Ensign, *Compulsory School Attendance*, 20.
4. Butts and Cremin, *A History of Education*, 102.
5. Ibid., 102.
6. Ibid., 102–103.
7. Paul Peterson, "The New Politics of Choice," in *Learning from the Past: What History Teaches Us about School Reform,* ed. Diane Ravitch and Maris A. Vinovskis (Baltimore: JHU Press, 1995), 220.
8. Thomas D. Snyder, ed., "120 Years of American Education: A Statistical Portrait," *National Center for Education Statistics* (January 1993), 5;

Samuel Furman Hunt, *Orations and Historical Addresses* (Cincinnati: Robert Clarke Company, 1908), 297.

9. Robert L. Church and Michael W. Sedlak, *Education in the United States: An Interpretive History* (New York: Free Press, 1976), 13–20.

10. Ibid., 38.

11. David B. Tyack, ed., *Turning Points in American Educational History* (Waltham, MA: Blaisdell, 1967), 469; Snyder, ed., "120 Years of American Education," 27.

12. David L. Angus and Jeffrey E. Mirel, *The Failed Promise of the American High School, 1890–1995* (New York: Teachers College Press, 1999), 203.

13. Edwin Grant Dexter, *A History of Education in the United States* (New York: Macmillan, 1906), 178.

14. William M. French, *America's Educational Tradition: An Interpretive History* (Boston: DC Heath, 1964), 153.

15. Snyder, ed., "120 Years of American Education," 14.

16. James M. McPherson, *Drawn with the Sword: Reflections on the American Civil War* (New York: Oxford University Press, 1996), 15.

17. Snyder, ed., "120 Years of American Education," 6.

18. Nicholas J. Evans, "Indirect Passage from Europe," *Journal for Maritime Research* (June 2001), www.jmr.nmm.ac.uk/server/show/conJmrArticle .28/setPaginate/No, accessed May 5, 2010.

19. Church and Sedlak, *Education in the United States*, 70.

20. Ibid., 55.

21. William Boyd and Edmund King, *The History of Western Education* (New Jersey: Barnes and Noble Press, 1975), 307; Yasemin Nuhoglu Soysal and David Strang, "Construction of the First Mass Education Systems in Nineteenth-Century Europe," *Sociology of Education* 62, no. 4 (October 1989): 278.

22. Horace Mann, "Report for 1843," in *Annual Reports of the Secretary of the Board of Education of Massachusetts for the Years 1839–1844,* ed. Horace Mann (Boston: Lee and Shepard, 1891), 303.

23. James Earl Russell, *German Higher Schools: The History, Organization and Methods of Secondary Education in Germany* (New York: Longmans, Green, 1899), 79, http://books.google.com/books?id=JMYNAAAAYAAJ &pg=PA108&dq=prussian+school+system#v=onepage&q=prussian %20school%20system&f=false, accessed May 5, 2010.

24. Angela Little, "Education for All: Multigrade Realities and Histories," in *Education for All and Multigrade Teaching: Challenges and Opportunities*, ed. Angela Little (New York: Springer, 2007), 17.

25. Christopher J. Lucas, *Our Western Educational Heritage* (New York: Macmillan, 1972), 516.

26. Michael S. Katz, *A History of Compulsory Education Laws* (Bloomington, IN: Phi Delta Kappa Bicentennial Series, 1976), 17.

27. "Enforced Education," *New York Times*, January 23, 1876.

28. William T. Harris, *Report of the Commissioner of Education for the Year 1889–90* (Washington, DC: Government Printing Office, 1893).

29. Katz, *A History of Compulsory Education Laws*, 19.

30. Henry Barnard et al., *Report of the Commissioner of Education for the Year 1888–1889* (Washington, DC: Government Printing Office, 1891), 517.

31. Ibid., 524.

32. Katz, *A History of Compulsory Education Laws*, 18.

33. Carl F. Kaestle, *Pillars of the Republic: Common Schools and American Society, 1780–1860* (New York: Hill and Wang, 1983), 107.

34. Hugh D. Hindman, *Child Labor: An American History* (New York: M. E. Sharpe, 2002), 32.

35. Ensign, *Compulsory School Attendance*, 235.

36. Hindman, *Child Labor*, 49.

37. Ira Katznelson and Margaret Weir, *Schooling for All: Class, Race, and the Decline of the Democratic Ideal* (Berkeley: University of California Press, 1988), 71–72.

38. William Maxwell Burke, "History and Functions of Central Labor Unions," *Studies in History, Economics, and Law* 12 (1899): 56.

39. Hindman, *Child Labor*, 59.

40. U.S. Department of State, *Abstract of the Returns of the Fifth Census* (Washington, DC: Duff Green, 1839), 47.

41. This data was calculated by adding together the totals from the Department of Homeland Security, *2007 Yearbook of Immigration Statistics* (Washington DC: Office of Immigration Statistics, 2008), 6.

42. Ibid.

43. Horace Mann, *Lectures on Education, 1855* (Boston: Ide & Dutton, 1855), 56.

44. Church and Sedlak, *Education in the United States,* 70.

45. "The Emigration from Europe," *New York Times,* August 2, 1876, http://query.nytimes.com/gst/abstract.html?res=9B07EEDB143CE63ABC4A53DFBE66838D669FDE, accessed May 5, 2010.

46. "Enforced Education," *New York Times.*

47. Patricia Albjerg Graham, *Schooling America: How the Public Schools Meet the Nation's Changing Needs* (New York: Oxford University Press, 2005), 11.

48. Church and Sedlak, *Education in the United States,* 80.

49. "Religion in the Public Schools," *New York Times,* November 18, 1878.

50. *The Memorial Volume: A History of the Third Plenary Council of Baltimore, November 9–December 7, 1884* (Baltimore: Baltimore Publishing Company, 1885), 33.

51. "New Catholic Decrees: The Work of the Recent Plenary Council in Baltimore," *New York Times,* March 25, 1886.

52. Joseph P. Viteritti, *Choosing Equality: School Choice, the Constitution, and Civil Society* (Washington, DC: Brookings Institution Press, 1999), 152.

53. Ibid., 18.

54. Ibid., 155.

55. *Pierce v. Society of the Sisters of the Holy Names of Jesus and Mary,* 268 U.S. 510 (1925), Supreme Court of the United States, 1925.

56. Ibid.

57. Ibid.

58. Joseph P. Viteritti, "Blaine's Wake: School Choice, The First Amendment, and State Constitutional Law," *Harvard Journal of Law & Public Policy* 21, no. 3 (1998): 657–718.

59. David K. Barnhart and Allan A. Metcalf, *America in So Many Words: Words That Have Shaped America* (Boston: Houghton Mifflin, 1997), 206–207.

60. Ibid., 206.

61. Stephen Macedo, *Diversity and Distrust: Civic Education in a Multicultural Democracy* (Cambridge, MA: Harvard University Press, 2000), 263.

62. Florida State Constitution, Article IX, Section 1.

63. Frederick Hess and Andrew Rotherham, "Restrictive Uniforms," *Tech Central Station,* January 24, 2006, www.educationsector.org/analysis/analysis_show.htm?doc_id=342793, accessed May 5, 2010.

64. Kari Lydersen, "Preserving Languages Is about More Than Words," *Washington Post,* March 16, 2009, A07.

65. John Stuart Mill, *On Liberty* (New York: Longmans, Green, 1921), 63.

66. Based on author's calculations, U.S. Department of Education, National Center for Education Statistics, *Digest of Education Statistics 2008* (March 2009), 98, http://nces.ed.gov/pubs2009/2009020.pdf, accessed May 5, 2010.

67. Ibid., 53.

68. Chester Finn Jr., *Troublemaker: A Personal History of School Reform since Sputnik* (Princeton, NJ: Princeton University Press, 2008), 284.

69. Martin West and Ludger Woessmann, "Which School Systems Sort Weaker Students into Smaller Classes? International Evidence," *European Journal of Political Economy* 22, no. 4 (December 2006): 944–968, www.cesifo-group.de/DocCIDL/cesifo1_wp1054.pdf, accessed May 5, 2010.

70. Dan Goldhaber, "Lessons from Abroad: Exploring Cross-Country Differences in Teacher Development Systems and What They Mean for U.S. Policy," in *Creating a New Teaching Profession,* eds. Dan Goldhaber and Jane Hannaway (Washington, DC: Urban Institute, 2009), 89.

71. Terry M. Moe and John E. Chubb, *Liberating Learning: Technology, Politics, and the Future of American Education* (San Francisco: Wiley, 2009), 127.

72. Ibid., 132.

73. Ibid., 133.

74. National Conference of State Legislatures, "Compulsory School Age Requirements," February 2006, http://www.ncsl.org/print/educ/CompulsorySchAgeChart.pdf, accessed May 5, 2010.

75. Snyder, ed., "120 Years of American Education," 6.

76. Ethan Yazzie-Mintz, *Voices of Students on Engagement: A Report on the 2006 High School Survey of Student Engagement* (Bloomington, IN: Center for Evaluation and Education Policy at Indiana University, 2007), 5.

77. Dana Markow and Marc Schneer, "The MetLife Survey of the American Teacher, 2002: Student Life—School, Home & Community" (New York: Metropolitan Life Insurance Company, 2002), 53.

78. Helen M. Marks, "Student Engagement in Instructional Activity: Patterns in the Elementary, Middle and High School Years," *American Educational Research Journal* 37, no. 1 (2000): 155–156.

79. Ibid., 153-184.
80. Theodore Sizer, *Horace's Compromise: The Dilemma of the American High School* (New York: Houghton Mifflin, 1984).
81. Murray N. Rothbard, *For a New Liberty: The Libertarian Manifesto* (Auburn, AL: Ludwig von Mises Institute, 2006), 146.
82. David B. Tyack, *Seeking Common Ground: Public Schools in a Diverse Society* (Cambridge, MA: Harvard University Press, 2003), 20.
83. David Whitman, *Sweating the Small Stuff: Inner-City Schools and the New Paternalism* (Washington, DC: Thomas B. Fordham Institute Press, 2008).

5. The Progressives and the Quest for Universality

1. Jonathan Zimmerman, *Whose America? Culture Wars in the Public Schools* (Cambridge, MA: Harvard University Press, 2002).
2. John E. Chubb and Terry Moe, *Politics, Markets, and America's Schools* (Washington, DC: Brookings Institution Press, 1990), 141.
3. The faddism phenomenon in America's schools has been studied by educationists and sociologists alike. For example, Amy Binder, in 2004's *Contentious Curricula* (Princeton, NJ: Princeton University Press), documented the rise and fall of two movements—afrocentrism and creationism—to better understand the mechanisms and motivations behind the large-scale curriculum movements of the 1980s and 1990s.
4. Diane Ravitch, *Left Back: A Century of Battles over School Reform* (New York: Touchstone, 2000), 328.
5. Ibid., 440.
6. Ibid., 443.
7. Dan Koretz, "Using Student Assessments for Educational Accountability," in *Improving America's Schools,* eds. Eric Alan Hanushek and Dale Waeldeau Jorgenson (Washington, DC: National Academies Press, 1996), 171-194.
8. Frederick Winslow Taylor, *The Principles of Scientific Management* (New York: Harper & Brothers, 1911).
9. David B. Tyack, *The One Best System: A History of American Urban Education* (Cambridge, MA: Harvard University Press, 1974), 30.
10. Ibid.

11. George H. Martin, "Comparison of Modern Business Methods with Educational Methods," *Journal of Proceedings and Addresses of the National Education Association of the United States* (Winona, MN: National Education Association, 1905), 321.

12. George Herbert Betts, *Social Principles of Education* (New York: Charles Scribner's Sons, 1912), 86.

13. Paul Hanus, "Improving School Systems by Scientific Management," *Journal of Proceedings and Addresses of the National Education Association of the United States* (Winona, MN: National Education Association, 1913), 248.

14. Tyack, *The One Best System*, 50.

15. Ibid., 66.

16. Plato, *The Republic of Plato*, trans. B. Jowett (London: Oxford University Press, 1881), 233.

17. Plato, "Protagoras," *The Dialogues of Plato*, trans. B. Jowett (New York: Random House, 1937), 96.

18. Thomas Jefferson, *Notes on the State of Virginia* (Richmond, VA: Chas H. Wynne, Printer, 1853), 157–158.

19. David L. Angus and Jeffrey E. Mirel, *The Failed Promise of the American High School, 1890–1995* (New York: Teachers College Press, 1999), 7.

20. Michael W. Apple, *Official Knowledge: Democratic Education in a Conservative Age* (New York: Routledge, 2000), 71.

21. Ibid., 16.

22. Jim B. Pearson and Edgar Fuller, *Education in the States: Nationwide Development since 1900* (Washington, DC: National Education Association, 1969), 15.

23. Arthur G. Wirth, "John Dewey's Design for American Education: An Analysis of Aspects of His Work at the University of Chicago, 1894–1904," *History of Education Quarterly* 4, no. 2 (June 1964): 101.

24. Theodore Sizer, *Secondary Schools at the Turn of the Century* (New Haven, CT: Yale University Press, 1964), 55.

25. Ellwood Cubberley, *Public Education in the United States: A Study and Interpretation of American Educational History* (Cambridge, MA: Riverside Press, 1947), 542–543.

26. National Education Association of the United States, *Report of the Committee of Ten on Secondary School Studies: With the Reports of the*

Conferences Arranged by the Committee (New York: American Book Company, 1894), 51–52.

27. Ibid., 52.
28. R. Freeman Butts and Lawrence A. Cremin, *A History of Education in American Culture* (New York: Holt, Rinehart, and Winston, 1953), 390.
29. Sizer, *Secondary Schools*, 106.
30. Cubberley, *Public Education in the United States*, 543.
31. Sizer, *Secondary Schools*, 146.
32. "Cardinal Principles of Secondary Education: A Report of the Commission on the Reorganization of Secondary Education, Appointed by the National Education Association," *Bulletin* 35 (Washington, DC: U.S. Department of the Interior, 1918), 9.
33. Lawrence A. Cremin, "The Revolution in American Secondary Education, 1893–1918," *Teachers College Record* 56 (1955): 307.
34. "Cardinal Principles of Secondary Education," 15.
35. Ibid., 21.
36. Ravitch, *Left Back*, 128–129.
37. Dennis Littky with Samantha Grabelle, *The Big Picture: Education Is Everyone's Business* (Alexandria, VA: Association for Supervision and Curriculum Development, 2004), 74.
38. Terrence E. Cook, "Rousseau: Education and Politics," *Journal of Politics* 37 (February 1975): 108.
39. Nel Noddings, *Philosophy of Education* (Boulder, CO: Westview Press, 1995), 18.
40. Christopher J. Lucas, *Our Western Educational Heritage* (New York: Macmillan, 1972), 531.
41. Gerald L. Gutek, *Education and Schooling in America* (Englewood Cliffs, NJ: Prentice-Hall, 1983), 31.
42. Ibid., 61–62.
43. George Wood, "A View from the Field: NCLB's Effects on Classrooms and Schools," in *Many Children Left Behind: How the No Child Left Behind Act Is Damaging Our Children and Our Schools*, ed. Deborah Meier and George Wood (Boston: Beacon Press, 2004), 35.
44. Elissa Gootman and David Herszenhorn, "Getting Smaller to Improve the Big Picture," *New York Times*, May 3, 2005.

45. "Core Knowledge K–8 Schools," Core Knowledge Foundation, http://teachingcontentisteachingreading.com/CK/schools/schools_list.htm, accessed May 5, 2010.

46. E. D. Hirsch Jr., "The 21st-Century Skills Movement," text of remarks from "What Is the Proper Role of Skills in the Curriculum" event at Common Core on February 24, 2009, www.commoncore.org/_docs/hirsch.pdf, accessed May 5, 2010.

47. Matthew Davis, "Diane Ravitch Defends the Academic Tradition," *Common Knowledge* 14 (2001), http://teachingcontent.org/CK/about/print/RavitchDefends.htm, accessed May 5, 2010.

48. Ravitch, *Left Back*, 16.

49. Donald N. Langenberg, *The Report of the National Reading Panel: Teaching Children to Read* (Washington, DC: National Reading Panel, 2000), 1, www.nichd.nih.gov/publications/nrp/upload/smallbook_pdf.pdf, accessed May 5, 2010.

50. See Valerie Strauss and Jay Mathews, "Extra Credit," *Washington Post,* April 25, 2000; Valerie Strauss, "Relying on Science in Teaching Kids to Read," *Washington Post,* February 26, 2002; Valerie Strauss, "Phonics Pitch Irks Teachers—U.S. Denies It's Pushing Commercial Products," *Washington Post,* September 10, 2002.

51. Langenberg, *Report of the National Reading Panel,* 15,

52. *Foundations for Success: The Final Report of the National Mathematics Advisory Panel* (Washington DC: U.S. Department of Education, 2008), xiii, www.ed.gov/about/bdscomm/list/mathpanel/report/final-report.pdf, accessed May 5, 2010.

53. Ibid., xiii.

54. Ibid., xix.

55. Tamar Lewin, "Report Urges Change in Teaching Math," *New York Times,* March 14, 2008, www.nytimes.com/2008/03/14/education/14math.htm, accessed May 5, 2010.

56. Grover J. Whitehurst and Michelle Croft, "Faith in Common Standards Not Enough," Brookings Institution, October 29, 2009, www.brookings.edu/opinions/2009/1029_standards_whitehurst.aspx, accessed May 5, 2010.

57. Lisa D. Delpit, "Education in a Multicultural Society: Our Future's Greatest Challenge," *Journal of Negro Education* 61 (Summer 1992): 237.

58. Andrew Dawson, "The Workshop and the Classroom: Philadelphia Engineering, the Decline of Apprenticeship, and the Rise of Industrial Training, 1878–1900," *History of Education Quarterly* 39 (Summer 1999): 144.

59. Emery Hyslop-Margison, "An Assessment of the Historical Arguments in Vocational Education Reform," *Journal of Career and Technical Education* 17 (Spring 2001): 24, http://scholar.lib.vt.edu/ejournals/JCTE/v17n1/pdf/hyslop.pdf, accessed May 5, 2010.

60. S. Alexander Rippa, "The Business Community and the Public Schools on the Eve of the Great Depression," *History of Education Quarterly* 4, (March 1964): 34.

61. Hyslop-Margison, "An Assessment of the Historical Arguments," 24.

62. Patricia Albjerg Graham, *Schooling America: How the Public Schools Meet the Nation's Changing Needs* (New York: Oxford University Press, 2005), 42.

63. Robert L. Church and Michael W. Sedlak, *Education in the United States: An Interpretive History* (New York: Free Press, 1976), 308.

64. Booker T. Washington, *Booker T. Washington's Own Story of His Life and Work* (Naperville, IL: J. L. Nichols and Co., 1915), 116.

65. Ibid., 118.

66. Karen Levesque, Doug Lauen, Peter Teitelbaum, Martha Alt, and Sally Librera, *Vocational Education in the United States: Toward the Year 2000*, National Center for Education Statistics (Washington, DC: U.S. Department of Education, 2000), 61.

67. Marie Cohen and Douglas J. Besharov, "The Role of Career and Technical Education: Implications for the Federal Government," Office of Vocational and Adult Education (Washington, DC: U.S. Department of Education, 2002), 16, www.eric.ed.gov/ERICWebPortal/contentdelivery/servlet/ERICServlet?accno=ED466939, accessed May 5, 2010.

68. Tom Loveless, *The Tracking Wars* (Washington, DC: Brookings Press, 1999), 36.

69. Ibid., 1.

70. Debra Viadero, "'Algebra-for-All' Push Found to Yield Poor Results," *Education Week,* February 9, 2010, www.edweek.org/ew/articles/2010/02/10/21algebra_ep.h29.html?tkn=VRWFLQqC2mgkHzGhm5J%2BiL VyP%2BLMu%2FbhopXV&cmp=clp-edweek, accessed May 5, 2010.

71. Ann Duffett and Steve Farkas, "Results from a National Teacher Survey," *High-Achieving Students in the Era of NCLB* (Washington, DC: Thomas B. Fordham Institute, 2008), 75, http://www.edexcellence.net/detail/news.cfm?news_id=732, accessed May 5, 2010.

72. Ibid., 76.

73. Ibid., 79.

74. "About TJ," Thomas Jefferson High School for Science and Technology, www.tjhsst.edu/abouttj/.

75. National Center for Education Statistics, *America's High School Graduates: Results from the 2005 NAEP High School Transcript Study* (Washington, DC: U.S. Department of Education, 2007); National Center for Education Statistics, *The Nation's Report Card: Reading 2007* (Washington, DC: U.S. Department of Education, 2007); National Center for Education Statistics, *The Nation's Report Card: Mathematics 2007* (Washington, DC: U.S. Department of Education, 2007).

76. Amit R. Paley, "Test Scores at Odds with Rising High School Grades," *Washington Post,* February 23, 2007.

77. Mitchell Landsberg, "Grades Are Rising but Learning Is Lagging, Federal Reports Find," *Los Angeles Times,* February 23, 2007.

78. Paley, "Test Scores at Odds."

79. Mark Schneider, "Math in American High Schools: The Delusion of Rigor," *AEI Education Outlook* (October 2009), http://www.aei.org/outlook/100074, accessed May 5, 2010.

80. Daniel de Vise, "To Be AP, Courses Must Pass Muster," *Washington Post,* March 25, 2007.

81. Ibid.

82. Ann Duffett and Steve Farkas, "Growing Pains in the Advanced Placement Program: Do Tough Trade-Offs Lie Ahead?" (Washington, DC: Thomas B. Fordham Institute, April 29, 2009), vii, http://www.edexcellence.net/index.cfm/news_advanced-placement-program-study, accessed May 5, 2010.

83. Cubberley, *Public Education in the United States,* 544.

84. Harold O. Rugg, *Twenty-Sixth Yearbook of the National Society for the Study of Education* (Bloomington, IL: Public School Publishing, 1927), 67.

85. W. C. Bagley, "Present-Day Minimal Essentials in United States History as Taught in the Seventh and Eighth Grades," in *Sixteenth Yearbook of*

the *National Society for the Study of Education: Second Report of the Committee on Minimal Essentials in Elementary-School Subjects* (Bloomington, IL: Public School Publishing, 1917), 144

86. B. B. Bassett, "The Content of the Course of Study in Civics," in *Seventeenth Yearbook of the National Society for the Study of Education: Third Report of the Committee on the Economy of Time in Education* (Bloomington, IL: Public School Publishing, 1919), 64.

87. Walter S. Monroe, "A Preliminary Report of an Investigation of the Economy of Time in Arithmetic," in *Sixteenth Yearbook of the National Society for the Study of Education: Second Report of the Committee on Minimal Essentials in Elementary-School Subjects* (Bloomington, IL: Public School Publishing, 1917), 119.

88. Butts and Cremin, *A History of Education,* 439.

89. Ellwood Cubberley, *Public Education in the United States: A Study and Interpretation of American Educational History* (Cambridge, MA: Riverside Press, 1947), 693.

90. Ibid., 694.

91. Stephen Murdoch, *IQ: A Smart History of a Failed Idea* (Hoboken, NJ: John Wiley & Sons, 2007), 76.

92. Butts and Cremin, *A History of Education,* 439.

93. Cubberley, *Public Education in the United States,* 694.

94. Ibid., 698.

95. Ibid.

96. Jay Mathews, "Just Whose Idea Was All This Testing?" *Washington Post,* November 14, 2006.

97. Stephen Jay Gould, *The Mismeasure of Man* (New York: W. W. Norton, 1981), 227.

98. Graham, *Schooling America,* 48.

99. Ibid., 49.

100. Ibid., 79.

101. Bird T. Baldwin, "The Normal Child: Its Physical Growth and Mental Development," *Popular Science* 85, no. 36 (December 1914): 567.

102. James Surowiecki, *The Wisdom of Crowds* (New York: Random House, 2004).

103. Irving Lester Janis, *Victims of Groupthink* (Boston: Houghton Mifflin, 1972), 9.

6. Teachers and Teaching

1. Larry Cuban, *How Teachers Taught: Constancy and Change in American Classrooms 1890–1990* (New York: Teachers College Press, 1993).

2. National Center for Education Statistics, "Fast Facts," http://nces.ed .gov/FastFacts/display.asp?id=372, accessed May 5, 2010.

3. Author's May 2010 calculation based on U.S. Census data.

4. Daniel Aaronson and Katherine Meckel, "The Impact of Baby Boomer Retirements on Teacher Labor Markets," *Chicago Fed Letter*, no. 254 (September 2008): 1, www.chicagofed.org/digital_assets/publications/ chicago_fed_letter/2008/cflseptember2008_254.pdf, accessed May 5, 2010.

5. Thomas D. Snyder, Sally A. Dillow, and Charlene M. Hoffman, *Digest of Education Statistics 2008* (Washington, DC: National Center for Education Statistics, 2009), 401, http://nces.ed.gov/pubs2009/2009020 .pdf, accessed May 5, 2010.

6. Martin Kintzinger, "A Profession but Not a Career? Schoolmaster and the *Artes* in Late Medieval Europe," in *Universities and Schooling in Medieval Society*, ed. William J. Courtenay, Jurgen Miethke, and David B. Priest (Leiden, The Netherlands: Brill Academic Publishers, 2000), 167.

7. Gerald L. Gutek, *Education and Schooling in America* (Englewood Cliffs, NJ: Prentice-Hall, 1983), 12.

8. Robert L. Church and Michael W. Sedlak, *Education in the United States* (New York: Free Press, 1976), 11.

9. Edwin Grant Dexter, *A History of Education in the United States* (New York: Macmillan, 1906), 65.

10. George S. Counts, *Education and American Civilization* (Westport, CT: Greenwood Press, 1952), 455.

11. Jonathan Zimmerman, *Small Wonder: The Little Red Schoolhouse in History and Memory* (New Haven, CT: Yale University Press, 2009), 28.

12. Joan Jacobs Brumberg, "The Feminization of Teaching: 'Romantic Sexism' and American Protestant Denominationalism," *History of Education Quarterly* 23, no. 3 (Autumn 1983): 379.

13. Susan B. Carter, "Occupational Segregation, Teachers' Wages, and American Economic Growth," *Journal of Economist History* 46, no. 2 (June 1986): 374.

14. R. Freeman Butts and Lawrence A. Cremin, *History of Education in American Culture* (New York: Holt, Rinehart and Winston, 1953), 284.
15. John L. Rury, "Who Became Teachers? The Social Characteristics of Teachers in American History," in *American Teachers: Histories of a Profession at Work*, ed. D. Warren (New York: Macmillan, 1989), 16–17.
16. Dexter, *A History of Education*, 453.
17. Brumberg, "The Feminization of Teaching," 379–384.
18. U.S. Census Bureau, "A Half-Century of Learning: Historical Statistics on Educational Attainment in the United States, 1940 to 2000," *Census 2000 PHC-T-41* (Washington, DC: U.S. Census Bureau, 2006), www .census.gov/population/www/socdemo/education/phct41.html, accessed May 5, 2010.
19. U.S. Census Bureau, "Sixteenth Census of the United States: 1940" (Washington, DC: U.S. Census Bureau, 1940), 6, www2.census.gov/ prod2/decennial/documents/33973538v2p1ch2.pdf, accessed May 5, 2010.
20. Ibid., 67, 69.
21. Chester M. Stephenson, "Married Female School Teachers," *Marriage and Family Living* 16, no. 3 (August 1954): 251.
22. Jonna Perrillo, "Beyond 'Progressive' Reform: Bodies, Discipline, and the Construction of the Professional Teacher in Interwar America," *History of Education Quarterly* 44, no. 3 (2004): 341, www.jstor.org.proxycu .wrlc.org/stable/3218026?seq=5, accessed May 5, 2010.
23. Dexter, *A History of Education*, 164.
24. Rury, "Who Became Teachers?" 27.
25. Carl F. Kaestle, *Pillars of the Republic* (New York: Hill and Wang, 1983), 123.
26. As cited in David B. Tyack, *The One Best System: A History of American Urban Education* (Cambridge, MA: Harvard University Press, 1974), 60.
27. Public Broadcasting Service, "*Only* a Teacher," documentary series produced by Claudia Levin, 2000. Specific quote cited in "Teaching Timeline" section of documentary, www.pbs.org/onlyateacher/timeline .html, accessed May 5, 2010.
28. Susanna Loeb and Michelle Reininger, "Public Policy and Teacher Labor Markets: What We Know and Why It Matters," *The Education Policy Center at Michigan State University* (April 2004), 40, http://eric.ed

.gov/ERICWebPortal/custom/portlets/recordDetails/detailmini.jsp?
nfpb=true&&ERICExtSearch_SearchValue_0=ED485592&ERICExt
Search_SearchType_0=no&accno=ED485592, accessed May 5, 2010.

29. Loeb and Reininger, "Public Policy and Teacher Labor Markets," 11.

30. U.S. Department of Labor: Women's Bureau, *Quick Stats on Women Workers, 2008,* www.dol.gov/wb/stats/main.htm, accessed May 5, 2010.

31. Loeb and Reininger, "Public Policy and Teacher Labor Markets," 18.

32. David Leal, "Assessing Traditional Teacher Preparation: Evidence from a Survey of Graduate and Undergraduate Programs," in *A Qualified Teacher in Every Classroom? Appraising Old Answers and New Ideas,* ed. Frederick Hess, Andrew Rotherham, and Kate Walsh (Cambridge, MA: Harvard Education Press, 2004), 101–117.

33. Jay Mathews, "When a Gifted Teacher Has to Jump through Hoops Just to Keep His Job, Change Is Needed," *Washington Post,* August 24, 2009, www.washingtonpost.com/wp-dyn/content/article/2009/08/23/AR2009082302154.html, accessed May 5, 2010.

34. Dan Goldhaber, "The Mystery of Good Teaching," *Education Next* 2, no. 1 (Spring 2002): 53.

35. Charles W. Jones, "An Early Medieval Licensing Examination," *History of Education Quarterly* 3, no. 1 (March 1963): 26–27.

36. Paul F. Grendler, "Schooling in Western Europe," *Renaissance Quarterly* 43, no. 4 (Winter 1990): 779.

37. Gerald L. Gutek, *Education and Schooling in America* (Englewood Cliffs, NJ: Prentice-Hall, 1983), 351.

38. Christopher J. Lucas, *Our Western Educational Heritage* (New York: Macmillan, 1972), 481.

39. Dexter, *A History of Education,* 398.

40. James G. Carter, "Outline of an Institution for the Education of Teachers," in *Normal Schools and Other Institutions, Agencies, and Means Designed for the Professional Education of Teachers,* ed. Henry Barnard (Hartford, CT: Case, Tiffany, 1851), 92.

41. Ellwood Cubberley, *Public Education in the United States* (Cambridge, MA: Houghton Mifflin, 1947), 375.

42. T. M. Stinnett, "Teacher Education, Certification, and Accreditation," in *Education in the States: Nationwide Development Since 1900,* ed. Edgar

Fuller and Jim Pearson (Washington, DC: Council of Chief State School Officers, 1969), 387.

43. Horace Mann, "Progress of Education in Maine," *Common School Journal* 8, no. 18 (September 1846): 273–279.

44. Stinnett, "Teacher Education, Certification, and Accreditation," 388.

45. Butts and Cremin, *History of Education*, 287, 449.

46. David B. Tyack, ed., *Turning Points in American Educational History* (Waltham, MA: Blaisdell, 1967), 418.

47. Ibid.

48. Andrew J. Rotherham and Sara Mead, "Back to the Future: The History and Politics of State Teacher Licensure and Certification," in *A Qualified Teacher in Every Classroom? Appraising Old Answers and New Ideas*, eds. Frederick M. Hess, Andrew J. Rotherham, and Kate Walsh (Cambridge, MA: Harvard Education Press, 2004), 21–22.

49. Kate Walsh and Sandi Jacobs, "Alternative Certification Isn't Alternative," National Council on Teacher Quality, September 2007, 13, http://www.nctq.org/p/tqb/docs/Alternative_Certification_Isnt_Alternative_20071113021230.pdf, accessed May 5, 2010.

50. National Board for Professional Teaching Standards, *What Teachers Should Know and Be Able to Do* (Arlington, VA: National Board for Professional Teaching Standards, 2002), 17, www.nbpts.org/UserFiles/File/what_teachers.pdf, accessed May 5, 2010.

51. Dexter, *A History of Education*, 37.

52. Jonna Perillo, "Beyond 'Progressive' Reform: Bodies, Discipline, and the Construction of the Professional Teacher in Interwar America," *History of Education Quarterly* 44, no. 3 (2004): 341.

53. Sol Cohen, "The Mental Hygiene Movement, the Development of Personality and the School: The Medicalization of American Education," *History of Education Quarterly* 23, no. 2 (Summer 1983): 125.

54. Perillo, "Beyond 'Progressive' Reform," 337.

55. Harvey W. Zorbaugh, "Mental Hygiene's Challenge to Education," *Journal of Educational Sociology* 5 (February 1932): 332.

56. "Analyzing the Schoolmarm," *Newsweek* 22, July 26, 1943, 78.

57. Percival M. Symonds quoted in *Teacher Assessment and the Quest for Teacher Quality: A Handbook*, ed. Mary Kennedy (San Francisco: John Wiley & Sons, 2010), 53.

58. Percival M. Symonds, "Dynamic Factors Contributing to Personality Formation in Teachers," *Education* 63 (1943): 616–626; "Analyzing the Schoolmarm," 78.

59. "Analyzing the Schoolmarm," 78.

60. Percival M. Symonds, "Reflections on Observations of Teachers," *Journal of Educational Research* 43, no. 9 (May 1950): 692.

61. Bruce B. Robinson, "Emotional Problems in the Administration of Educational Personnel," *Education* 75 (December 1954): 229.

62. Laurence D. Haskew, "Selection, Guidance, and Preservice Preparation of Students for Public-School Teaching," *Review of Educational Research* 22, no. 3 (June 1952): 175–181, 176. An earlier report of selection practices indicated that the "typical college and department of education take the students that come without utilizing any systematic screening process." From R. H. Eliassen and Robert L. Martin, "Teacher Recruitment and Selection during the Period 1944 through 1947," *Journal of Educational Research* 41, no. 9 (May 1948): 651.

63. Ruth A. Stout, "Selective Admissions and Retention Practices in Teacher Education," *Journal of Teacher Education* 8, in four parts (September 1957): 299–317; ibid. (December 1957): 422–432.

64. Frederick L. Patry, "Mental Hygiene Is First Need in the Selection of Teachers," *Nation's Schools* 27 (April 1951): 58.

65. Carroll M. Helm, "Teacher Dispositions as Predictors of Good Teaching," *Clearing House* 79, no. 3 (January/February 2006): 118.

66. Ibid.

67. Patricia H. Phelps, "The Dilemma of Dispositions," *A Journal of Educational Strategies, Issues and Ideas* 79, no. 4 (March–April 2006): 174.

68. Frederick M. Hess, "Schools of Re-education?" *Washington Post,* February 5, 2006, www.washingtonpost.com/wp-dyn/content/article/2006/02/03/AR2006020302603_pf.html, accessed May 5, 2010.

69. Carole Gupton, Mary Beth Kelley, Tim Lensmire, Bic Ngo, and Michael Goh, "Teacher Education Redesign Initiative Race, Culture, Class, and Gender Task Group," Foundation for Individual Rights in Education, July 16, 2009, www.thefire.org/public/pdfs/644d7eac9fea37165d1129cb1420163c.pdf?direct, accessed May 10, 2010.

70. "Victory for Freedom of Conscience as University of Minnesota Backs Away from Ideological Screening for Ed Students," Foundation for

Individual Rights in Education, December 23, 2009, www.thefire.org/article/11420.html, accessed May 10, 2010.

71. "Brooklyn College: Possible Investigation of Professor's Expression," Foundation for Individual Rights in Education, www.thefire.org/case/685.html, accessed May 10, 2010.

72. "Stanford University: Education Program Tries to Keep Outspoken Student from Enrolling, Demands Access to Private Blog," Foundation for Individual Rights in Education, www.thefire.org/case/799.html, accessed May 10, 2010.

73. National Council for Accreditation of Teacher Education, "NCATE Unit Standards," www.ncate.org/public/unitStandardsRubrics.asp?ch=4#stnd4, accessed May 10, 2010.

74. "Foundation for Individual Rights in Education Statement on National Council for Accreditation of Teacher Education's Encouragement of Political Litmus Tests in Higher Education," Foundation for Individual Rights in Education, June 5, 2006, www.thefire.org/article/7079.html, accessed May 10, 2010.

75. Goldhaber, "The Mystery of Good Teaching," 53.

76. "President Obama's Remarks on Education," *Wall Street Journal: Washington Wire Blog,* March 10, 2009, http://blogs.wsj.com/washwire/2009/03/10/obamas-remarks-on-education-2, accessed May 10, 2010.

77. Jean Protsik, "History of Teacher Pay and Incentive Reforms," paper presented at the Consortium for Policy Research in Education Conference on Teachers' Compensation (Washington, DC: November 1994), 7, https://www.eric.ed.gov/ERICWebPortal/contentdelivery/servlet/ERICServlet?accno=ED380894, accessed May 10, 2010.

78. Ibid., 5.

79. Butts and Cremin, *History of Education,* 135.

80. Protsik, "History of Teacher Pay," 6.

81. Allan Odden and Carolyn Kelley, *Paying Teachers for What They Know and Do: New and Smarter Compensation* (Newbury Park, CA: Corwin Press, 2002), 29.

82. Protsik, "History of Teacher Pay," 7.

83. Herbert A. Tonne, "Social Aspects of Equal Pay for Men and Women in Teaching," *Journal of Educational Sociology* 2, no. 2 (October 1928): 108–113, 109.

84. Cora B. Morrison, "Single Salary Schedules," *Journal of Proceedings and Addresses of the National Education Association of the United States* (1924): 484.

85. Lyle L. Morris, *The Single Salary Schedule: An Analysis and Evaluation* (New York: Columbia University Press, 1930), 42.

86. Odden and Kelley, *Paying Teachers for What They Know and Do*, 33.

87. Morrison, "Single Salary Schedules," 482.

88. Michael Podgursky and Matthew Springer, "Teacher Performance Pay: A Review," *Journal of Policy Analysis and Management* 26, no. 4 (2007): 912.

89. David Lipsky and Samuel Bacharach, "The Single Salary Schedule vs. Merit Pay: An Examination of the Debate," *Collective Bargaining Quarterly* 1, no. 4 (1983), 7.

90. Janet Hansen, "An Introduction to Teacher Retirement Benefits," paper presented at the "Rethinking Teacher Retirement Benefit Systems" conference, Vanderbilt University, Nashville, TN, February 19, 2009, www.performanceincentives.org/data/files/news/ConferencePapers2009 News/Hansen_Conference_2009.pdf, accessed May 10, 2010.

91. Employee Benefit Research Institute, "History of Pension Plans," March 1998, www.ebri.org/publications/facts/index.cfm?fa=0398afact, accessed May 10, 2010.

92. Hansen, "An Introduction to Teacher Retirement Benefits," 2.

93. Author's calculation based on survey of the 125 largest public pension funds in the United States as found in the National Association of State Retirement Administrators and the National Council on Teacher Retirement, *Public Fund Survey: Summary of Findings for FY 2007*, prepared by Keith Brainard, November 2008, www.publicfundsurvey.org/publicfundsurvey/pdfs/Summary_of_Findings_FY08.pdf, accessed May 10, 2010.

94. Michael Podgursky and Robert M. Costrell, "Peaks, Cliffs, & Valleys: The Peculiar Incentives of Teacher Pensions," *Education Next* (Winter 2008): 22.

95. Lily Eskelsen, panel address, "A Penny Saved Conference," American Enterprise Institute, Washington, DC, January 11, 2010.

96. Steven Brill, "The Rubber Room: The Battle of New York City's Worst Teachers," *New Yorker*, August 31, 2009, www.newyorker.com/reporting/2009/08/31/090831fa_fact_brill, accessed May 10, 2010.

97. Joseph Mayer Rice, "The Absurdity of Primary Education," *Annals of American History*, 1892, http://america.eb.com/america/print?articleId= 386382, accessed May 10, 2010.

98. "Tenure for Teachers," *Wall Street Journal*, March 21, 1972, 16.

99. Fred Hechinger, "Tenure: The Case For—And Against," *New York Times*, September 24, 1972.

100. Charl O. Williams, "Report of the Committee on Tenure," *Journal of Proceedings and Addresses of the National Education Association of the United States* (1921): 145–146.

101. Laurie Moses Hines, "Return of the Thought Police?" *Education Next* 7, no. 2 (Spring 2007): 62.

102. Ibid.

103. Karen L. Graves, *And They Were Wonderful Teachers: Florida's Purge of Gay and Lesbian Teachers* (Urbana: University of Illinois, 2009).

104. Williams, "Report of the Committee on Tenure," 148.

105. Committee on Tenure and Academic Freedom, *Teacher Tenure: Analysis and Appraisal* (Washington, DC: National Education Association, 1947), 5.

106. Ibid., 6–7.

107. Committee on Tenure, "Report of the Committee on Tenure," *Journal of Proceedings and Addresses of the National Education Association of the United States* (1948): 5.

108. George S. Reuter Jr., *Current Status of Teacher Tenure: A Research Department Survey* (Chicago: American Federation of Teachers, 1963), 2.

109. Patricia L. Marshall, Debra V. Baucom, and Allison L. Webb, "Do You Have Tenure, and Do You Really Want It?" *Clearing House* 71, no. 5 (May/June 1998): 302.

110. Richard A. Musemeche, *An Objective Study of Teacher Tenure— Nationwide and in Louisiana* (Baton Rouge: Louisiana State University, 1974), 2.

111. Frank Eltman, "Firing Tenured Teachers Isn't Just Difficult, It Costs You," *USA Today*, June 30, 2008.

112. Newark Public School District, Office of the General Counsel, *Certificate of Determination: Statement of Charges*, November 19, 2002 (Newark, NJ), 1–7, http://teachersunionexposed.com/Newark/downloads/docs/10.pdf, accessed May 10, 2010.

113. Frederick M. Hess and Martin West, *A Better Bargain: Overhauling Teacher Collective Bargaining for the 21st Century* (Cambridge, MA: Harvard University Press, 2006), 31.

114. Daniel Weisberg, Susan Sexton, Jennifer Mulhern, and David Keeling, *The Widget Effect* (Washington, DC: The New Teacher Project, 2009), http://widgeteffect.org/downloads/TheWidgetEffect.pdf, accessed May 10, 2010.

115. Jessica Levin, Jennifer Mulhern, and Joan Schunck, *Unintended Consequences* (Washington, DC: The New Teacher Project: 2005), 17–18, www.tntp.org/files/UnintendedConsequences.pdf, accessed May 10, 2010.

116. Robert J. Laubacher and Thomas W. Malone, "Flexible Work Arrangements and 21st Century Worker's Guilds," Initiative on Inventing the Organizations of the 21st Century, Massachusetts Institute of Technology, Sloan School of Management, working paper #004 (October 1997), http://ccs.mit.edu/21C/21CWP004.html, accessed May 10, 2010.

117. Ibid.

118. U.S. Department of Labor, Bureau of Labor Statistics, "Contingent and Alternative Employment Arrangements," Table 12, news release (Washington DC: Bureau of Labor Statistics, February 2005), 19, www.bls.gov/news.release/pdf/conemp.pdf, accessed May 10, 2010.

119. Susan N. Houseman, "The Policy Implications of Nonstandard Work Arrangements," W. E. Upjohn Institute for Employment Research (Fall 1999), www.dol.gov/oasam/programs/history/herman/reports/futurework/conference/staffing/flexible_table1_text.htm, accessed May 10, 2010.

120. Author's calculation based on Bureau of Labor Statistics, "Occupational Employment and Wages, 2008," Table 1, May 1, 2009, www.bls.gov/news.release/pdf/ocwage.pdf, accessed May 10, 2010.

7. Some Reassembly Required

1. David B. Tyack, *The One Best System: A History of American Urban Education* (Cambridge, MA: Harvard University Press, 1974).

2. National Center for Education Statistics, *Schools and Staffing Survey,* Table 1: Number of students, teachers, schools, principals, school libraries, and districts, by school type and selected school characteristics:

2003–2004 (Washington, DC: US Department of Transportation, 2004), http://nces.ed.gov/surveys/sass/tables/sass_2004_01.asp/, accessed May 5, 2010.

3. David Berliner and Bruce Biddle, *The Manufactured Crisis: Myths, Fraud, and the Attack on America's Public Schools* (New York: Basic Books, 1996), xii.

4. Loie Fecteau, "Experts Differ on Vouchers," *Albuquerque Journal*, May 8, 1999, www.abqjournal.com/cgi-bin/decision.pl?attempted= www.abqjournal.com/news/xgr99/1legis05-08.htm/, accessed May 5, 2010.

5. Benjamin Barber, *A Passion for Democracy: American Essays* (Princeton, NJ: Princeton University Press, 2000), 225.

6. Diane Ravitch, "Education and Democracy," in *Making Good Citizens: Education and Civil Society*, ed. Diane Ravitch and Joseph Viteritti (New Haven, CT: Yale University Press, 2003), 19.

7. Ibid.

8. John Stuart Mill, *On Liberty* (London: Oxford University Press, 1913), 62–63.

9. Charles Glenn, "Protecting and Limiting School Distinctiveness: How Much of Each?" in *School Choice: The Moral Debate*, ed. Alan Wolfe (Princeton, NJ: Princeton University Press, 2003), 173.

10. Dennis Meuret, "School Choice and Its Regulation in France," in *Educating Citizens: International Perspectives on Civic Values and School Choice*, ed. Patrick Wolf and Stephen Macedo (Washington, DC: Brookings Institution Press, 2004), 238.

11. Lutz Reuter, "School Choice and Civic Values in Germany," in *Educating Citizens: International Perspectives on Civic Values and School Choice*, ed. Patrick Wolf and Stephen Macedo (Washington, DC: Brookings Institution Press, 2004), 224.

12. Ibid.

13. Patrick Wolf, "School Choice and Civic Values," in *Getting Choice Right: Ensuring Equity and Efficiency*, ed. Julian Betts and Tom Loveless (Washington, DC: Brookings Institution Press, 2005), 212.

14. Ibid., 214–215.

15. Jay P. Greene, "Civic Values in Public and Private Schools," in *Learning from School Choice*, ed. Paul E. Peterson and Bryan C. Hassel (Washington, DC: Brookings Institution Press, 1998), 101.

16. Jeffrey R. Henig, *Rethinking School Choice: Limits of the Market Metaphor* (Princeton, NJ: Princeton University Press, 1994), 215.

17. Mark Twain, *Following the Equator: A Journey around the World* (Hartford, CT: American Publishing, 1901), 295.

18. Lisa Graham Keegan, "What Is Public Education?" *City Journal,* Autumn 2000, www.city-journal.org/html/10_4_what_is_public_edu.html/, accessed May 5, 2010.

19. Matt Miller, "First, Kill All the School Boards," *Atlantic Monthly,* January/February 2008, www.theatlantic.com/doc/200801/miller-education/, accessed May 5, 2010.

20. William Howell, *Besieged: School Boards and the Future of Education Politics* (Washington, DC: Brookings Institution Press, 2005), 1.

21. Tyack, *The One Best System,* 33.

22. Ibid., 37.

23. Ibid., 127.

24. Ibid., 89–90.

25. Joseph Viteritti, "Why Governance Matters," in *When Mayors Take Charge,* ed. Joseph Viteritti (Washington, DC: Brookings Institution Press, 2009), 2.

26. Carl Campanile, "Bam Backs Mike School Rule: Ed. Czar's Message to Albany," *New York Post,* March 30, 2009, www.nypost.com/p/news/politics/bam_backs_mike_school_rule_oL38ZA3NwxxoWnBELBh PXP, accessed May 5, 2010.

27. Joseph Viteritti, "The End of Local Politics?" in *Besieged: School Boards and the Future of Education Politics,* ed. William G. Howell (Washington, DC: Brookings Institution Press, 2005), 321.

28. Christopher R. Berry, "School District Consolidation and Student Outcomes: Does Size Matter?" in *Besieged: School Boards and the Future of Education Politics,* ed. William G. Howell (Washington, DC: Brookings Institution Press, 2005), 56.

29. Tyack, *The One Best System,* 25.

30. National Center for Education Statistics, *Digest of Education Statistics, 2001* (Washington, DC: U.S. Department of Education, 2002).

31. *Milliken v. Bradley,* 418 U.S. 717 (1974).

32. Miller, "First, Kill All the School Boards."

33. Jennifer Hochschild, "What School Boards Can and Cannot (or Will Not) Accomplish," in *Besieged: School Boards and the Future of Education*

Politics, ed. William G. Howell (Washington, DC: Brookings Institution Press, 2005), 330.

34. Eric Brunner, Sung-Woo Cho, and Randall Reback, "How Does School Choice Impact Residential Selection?" National Center for the Study of Privatization in Education, Occasional Paper no. 184 (New York: Columbia University, 2010), http://campaign.constantcontact.com/render ?v=001rq5EDIUvnj6CGzcwvdFrKayVoG2M3uUc9YFmYRMPBz 5v3EecKfr2A3AljYLPEWakxm5wc_-_QrS4eVH-_y_3vxoHfWSD kxJRcv_xhz59lnI%3D/, accessed May 5, 2010.

35. David Mowery and Nathan Rosenberg, *Paths of Innovation* (Cambridge, UK: Cambridge University Press, 1999), 50.

36. Arlene Eakle and Johni Cerny, *The Source: A Guidebook of American Genealogy* (Orem, UT: Ancestry Publishing, 1984), 388.

37. "History of the Sears Catalog," Sears Archives, www.searsarchives.com/ catalogs/history.htm/, accessed May 5, 2010.

38. Paul Hill, "Change the Rules," *Blueprint Magazine* 21, March/April 2003, www.dlc.org/ndol_ci.cfm?contentid=251499&kaid=110&subid=181/, accessed May 5, 2010.

39. Bill Gates, Prepared Remarks to National Governors Association, Washington, DC, February 26, 2005, www.nga.org/cda/files/eso5gates .pdf/, accessed May 5, 2010.

40. Ellwood P. Cubberley, *Public Education in the United States* (Boston: Houghton Mifflin, 1919), 5.

41. Patricia Albjerg Graham, *Schooling America: How the Public Schools Meet the Nation's Changing Needs* (New York: Oxford University Press, 2005), 37.

42. Ibid., 35.

43. National Center for Education Statistics, *2004 Digest of Education Statistics,* Table 56 (Washington, DC: U.S. Department of Education, 2004), http://nces.ed.gov/programs/digest/d04/tables/dt04_056.asp/, accessed May 5, 2010.

44. David L. Angus and Jeffrey E. Mirel, *The Failed Promise of the American High School 1890–1995* (New York: Teachers College Press, 1999), 45; Cubberley, *Public Education,* 627.

45. Cubberley, *Public Education.*

46. National Center for Education Statistics, *2004 Digest,* http://nces.ed .gov/programs/digest/d04/tables/dt04_056.asp/, accessed May 5, 2010.

47. Ibid., Table 102, http://nces.ed.gov/programs/digest/d04/tables/dt04_102.asp/.

48. Carl F. Kaestle, *Pillars of the Republic* (New York: Hill and Wang, 1983), 119–120.

49. Graham, *Schooling America*, 36.

50. Ibid., 36–37.

51. Gerald R. Gutek, *A History of the Western Educational Experience* (Prospect Heights, IL: Waveland Press, 1995), 466–467.

52. Angus and Mirel, *The Failed Promise of the American High School*, 199.

53. Gutek, *A History of the Western Educational Experience*, 494.

54. Arthur G. Powell, Eleanor Farrar, and David K. Cohen, *The Shopping Mall High School: Winners and Losers in the Educational Marketplace* (Boston: Houghton Mifflin, 1985), 8.

55. Tom Vander Ark, speech given at the Gates Foundation, March 14, 2002, www.gatesfoundation.org/speeches-commentary/Pages/tom-vander-ark-2002-education-counseling.aspx/, accessed May 5, 2010.

56. William M. French, *America's Educational Tradition: An Interpretive History* (Boston: D.C. Heath, 1964), 167; Graham, *Schooling America*, 110.

57. Tom Toch, *High Schools on a Human Scale: How Small Schools Can Transform American Education* (Boston: Beacon Press, 2003).

58. National Center for Education Statistics, *Digest of Education Statistics 2007*, Table 32 (Washington, DC: U.S. Department of Education, 2004), http://nces.ed.gov/programs/digest/, accessed May 5, 2010.

59. David Farbman and Claire Kaplan, *Time for a Change: The Promise of Extended-Time Schools for Promoting Student Achievement* (Boston: Massachusetts 2020, 2005), 8.

60. "Prisoners of Time," *Report of National Education Commission on Time and Learning* (Washington, DC: U.S. Department of Education, 1994), www2.ed.gov/pubs/PrisonersOfTime/Prisoners.html/, accessed May 5, 2010.

61. Charles Ballinger and Carolyn Kneese, *School Calendar Reform: Learning in All Seasons* (Lanham, MD: Rowman & Littlefield Education, 2006), 38.

62. Kenneth M. Gold, *School's In: The History of Summer Education in American Public Schools* (New York: Peter Lang, 2002), 3.

63. Ballinger and Kneese, *School Calendar Reform*, 33.

64. Ibid., 33–34.

65. Gold, *School's In*, 108.
66. "Vacations for Teachers," *New York Times*, May 26, 1870, 4.
67. Joel Weiss and Robert S. Brown, "Telling Tales over Time: Constructing and Deconstructing the School Calendar," *Teachers College Record* 105, no. 9 (December 2003): 1744.
68. Ibid., 1743.
69. Ibid., 1746.
70. Hilary Pennington, "Expanding Learning Time in High Schools" (Washington, DC: Center for American Progress, October 2006), 4–5.
71. Diana Jean Schemo, "Failing Schools See a Solution in Longer Day," *New York Times*, March 26, 2007, 1.
72. Karl Alexander, Linda Olson, and Doris Entwisle, "Lasting Consequences of the Summer Learning Gap," *American Sociological Review* 72 (April 2007): 175.
73. Donald Hernandez, *America's Children: Resources from Family, Government, and the Economy* (New York: Russell Sage Foundation, 1995), 104.
74. Jane Waldfogel, "School's Out—What's a Working Parent To Do?" *Baltimore Sun*, June 22, 2006.
75. Jeffrey Capizzano, Sarah Adelman, and Matthew Stagner, "What Happens when the School Year Is Over? The Use and Costs of Child Care for School-Age Children during the Summer Months," *Occasional Paper* 58 (Washington, DC: Urban Institute, 2002), 6.
76. Ibid., 14.
77. Ballinger and Kneese, *School Calendar Reform*, 81, 96.
78. David Tyack and William Tobin, "The 'Grammar' of Schooling: Why Has It Been So Hard to Change?" *American Educational Research Journal* 31, no. 3 (1994): 453–479.

8. Finding a New Path

1. Robert L. Church and Michael W. Sedlak, *Education in the United States* (New York: Free Press, 1976), 81.
2. Arthur L. Stinchcombe, *Stratification and Organization* (Cambridge, UK: Cambridge University Press, 1986), 196.
3. Lawrence Arthur Cremin, *Popular Education and Its Discontents* (New York: Harper and Row, 1990), viii.

4. Diane Ravitch, *Left Back: A Century of Battles over School Reform* (New York: Touchstone, 2000), 13.

5. Richard Rothstein, *The Way We Were? The Myths and Realities of America's Student Achievement* (New York: Century Foundation Press, 1998), 19.

6. Maria Glod, "Budget Outlines Funding for Teacher Merit Pay Programs," *Washington Post*, May 7, 2009, www.washingtonpost.com/wp-dyn/con tent/article/2009/05/07/AR2009050703786.html, accessed May 5, 2010.

7. According to author's calculation; Frederick M. Hess, "To Fix Education, School Hours and Money Need to Be Better Spent," *U.S. News & World Report*, April 27, 2009, www.usnews.com/articles/opinion/2009/ 04/27/to-fix-education-school-hours-and-money-need-to-be-better -spent.html, accessed May 5, 2010.

8. U.S. Department of Education, *Race to the Top Fund: Notice of Proposed Priorities, Requirements, Definitions, and Selection Criteria*, July 29, 2009, www.ed.gov/legislation/FedRegister/proprule/2009-3/072909d.html, accessed May 5, 2010.

9. Eric A. Hanushek, John F. Kain, and Steven G. Rivkin, "Why Public Schools Lose Teachers," *Journal of Human Resources* 39, no. 2 (2004): 326–354.

10. Thomas Smith and Richard Ingersoll, "Reducing Teacher Turnover: What Are the Components of Effective Induction?" *American Educational Research Journal* 41, no. 3 (2004): 687–714.

11. Ellen Condliffe Lagemann, *The Elusive Science: The Troubling History of Education Research* (Chicago: Chicago University Press, 2002); Larry Cuban, *How Teachers Taught: Constancy and Change in American Classrooms, 1890–1990* (New York: Teachers College Press, 1993).

12. Margaret A. Nash, *Women's Education in the United States, 1780–1840* (New York: Palgrave Macmillan, 2005), 113.

13. Patricia A. Palmieri, "From Republican Motherhood to Race Suicide: Arguments on the Higher Education of Women in the United States, 1820–1920," http://ed-share.educ.msu.edu/scan/ead/mabokela/document9 .pdf, accessed May 5, 2010.

14. Leonard P. Ayers, "The Economy of Time Thru Testing the Course of Study and Time Allotment," *Journal of Proceedings and Addresses of the National Education Association of the United States* (1913): 246.

15. Gary W. Phillips, "Linking NAEP Achievement Levels to TIMSS" (Washington, DC: American Institutes for Research, 2007), 9.

16. Maris A. Vinovskis, *History and Educational Policymaking* (New Haven, CT: Yale University Press, 1999).

17. Jonathan Gatlin, *Bill Gates: The Path to the Future* (New York: Avon Books, 1999), 39.

18. Christopher Cerf and Victor Navasky, *The Experts Speak: The Definitive Compendium of Authoritative Misinformation* (New York: Pantheon Books, 1984), 231.

19. Kevin Maney, "Tech Titans Wish We Wouldn't Quote Them on This Baloney," *USA Today*, July 5, 2005, http://www.usatoday.com/money/industries/technology/maney/2005-07-05-famous-quotes_x.htm, accessed May 5, 2010.

20. Mark J. Plotkin and Michael Shnayerson, *The Killers Within: The Deadly Rise of Drug-Resistant Bacteria* (London: Little, Brown, 2003), 18.

21. Kathleen Kennedy Manzo, "Students Taking Spanish, French; Leaders Pushing Chinese, Arabic," *Education Week*, March 28, 2006, www.edweek.org/ew/articles/2006/03/29/29mismatch.h25.html, accessed May 5, 2010.

22. Douglas M. Knight, ed., *The Federal Government and Higher Education* (Englewood Cliffs, NJ: Prentice-Hall, 1960), 41–46; Julia Gibson Kant, "Foreign-Language Offerings and Enrollments in Public and Nonpublic Secondary Schools, Fall 1968" (New York: Modern Language Association of America, 1970), 12.

23. Manzo, "Students Taking Spanish, French."

24. Scott E. Page, *The Difference: How the Power of Diversity Creates Better Groups, Firms, Schools, and Societies* (Princeton, NJ: Princeton University Press, 2008).

25. Patricia Albjerg Graham, *Schooling America: How the Public Schools Meet the Nation's Changing Needs* (New York: Oxford University Press, 2005), 176.

Epilogue

1. Andrew Delbanco, "Dreams of Better Schools," *New York Review of Books* 56 (2009), www.nybooks.com/articles/23377?, accessed May 5, 2010.

2. Jeanne H. Ballantine and Joan Z. Spade, *Schools and Society: A Sociological Approach to Education* (Thousand Oaks, CA: Sage, 2008), 280.

3. Caroline Hoxby, "If Families Matter Most, Where Do Schools Come In?" in *A Primer on America's Schools,* ed. Terry Moe (Stanford, CA: Hoover Institution Press, 2001), 104.

4. Milton Friedman, "The Role of Government in Education," in *Economics and the Public Interest,* ed. Robert A. Solo (New Brunswick, NJ: Rutgers University Press, 1955).

5. Bureau of Labor Statistics, "Number of Jobs Held, Labor Market Activity, and Earnings Growth among the Youngest Baby Boomers: Results from a Longitudinal Survey," Bureau of Labor Statistics, June 27, 2008, www.bls.gov/news.release/pdf/nlsoy.pdf, accessed May 5, 2010.

6. U.S. Department of Education, "Supplement Not Supplant Provision of Title III of the ESEA" (Washington, DC: U.S. Department of Education), www2.ed.gov/programs/sfgp/supplefinalattach2.pdf, accessed May 5, 2010.

7. Larry Cuban, *Oversold and Underused: Computers in the Classroom* (Cambridge, MA: Harvard University Press, 2003).

8. Clayton M. Christensen and Michael B. Horn, "How Do We Transform Our Schools?" *Education Next* 8 (Summer 2008), http://educationnext.org/how-do-we-transform-our-schools/, accessed May 28, 2010.

9. U.S. Treasury, "Health Savings Accounts (HSAs)," www.ustreas.gov/offices/public-affairs/hsa/, accessed on May 5, 2010.

Acknowledgments

This has been a project of several years, pursued intermittently alongside the other obligations and engagements that distract any academic engaged in the world of policy. Over that time, I have accumulated many debts. I owe a special gratitude to those friends and colleagues who have helped me along the way as I have worked on this manuscript. I would like to express my particular appreciation for the friendship and insights provided by Jennifer de Forest, Chester Finn Jr., Dan Goldhaber, Jane Hannaway, Jeff Henig, Tom Loveless, Henry Olsen, Mike Petrilli, Diane Ravitch, and Andrew Rotherham. Inclusion here does not, of course, indicate that any of these individuals endorse any part of the argument that follows; only that their thinking or their generosity has informed my own efforts.

This book draws upon a variety of research and scholarship I have pursued in the past several years. Those efforts have been generously supported by a number of funders, including particularly the Smith Richardson Foundation and the Bill & Melinda Gates Foundation. I have also benefited from the opportunity to present elements of the argument in various scholarly and popular outlets, including *Education Next, Journal of Teacher Education, American Journal of Education, Educational Policy, Phi Delta Kappan, U.S. News & World Report,* and the *Washington Post,* and owe thanks to the readers of those publications for their generous thoughts and suggestions. I have also spoken on elements of this manuscript in scores of forums and am equally appreciative of the feedback I received in those forums.

I owe a debt of gratitude to the many individuals who have assisted with the writing and research for this volume over time, as it went through multiple incarnations. I would like to thank my research assistants Hilary Boller, Raphael Gang, Thomas Gift, Morgan Goatley, Rachel Hoff, Emily

Kluver, Daniel Lautzenheiser, and Jenna Schuette for their tireless editing and research. I'd also like to thank dedicated interns like Jessica Farace, Gregory Franke, Bridget Hahn, Ben Hyman, Steve Lecholop, Claire Moore, Peter Mui, Emily Patch, Julia Payson, Erin Riley, Michael Ruderman, Adam Schaeffer, Arushi Sherma, Melissa Silvers, and Shane Wilson for their efforts, as well as William Stull and Danielle Allen for their expert feedback.

I'd like to offer particular thanks to Rosemary Kendrick, Olivia Meeks, and Juliet Squire for the extraordinary work they did in coordinating the research, keeping the project moving during hectic times, and providing essential feedback and insight in the drafting and preparation of the manuscript. And I'd like to thank my editor, Elizabeth Knoll, for her invaluable guidance and support.

Finally, I'd particularly like to express my appreciation to the American Enterprise Institute for providing the warmest, most supportive intellectual and scholarly environment I could desire. I want to offer my deepest thanks to AEI's former president, Chris Demuth, and to its current president, Arthur Brooks, for their unwavering support and for providing an intellectual home where I find myself free to speak the truth that I see.

—Frederick M. Hess

Index